Managerial Flow ·

When globalization affects jobs and economies, policy makers strive to plan, design, and implement actions to support their communities and businesses. Furthermore, local development policies are at the core of international cooperation programs or more in general represent a challenge for emerging countries. They could refer to infrastructure, entrepreneurship innovation, or urban renewal. However, more frequently than not, development policies, which involve different institutional levels and public and private players, fail because of poor implementation management. This research book presents a managerial approach (the so-called Managerial Flow) that could help the closure of gaps that hamper an efficient and effective policy execution.

The managerial flow model observes the phenomenon of policy implementation for economic development through managerial lens. In the book, the research team has empirically identified five gaps in practice whereupon public policy implementation falls down. As a response Managerial Flow model outlines sets of managerial actions that can be adopted to facilitate a clear "flow" from policy development through to implementation.

This book expands on the Managerial Flow model and acts as both a practical guide to stimulate evidence-based policy implementation in governments and as theoretical contribution to policy and strategy execution.

Written for researchers and academics, this book begins by outlining the theoretical foundations of Managerial Flow and moves to unpack application and cases, based in different sectors and countries, in order to discuss and show how the Managerial Flow approach can concretely support managers in the implementation of economic development policies. It reviews and discusses how the managerial flow could be relevant in the implementation of a set of sectorial policies and uses the managerial flow concept to analyze cases of economic development and to establish lessons for broader management scope.

Veronica Vecchi is SDA Professor of Public Management and Policy at SDA Bocconi, Bocconi University School of Management.

Ben Farr-Wharton is in the final stages of achieving his doctoral thesis at Southern Cross Business School. His doctoral research focuses on the impact of social networks, business acumen, and performance for people working within the creative industries.

Rodney Farr-Wharton is Program Leader, Entrepreneurship, and Senior Lecturer, Innovation and Entrepreneurship, at Faculty of Business, University of the Sunshine Coast.

Manuela Brusoni is Senior SDA Professor of Public Management and Policy at SDA Bocconi, Bocconi University School of Management.

Routledge Advances in Management and Business Studies

For a full list of titles in this series, please visit www.routledge.com

Managerial Flow

Edited by Veronica Vecchi,
Ben Farr-Wharton, Rodney
Farr-Wharton, and Manuela Brusoni

Routledge
Taylor & Francis Group

NEW YORK AND LONDON

First published 2015
by Routledge
711 Third Avenue, New York, NY 10017

and by Routledge
2 Park Square, Milton Park, Abingdon, Oxon OX14 4RN

*Routledge is an imprint of the Taylor & Francis Group,
an informa business*

Library of Congress Cataloging-in-Publication Data
Managerial flow / edited by Veronica Vecchi, Ben Farr-Wharton, Manuela
    Brusoni, Rodney Farr-Wharton.
    pages cm. — (Routledge advances in management and business studies ; 61)
    Includes bibliographical references and index.
    1. Industrial management. 2. Management. I. Vecchi, Veronica.
    HD31.2.M36 2015
    658—dc23
    2014045550

ISBN: 978-0-415-74945-9 (hbk)
ISBN: 978-1-315-79611-6 (ebk)

Typeset in Sabon
by Apex CoVantage, LLC

This book is dedicated to:

Mami, Papi, and Sole, by Veronica
Eloisa, by Ben
Yvonne, by Rod
Ulisse and Pcnelope, by Manuela

Contents

PART III
Economic Development and Managerial Flow

PART IV
Clusters, Entrepreneurship, and Managerial Flow

PART V
Investments, Public–Private Partnerships, and
Managerial Flow

Figures

Tables

Preface

*Elio Borgonovi, Professor of Public Management
at Bocconi University, Italy*

The economy, and society generally, is more complex, uncertain, and con-tradictory than ever before. Moreover, people seem to show lower ethical values and decreasing trust toward each other. Additionally credibility in institutions, both public and private, has decreased in the last two decades. Private firms and market rules and dynamics are no longer able to create jobs and development. Despite their best intentions, governments and public authorities are often, if not always, considered inefficient and unable to guar-antee welfare conditions and to sustain economic and societal development.

How can this situation be challenged? Joint public–private efforts to pro-mote, support, enhance, and incentivize economic development and social growth have been conceived as a possible answer. However, there is evi-dence that these collaborations are not easily implemented and often fail. The contributors of this book try to explain why failures happen and how to overcome them. The key reason they agree on is summarized in the frame of managerial gaps. This framework is based on two pillars: On the one hand, the private management culture is far away from understanding pub-lic interest goals; on the other hand, public authorities are still conditioned by the bureaucratic model, notwithstanding the New Public Management approach introduced in many countries since the 1980s, and later on the Public Governance approach.

A main pitfall of these methods remains in their simplistic transfer, to the public sector at large, principles, criterion, methodologies, and techniques consolidated in private firms and in the market arena without rethinking the relations between pubic interest goals and effective approaches to pursue them. The Managerial Flow framework connects the culture and decision-making and implementation processes of both public and private sectors and therefore is a reference point for supporting the collaboration of public and private operators, putting at the core the concrete design and imple-mentation of projects and initiatives useful to stimulate cross-learning and mutual trust, facilitate interactions and promote convergence toward win-win solutions rather than win-lose solutions—or even lose-lose solutions.

Hence, Managerial Flow is developed according to the public policy cycle on the one hand, and to the mission/vision/strategy cycle on the other.

Analysis of the economic, social, political, and institutional environment is the starting point of policy analysis, while the definition of a mission/vision consistent with the economic, social, political, and institutional environment is the starting point for private firms. The formulation of policy and strategy alternatives is the second phase for public administration as well as for businesses. The third phase is the evaluation/decision of public policies on the basis of cost-benefit, cost-effectiveness, cost-quality criteria, and evaluation/decision of the individual firm's strategy on the basis of profit maximization or stakeholder rewards theory. The fourth phase, implementation, means to define concrete objectives, plans, and resource allocation in both sectors. However, resources are collected differently: from taxes or public debt for governments, whereas, for private firms, from market prices, equity and capital markets. The last phase is the impact evaluation that for private firms means mainly or exclusively to monitor the effectiveness of the strategy in terms of profit, stakeholder rewards, market shares, competitiveness; while for public authorities means to monitor social value creation, distribution, and equity effects.

As the myth of a self-regulating market has vanished and the heterogeneity of social groups emerged, higher contradictions characterized economy and society, while a fall of credibility between public and private institutions is bringing about an exponential reduction of the social capital represented by trust.

A lack of trust is also an outcome of the one-dimensional criterion that prevailed during the 20th century. Adam Smith, the founder of modern economy, built his theory on the concept of self-interest; as such he clearly stated that no economic relation and market could properly function without moral sentiments, beliefs, and values. Over time this framework was simplified and the rational choice theory imposed the profit maximization/optimization as the unique criterion, while scientific management focused on technical and economic efficiency. Thus governments experimented with a trend toward one-dimensional criterion of choice. The separation between politics (definition of objectives) and administration (instrumental activity to pursue them) was complemented by the bureaucratic model proposed by Max Weber as a neutral, impartial, objective organization behavior.

Today, indeed, a one-dimensional approach is no longer sustainable in a complex and uncertain environment. Therefore, to capture this multidimensionality, the Managerial Flow framework is grounded in a mix of theories. The first pillar, the interinstitutional relation theory, explains that economic development and social growth can no longer be the outcome of a policy driven only by firms/companies, nor it can be simply promoted by "good" public policies. Co-evaluation of environment, innovation, co-decision of public policies and firms' strategies, co-implementation and co-evaluation of the impact are required to achieve the expected outcomes. The second pillar is the change theory, because Managerial Flow is complemented by the gap analysis. Moreover, change is not simply an action of deciding goals, but rather a process of investigating how to achieve such goals and who is responsible for their execution. Through the gap analysis, managers and policy makers can understand how to remove the obstacles or constraints that hinder the change process. The gap analysis is also helpful to understand which organizations or people are ready to change and, consequently, to elaborate a fruitful strategy to motivate and convince them that a win-win change is possible. The third pillar is the dynamics theory. Actually, managerial flow and gap analysis are not simply the comparison of the present situation against a better one, but they also define the steps to be taken. The fourth pillar is the multidimensional criteria choice. To reach a convergence acceptable for both parts, equilibrium must be guaranteed among efficiency, effectiveness, economic sustainability, and legal and equity criteria. Firms are focused on the first three, while governments are focused on the last two.

The aim of this book is to disseminate the Managerial Flow approach and to stimulate applications and further developments. One of the next steps is certainly the definition of a set of metrics to evaluate in quantitative terms the managerial gaps, as "only what can be measured can be actually improved."

A Note from the Editors

What creates economic development? This question is the focus of much debate and deliberation from scholars past and present. The fields of economics and regional studies emphasize the need for regions to exploit their natural and human-made capital. However, it may be not enough. Our own research calls for a more managed and coordinated approach to growth initiatives that facilitate meaningful partnerships between business and governments. Furthermore, we believe that a good policy or program also depends on the implementation process. Therefore to design and implement successful economic development initiatives based on such partnerships, a Managerial Flow is required: in other words, a managerial approach, which flows across different institutional levels and organizations, as a common background to sustain interactions between businesses and governments.

In this book we provide a set of novel, and globally relevant, tools and perspectives that regional development practitioners and scholars can employ to more adequately understand, investigate, and execute growth initiatives. Growth initiatives typically take the form of *innovation capacity building programs* (including industry clustering), *entrepreneurial development strategies, sectoral growth interventions* and *public–private partnerships* that seek to build and maintain core (hard and soft) infrastructure.

The book, comprising fifteen chapters, is thus grouped in five parts. The first three chapters of the book begin by contextualizing, linking, and finally distinguishing the Managerial Flow framework from the cannon of regional development theories. The proceeding three chapters provide an appraisal of *innovation capacity building programs* in Australia, Singapore, and China respectively, through the lens of Managerial Flow. Chapters 6 through 9 investigate specific *sectoral growth interventions* involving public and private actors in Australia and post-conflict Bosnia. Chapters 10 to 12 focus on cases of *entrepreneurial development strategies* from Tunisia, Northern Ireland, and Australia. The final chapters of the book present key lessons comprising a Managerial Flow perspective of *public–private partnerships* with cases drawn from Italy and the Netherlands.

This book is a significant milestone in the global diffusion of the Managerial Flow concept to date, rooted in the academic and professional experiences of the authors, shared, systematized, and exalted within several editions of the Academy of Management and IRSPM (International Research Society for Public Management), which offered platforms to allow the concept to grow and expand over a series of five years. However, as the framework now is achieving considerable popularity in practice, research, and policy, we must be sure to thank all those who have created and nurtured its development. Thus, in the first instance, the editorial team would like to acknowledge all the authors and managers, from the public and private sector, who allowed us to experiment the Managerial Flow, to develop on the filed research, and shared with us thoughtful ideas and experiences. We would like also to thank the Singapore Management Review for supporting the very first special edition (2011) on Managerial Flow and we acknowledge the support of Routledge and David Varley, who supported the development of this book. We offer our heartfelt thanks to all those who have contributed to this book, with special acknowledgment attributed to the preface author—Elio Borgonovi, and chapter author—Yvonne Brunetto who continually supported, meaningfully challenged, and perpetually celebrated the rise of Managerial Flow. Finally, we thank you the reader. Your own application, appraisal, and synthesis of the Managerial Flow concept has the power to positively impact on the outcomes of regional development. Thank you all and happy reading!

Part I
Introduction and Overview

1 Closing the Gaps of the Successful Implementation of Local Development Policies

The Managerial Flow Approach

Veronica Vecchi and Manuela Brusoni

THE JOURNEY TO MANAGERIAL FLOW

In recent years the capacity to execute programs and projects has drawn the attention of academics and professionals, who highlight its relevance for the success of any given implementation process (Bossidy & Charan, 2002; Hrebiniak, 2013; Martin, 2010; Neilson, Martin, & Powers, 2008).

Our work has been informed by requests from public-sector managers to understand why, in a context in which there are clear development goals, a set of defined supranational- or national-level priorities often fail to be correctly or fully implemented at a local level. There is a type of "transmission bottleneck" that reduces the local effectiveness to interpret, align, and implement programs that contribute to the fulfilment of those national objectives in the target areas or communities (Ansell & Gash, 2007).

The excessive focus on policy planning has originated the so-called knowing–doing gap, where the emphasis is on efficient policy design at the expense of policy operation (Pfeffer & Sutton, 2013). Mason and Brown (2011) report that literature is often vague and does not provide specific guidance for the execution of policies but, rather, the tendency is to focus on "what not to do." Furthermore, McGuire (2000) calls for more complete, empirical studies to support managers and professionals involved in the implementation of local development policies. Although inspired by international literature, our work first started in Italy.

From 2006 to 2009, within our teaching and research activity at Bocconi University School of Management, Milan, Italy, we engaged more than 150 local Italian public and private managers involved in regional development programs, working in 65 organizations[1] (Vecchi, Brusoni, & Borgonovi, 2014).

In that period, the observation of more than 100 cases, informed by literature, generated a continual evaluation cycle that helped us to shape the conceptual framework for the assessment of process failures in the local implementation of economic development policies, which we called Managerial Flow (Eisenhardt, 1989). It was first applied in an experiment conducted in 2009–2010 within the Reggio Emilia province plan for crisis recovery (Vecchi & Brusoni, 2012).

This policy implementation process assessment toolbox was then further improved in 2010 through an Academy of Management (AoM) Professional Development Workshop (PDW), organized by the Public and non Profit Division, titled "Passion for Enterprises and Competitiveness: The Managerial Flow of Public Policies." A further two PDWs were organized in 2011 and 2012 AoM conferences in order to refine the conceptual framework, to collect cases and evidence worthy of analysis using the Managerial Flow toolbox, and to get a clearer idea of its international relevance and validity. The 2013 AoM symposium and the 2013–2014 International Research Society for Public Management panels dedicated to the Managerial Flow concept provided the opportunity to finalize the chapters that form this book through a process of informed critique and academic scrutiny.

THE MANAGERIAL FLOW APPROACH

Our research journey, which was originally based on case observation, analysis, and pilot testing, highlighted that the effective implementation of local development policies could be reduced or hampered by the existence of rather specific and well-defined managerial "gaps," related to five dimensions: strategy, governance, selection, coordination and integration, and communication and knowledge (Brusoni, Crugnola, & Vecchi, 2007; Brusoni & Vecchi, 2010; Vecchi & Brusoni, 2012; Vecchi et al., 2014):

1. **Strategy** emerges when public programs are defined on the basis of short-term expectations, current fashions, "announcement effects" or solely to allocate financial resources that otherwise could be diverted towards other policies or programs (Hospers, Desrochers, & Sautet, 2008; Malecki, 1984; Rubin & Zorn, 1985). Consequently, they lack a meaningful definition of performance indicators.
2. **Governance** refers to problems when multiple public agencies and stakeholders work together, with different mandates and without a common goal, thus bringing overlapping initiatives and confusion over roles, responsibility and accountability (Ansell & Gash, 2007; Ansell, 2000).
3. **Selection** emerges when resources and efforts, scarcer that ever, are allocated without appropriateness under the fairness illusion. The gap also emerges from the difficulties in designing coherent projects to be supported or funded and monitored. This is particularly true with reference to entrepreneurship programs (Mason & Brown, 2011).
4. The **coordination and integration** gap emerges when a lack of leadership, reciprocity, legitimacy and trust in the interorganizational activities reduces the integration of public and private financial and human resources (Ansell, 2000; O'Toole, 1997).

5. The **communication and knowledge** gap refers to asymmetric information flow and reciprocal knowledge gaps that push players to operate on different wavelengths, focusing only on their own silos (O'Toole, 1995).

Gaps may be considered from two different perspectives: retrospective and prospective. In other words, they can be useful to analyze a specific context in which local development policies were, or are going to be, implemented.

Within a retrospective perspective, gaps are useful to analyze ex post the implementation of a policy in order to understand room of improvements or empowerment and to generate lessons learned related to organizational and managerial processes and tools applied.

Within a prospective perspective, the analysis of gaps is useful in developing effective measures to close them. Closing gaps is achieved through the development of new policies and programs that are calibrated with the goals that are to be reached.

The Managerial Flow process involves "managerial decisions and actions" that, when put in place within one or more institutions, generate "managerial assets." Managerial assets are the milestones and enabling factors that bridge one or more perceived gaps. As managerial actions and assets are dynamic and co-related factors, their synergistic interaction facilitate a sort of flow, which supports the design and execution of programs and projects at the local level.

Managerial actions are carried out by different local actors and are a circular flow of actions based on the following:

- Context analysis (needs and expectations analysis; review of the existing programs, policies, best and worst practices; stakeholders analysis; Bennett & Robson, 2003)
- Planning and execution of pilot actions, useful to reach small wins able to reinforce commitment and collaboration and to test the reliability of the designed development plan (Chrislip & Larson, 1994; Fawcett et al., 2000; Warner, 2006)
- Monitoring and assessment, in order to understand if the pilot action generated some results, how the players interacted, if adjustments took place
- Scaling the pilot action so that the policy can be implemented at large in a certain community

Managerial assets could be considered as the following:

- Knowledge about the problems and awareness about possible solutions to reach a technical credibility and to take informed, credible, convincing, and common decisions (Ryan, 2001; Vangen & Huxham, 2003)
- Legitimacy and leadership toward local partners but moreover toward businesses, which are the main beneficiaries of local development

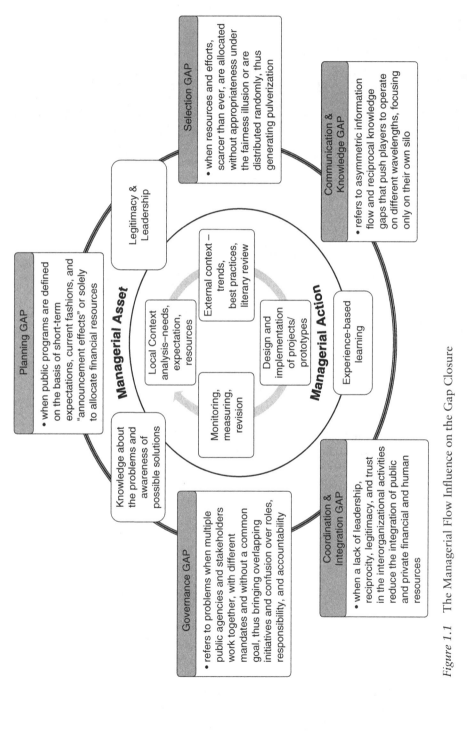

Figure 1.1 The Managerial Flow Influence on the Gap Closure

policies (Alexander, Comfort, & Weiner, 1998; Imperial, 2005; Murdock, 2005)
- Experience-based learning useful to plan and implement future actions and to stimulate a collaborative learning process (Daniels & Walker, 2001)

Figure 1.1 schematizes the link between managerial actions, managerial assets, and gaps.

3. MANAGERIAL FLOW IN ACTION

To further explain the managerial flow framework, we apply the model to three cases:

- Re'up—a program launched by Reggio Emilia province to sustain youth employment
- Milan Expo 2015—to support Milan neighborhood authorities to get the most from the World Exposition event
- Basilicata Region—to develop capacity to execute the cohesion policy program for 2014 through 2020 funded by European Union structural funds

Reggio Emilia Start-Ups Design and Implementation

The Province of Reggio Emilia is one of the richest and most developed regions in Italy. In 2009 this region faced an unemployment rate, that had risen by 88%, including a doubling of youth unemployment to 30%.

The provincial government of Reggio Emilia developed a local program, *Reggio Emilia Beats the Crisis*, and sought to involve all the local stakeholders to rapidly identify needs and solutions to support businesses and families during this economic crisis. The province agreed to plan and implement one component of the plan according to the Managerial Flow approach. It was therefore applied to Re'up, short for "Reggio Emilia start-ups." Re'up was designed not as an initiative to subsidize business start-ups but, rather, as a coaching process to support new and aspiring entrepreneurs in the development of their business idea. Specific and personalized coaching was offered to start-ups in order to strengthen business ideas, their feasibility, and their commercializability. Ten business ideas were selected from a pool of 20 using typical commercial assessment methodologies applied by venture capitalists to avoid adverse selection that can occur under a pure public evaluation process. At the end of the program, the entrepreneurs received a grant from the province based on their business plans, the results achieved to date, and development goals. In addition to the business coaching and skill development, participants were offered a contact with potential investors (industrial and financial), with the Italian Business Angels Network, the Italian Association of Venture Capital and Private Equity, and other potential partners relevant to the development of their business activities.

When defining the goals and the expected results of the program, it was very important to agreed-on, shared performance indicators among stakeholders. Not all the project ideas could be selected; not all the proposals would have turned into true start-ups; not all of them would have attracted equity investments. Notably, 7 of 10 projects became an enterprise, and overall, Re'up generated 70 new jobs. Six businesses were still in operation after 3 years.

These results, and the continuation of youth unemployment, led the provincial government to launch a second round in 2012. Thirty-eight business ideas were received, and 15 of them were selected to be developed within a program, which was slightly modified based on the feedback from the first edition.

Table 1.1 shows a synthesis of the managerial actions undertaken by the province, the milestones generated (managerial assets), and their relation with the gaps closure.

Table 1.1   Actions and Milestones and Their Relation With the Gaps Closure in the Case "Re'up of the Province of Reggio Emilia"

Reggio Emilia province managerial actions	Milestones achieved (assests)	Gap
Analysis of the local enterprises needs with the support of local stakeholders (grouped through the Stakeholder Table Initiative)	Taking stock of all the elements to set up Re'up as pilot action to support innovation and entrepreneurship in a new way, through services, i.e., coaching and training for selected enterprises	**Strategy**
Analysis of European policy plans		
Literary review		
Research through the main experiences		
Pilot action design and technical coordination made by the province task force, formed by national expert, with proven experiences	Technical effectiveness in order to reach the planned goals and thus to increase the province's legitimacy	**Governance**
Sharing Re'up pilot action with local stakeholders	No overlaps with other actions planned by the regions or by local institutions, whose representative are involved in the Stakeholder Table Initiative	

(*Continued*)

Table 1.1 (Continued)

Reggio Emilia province managerial actions	Milestones achieved (assests)	Gap
Involvement of investors' representatives (associations of business angels and venture capital funds) in the enterprises selection (candidates)	Selection of enterprises with high potentialities (high flyers) to be supported through Re'up	Selection
Selection of candidates through business plans assessment		
Involvement of potential investors (local banks, business angles, local entrepreneurs) during the enterprises coaching	Bridging demand and supply of investments. Taking stocks of feedbacks on business plans (even informal)	Coordination and Integration
Involvement of experts to design and manage Re'up	Coaching and training reshaping during Re'up	Communication and Knowledge
Continuous monitoring of the enterprises needs and learning assessment	Customized support to enterprises	
	Taking stocks of feedbacks to plan the second edition and further actions	

Getting the Most From Expo 2015: The Implementation of Local Development Projects in Surrounding Communities

Here we present an application of the managerial flow as a possible methodology for local authorities neighboring the city of Milan, which is hosting the World Exposition (Expo) in 2015, in order to develop projects and initiatives able not only to attract the tourism generated by the mega event (20 million of visitors are expected) but, above all, to create long-lasting development opportunities (Vecchi et al., 2014).

Table 1.2 outlines the managerial flow gaps relevant to the Milan neighborhood,[2] and Table 1.3 outlines some possible questions useful to stimulate among stakeholders the definition and implementation of managerial actions to close gaps. Furthermore, they generate those assets necessary to sustain the successful implementation of local development projects to get the most from the Expo event and to extend its effects beyond it.

3.3 Capacity Building for the Implementation of an EU Cohesion Policy in Basilicata Region

Contrary to the first two cases, here the identified gaps have been applied retrospectively to the Basilicata region, in the south of Italy. The region decided

Table 1.2 Gaps Affecting the Expo 2015 Surrounding Communities (as of December 2012)

Gap	Specific features in the Expo 2015 surrounding communities
Planning	Expo related development plan too broad and general
	Lack of public grants which generally drive the planning activity
Governance	Lack of coordination put in place by intermediate public authorities (such as the provinces)
	Lack of local leaders—champions
	High number and fragmented stakeholders
Selection	Too wide a number of initiatives put in pipeline by local authorities
	Lack of "evergreen" flagship initiatives, to be developed during the Expo event and relevant even after its end
Coordination and Integration	Weak and problematic coordination among the provinces, the Expo Organizational Committee, and the local stakeholders
Communication and Knowledge	Lack of knowledge of managerial practices put in place in previous and similar initiatives, their success factors and weaknesses
	Lack of awareness about expectations and point of view of local actors, which are the main players involved in the execution of initiatives for visitors/tourists

Table 1.3 Possible Managerial Assets to Put in Place to Close the Gaps

Managerial action	Possible questions to set the managerial actions
Local context analysis: expectation, needs, assets	Local development programs are still attractive and coherent?
	Which resources could be attracted/invested?
	Which are the stakeholders? What is the level of commitment?
	Are local businesses able to exploit/get the most from the Expo event?
Analysis of external environment: trends, experiences, practices	How other communities and local authorities are planning initiatives for the Expo?
	Which are the lessons learned from the previous mega-event experiences?
Design and execution of pilot initiatives	Which initiatives can be developed as a test, involving different partners also trying to capture the first touristic flows that the event is generating?
	Which initiatives can be developed as "evergreen," to be maintained even after the Expo event?
	How to sell its own touristic offer?
Monitoring, assessment and revision	How to measure the performance of the development plan?
	Which lessons could be learned from the pilot initiative(s)?
	How to redirect the future actions?
	Which goals in the medium term?

to apply the Managerial Flow concept in order to pursue the capacity-building goals set by the European Commission within the new Cohesion Policy Framework (2014–2020). The European Union Cohesion Policy is aimed at support the growth and competitiveness of European regions in order to reduce economic and social disparities and to tackle the main social and economic issues.

A group of stakeholders, involved in the design and implementation of local development programs and projects during the previous cohesion policy framework, from 2007 to 2013, were asked to outline conditions, competences, processes, and tools that would close the gaps and to achieve the set goals or to determine the reasons why gaps remained open and outcomes failed to be achieved. Specifically, stakeholders were asked to address the following issues:

• Existing gaps prior to the commencement of the development program/project
• Solution put in place to solve the criticalities (stakeholders are required to gather them within the five gaps)
• The management tools, procedures, and processes put in place to implement the solutions envisaged
• The degree of effectiveness of the solution and or tools, processes, and procedures

This process helped the region to develop a capacity-building process, leveraging the lessons learned from good and critical practices and cases, and to define a set of procedures, processes, and managerial actions to be disseminated among local public and private players to generate the assets necessary to sustain the effective implementation of the 2014–2020 Cohesion Policy.

DISCUSSION AND CONCLUSION

Managerial Flow provides a useful framework to help managers to understand gaps that could hamper their efforts and orient their actions in order to better invest resources, to reinforce collaboration, and to design and implement actions able to generate results coherent with specific local development and competitiveness needs. Public authorities and local stakeholders can no longer afford the misallocation of resources, which are even more curtailed, and a disestablishment generated by the ineptitude to generate results, even in the short term.

In this book, our travel companions took the challenge to use the Managerial Flow approach as a framework to explain good or critical experiences within different jurisdictions, geographic areas, and sectors.

NOTES

1. The typological breakdown of these organizations is as follows: regions (7), regional financial agencies (4), provinces (8), municipalities (17), chambers of commerce (8), business associations (8), development agencies (9), and incubators and technology parks (4).
2. Gaps have been outlined on the basis of interviews made to local politicians in 2012, in charge of developing initiatives related to the Expo event, from the six main cities (county seats) surrounding Milan.

REFERENCES

Alexander, J. A., Comfort, M. E., & Weiner, B. J. (1998). Governance in public-private community health partnerships: A survey of the Community Care Network^{SM} demonstration sites. *Nonprofit Management and Leadership*, 8(4), 311–332.

Ansell, C. (2000). The networked polity: Regional development in Western Europe. *Governance*, 13(2), 279–291.

Ansell, C., & Gash, A. (2007). Collaborative governance in theory and practice. *Journal of Public Administration Research and Theory*, 18(4), 543–571.

Bennett, R., & Robson, P. (2003). Changing use of external business advice and government supports by SMEs in the 1990s. *Regional Studies*, 37(8), 795–811.

Bossidy, L., & Charan, R. (2002). *Execution*. New York, NY: Crown Business.

Brusoni, M., Crugnola, P., & Vecchi, V. (2007). Forum: Promuovere la competitività. Quale ruolo per la Pubblica Amministrazione? *Economia & Management*, 6, 14–25.

Brusoni, M., & Vecchi, V. (2010). Forum: Competitività, innovazione e imprenditorialità nelle amministrazioni pubbliche. *Economia & Management*, 6, 9–17.

Chrislip, D., & Larson, C. (1994). *Collaborative leadership: How citizens and civic leaders can make a difference*. San Francisco, CA: Jossey-Bass. Retrieved from http://scholar.google.it/scholar?q=Collaborative+leadership%3A+How+citizens+and+civic+leaders+can+make+a+difference&btnG=&hl=it&as_sdt=0%2C5#0

Daniels, S., & Walker, G. (2001). *Working through environmental conflict: The collaborative learning*. Retrieved from http://works.bepress.com/steven_daniels/30/

Eisenhardt, K. M. (1989). Building theories from case study research. *Academy of Management Review*, 14(4), 532–550.

Fawcett, S. B., Francisco, V. T., Hyra, D., Paine-Andrews, A., Schultz, J. A., Russos, S., . . . Evensen, P. (2000). Building healthy communities. In A. Tarlov (Ed.), *Society and population health reader: State and community applications*. (pp. 75–93). New York: The New Press.

Hospers, G.-J., Desrochers, P., & Sautet, F. (2008). The next Silicon Valley? On the relationship between geographical clustering and public policy. *International Entrepreneurship and Management Journal*, 5(3), 285–299.

Hrebiniak, L. (2013). *Making strategy work: Leading effective execution and change*. Upper Saddle River, NJ: Pearson Prentice Hall.

Imperial, M. T. (2005). Using collaboration as a governance strategy: Lessons from six watershed management programs. *Administration & Society*, 37(3), 281–320.

Malecki, E. J. (1984). High technology and local economic development. *Journal of the American Planning Association*, 50(3), 262–269.

Martin, R. (2010). The execution trap. *Harvard Business Review*, 8(7–8), 64–71.

Mason, C., & Brown, R. (2011). Creating good public policy to support high-growth firms. *Small Business Economics*, 40(2), 211–225.

McGuire, M. (2000). Collaborative policy making and administration: The operational demands of local economic development. *Economic Development Quarterly, 14*(3), 278–293.

Murdock, B. S. (2005). Stakeholder participation in voluntary environmental agreements: Analysis of 10 Project XL case studies. *Science, Technology & Human Values, 30*(2), 223–250.

Neilson, G., Martin, K., & Powers, E. (2008). The secrets to successful strategy execution. *Harvard Business Review, 86*(6), 60.

O'Toole, L. J. (1995). Rational choice and policy implementation: Implications for interorganizational network management. *The American Review of Public Administration, 25*(1), 43–57.

O'Toole, L. J. (1997). Implementing public innovations in network settings. *Administration & Society, 29*(2), 115–138.

Pfeffer, J., & Sutton, R. (2013). *The knowing-doing gap: How smart companies turn knowledge into action.* Cambridge, MA: Harvard Business Press.

Rubin, B., & Zorn, C. (1985). Sensible state and local economic development. *Public Administration Review, 45*(2), 333–339.

Ryan, C. M. (2001). Leadership in collaborative policy-making: An analysis of agency roles in regulatory negotiations. *Policy Sciences, 34*(3–4), 221–245.

Vangen, S., & Huxham, C. (2003). Nurturing collaborative relations Building trust in interorganizational collaboration. *The Journal of Applied Behavioral Science, 39*(1), 5–31.

Vecchi, V., & Brusoni, M. (2012). The managerial flow of public local development policies a conceptual framework. *Singapore Management Review, 34*(Suppl. 2), 5–20.

Vecchi, V., Brusoni, M., & Borgonovi, E. (2014). Public authorities for entrepreneurship: A management approach to execute competitiveness policies. *Public Management Review, 16*(2), 256–273.

Warner, J. F. (2006). More sustainable participation? Multi-stakeholder platforms for integrated catchment management. *International Journal of Water Resources Development, 22*(1), 15–35. doi:10.1080/07900620500404992

2 Evaluating the Potential Impact of Development Policies

Rod Farr-Wharton, Ben Farr-Wharton, and Yvonne Brunetto

Many Western governments have defined their role in economic development policy as ensuring that policies and infrastructure promote private-sector activity that fosters economic growth based on market forces. This situation suggests government is limited to reducing policy intervention and bureaucracy to enhance the ability of the private sector to invest, innovate, and employ. If this premise is accepted, then the public-sector role becomes one of correcting market failures, through investment in pure science, education, and infrastructure, for example:

> Government on its own cannot create growth. It is the decisions of business leaders, entrepreneurs and individual workers, which build our economy. What the Government can do is provide the conditions for success to promote a new economic dynamism—harnessing our economic strengths, removing the barriers which prevent markets from supporting enterprise, and putting the private sector first when making decisions on tax, regulation and spending.
>
> (Department for Business Innovation &
> Skills and Her Majesty's Treasury,
> 2011, p. 6)

Similarly, the Small Business Act of the European Union (EU) states in a 2008 review that

> in the Commission's opinion the mid-term review of the EU's Modern SME [small to medium-sized enterprise] policy from 2005 to 2007 showed that both the Member States and the EU have made progress in creating an SME-friendlier business environment. The Commission has made real efforts to cut red tape for SMEs and has significantly increased the SME focus in major EU support programmes for 2007–2013.
>
> (Borbás, 2009, p. 374)

Therefore, it appears that many Western governments have adopted a role of focusing on improving the effectiveness of economic policy and ensuring that public funds are more effectively expended.

WHERE DOES GROWTH-ENHANCING DEVELOPMENT COME FROM?

Past research provides a pathway for understanding how growth enhances development. For example, in the 1950s it was shown by Abramovitz and Solow that the public-sector process of determining the impact of policy by measuring capital and labor inputs could not account for 90% of economic growth in an advanced industrialized country such as the UK (Abramovitz, 1956; Solow, 1956).

Instead of rejecting this model of growth, policy administrators just added more variables such as technological development to improve the 10% correlation condition; Solow's (1956) theory became known as the "exogenous growth theory" because the variable for technology was inserted exogenously, as a time-dependent trend. Later, the "endogenous" or "new growth" theory was developed to account for the endogenous outcome of investment in variables such as research and development (R&D) and human capital formation.

In the Solow (1956) model, it was assumed that for every additional unit of capital invested, there was a diminishing rate of return, but with the new growth theory, there was an increased return on extra units of capital invested in human capital and technology development. This, in turn, helped explain why different types of dynamic activity, such as automotive manufacture and aircraft manufacture, gave participating businesses and countries a strong competitive advantage through increased productivity through tacit learning.

Furthermore, and as expected, the impact of innovation on growth varies for different types and sizes of businesses, which in turn, has important implications for the many different policies that target support for SMEs. The commonly held belief by government is that small firms are responsible for growth, and although this is partly true, it is only some high-growth small businesses that actually make a difference (NESTA, 2011): A small minority of firms engages in high growth activities, although many of these firms are small in size. The problem is that many government policies aim at targeting incentives and benefits for all SMEs, with the aim of making the economy more innovative and productive; however, the policy is poorly targeted.

THE POLICY CYCLE

"Policy" can include a great number of things across a wide spectrum. This includes things such as ideas communicated during a policy speech, to "a series of interlocking steps, a dialogue between procedures and substance" resulting in partial or total implementation by public sector employees or agency staff (Bridgman & Davis, 2003). It is then the role of governments, agencies, and sometimes organizations to develop strategies for implementation in line with the policies. The aim of government policy is usually to develop policy that support business growth, including polices to assist them with exporting and policies aimed at promoting collaboration among businesses. However, previous research has identified that policy implementation depends on the interpretation of the original message, resource availability, and the existing organizational culture. Poorly defined policies, and/or poorly resourced policies are rarely implemented (Stewart, 2012). Consequently, the original policy objectives are often modified during the implementation phase (Brunetto & Farr-Wharton, 2005; Stewart, 2012).

As decision making has become more complex in public-sector organizations, there has been an increasing need to demonstrate a more formal process of public policy development. Such a process could be used to help new Members of Parliament and new public sector employees to quickly adopt a proven technique and therefore limit wasted time. Early descriptions of this "policy cycle," by Lasswell (1951) and Dror (1968), suggest three phases of the policy process:

- Policy Decision: The present government recognizes the need for a particular policy to be developed and implemented.
- Policy Development: The government undertakes a process of refinement and development of the policy.
- Policy Implementation: The policy is deployed and evaluated for its effectiveness and efficient use of public funds.

Each phase has separate prime activities as shown in Figure 2.1.

This process, however, is not necessarily rational or sequentially staged with a clear beginning and a defined ending. Also, policies are constantly reviewed, subject to dynamic administrative processes, modified, and even terminated in mid-stride. Hence, the stages are often subject to jumps across the cycle and entangled in an ongoing process of priority review. Furthermore, any new policy develops in a political environment of existing policies and will probably modify, change, or supplement older policies and even/or contradict them (Hogwood & Peters, 1983).

New policies tend to create side effects and become the causes of future policy issues not accounted for in the original implementation; for example, a tax on carbon emissions reduces competitiveness of SMEs.

Policy Decision: Problem Recognition and Issue Selection

Policy making presupposes some issue that is unresolved and requires intervention by the public sector to mitigate the effect of that issue on society.

This recognized issue, or problem, will need to be assessed for public benefit and then placed on the government's action agenda. Both issue recognition and its becoming an agenda item are intrinsically political processes in

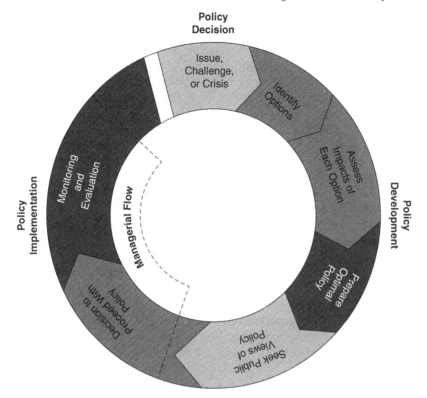

Figure 2.1 The Policy Cycle

which political attention is attached to it and any subsets of all possible relevant "knock-on" policy issues that might arise during the process. Aligning a policy decision with an agenda forces the development of policy strategies and instruments to facilitate implementation.

Policy Development

During this stage of the policy cycle, expressed problems, proposals, and demands are transformed into government options. This includes policy formulation, the definition of objectives, and the consideration of different alternatives. Three options are available for policy development, and these are known as policy instruments.

Policy instruments are the mechanisms policy makers have available to, in theory, influence a positive change to a society and include the following:

- Regulatory instruments: including laws, rules, prohibitions, licenses
- Financial instruments: including subsidies, taxes and tax deductions, user fees, certain types of budgetary expenditure

- Informational instruments: including advertising campaigns, information booklets, or use of the information technology

In many countries, the application of any policy instrument requires a legal underpinning such as a law or regulation in order to be implemented. For this reason, this chapter focuses on impact assessment in the context of legal instruments.

Policy Implementation

The decision on a specific course of action and the adoption of a program does not guarantee that the implementation actions will strictly follow the intended aims and objectives. Policy implementation is more or less "what happens between the establishment of an apparent intention on the part of the government to do something, or to stop doing something, and the ultimate impact in the world of action" (O'Toole, 2000, p. 266).

Policy implementation outcomes are assumed to come from the "top down" (from the minister and senior policy makers through to government employees, who implement the policy exactly as the policy makers intended), the "bottom up" (when government employees at the coalface implement what they believe to be the policy intention to the extent that resourcing and other policy and organizational agendas allow, along with their own preferences based on their experiences and knowledge), or through mixed-model (which combines the two approaches) approaches (Stewart, 2012).

From the perspective of top-down theorists, policies are developed by senior personnel, and implementers implement the policy completely to achieve the stated aims (Sabatier, 2007). Top-down factors usually examined include the quality of the policy objectives, the funding model, and the extent to which the substance of policy is supported by different levels of government (federal, state, and local). The top-down approach argues that government employees implement policies; however, this belief is not supported by the evidence presented by bottom-up-implementation researchers.

Instead, bottom-up implementation researchers believe that public-sector employees influence policy by the way they prioritize and interpret policies and design organizational strategies to implement the polices (Stewart, 2012). In particular, Stewart (2012) argues that unless implementers are willing to implement the policy, there is no way the policy will be implemented. Furthermore, bottom-up-implementation researchers argue that despite increased accountability, implementation outcomes are still dependent on the knowledge and decision making of collections of individual government employees (May & Winter, 2009). Other researchers use a combination of top-down and bottom-up approaches to explain implementation outcomes. Page (2010) framework fits into this category of implementation explanations. Page's (2010) lens perceives outcomes as a reflection of four components (*principles, policy lines, measures,* and *practices*). In summary, there is no perfect model for explaining implementation; however, there are emerging themes that appear important across most implementation literature. For example, implementation requires the "chain of command" to have perfect communication and to understand the mind of the policy formulators. Because this ideal can probably never be met and even controlled for through objectives, programs, laws, and training, the original policy will be subject to change and distortion or full implementation delayed or blocked.

An ideal process of policy implementation would include the following core elements:

- Specification of the implementation details (i.e., who has responsibility for the implementation and how will it be implemented? How should the new laws be interpreted?)
- Allocation of resources (how are budgets distributed? Which personnel will execute the program? Which units of an organization will be in charge for the execution?)
- Decisions (who is responsible for the ongoing decisions required for the implementation such as regulatory instruments, including rules, prohibitions, licenses, etc.; financial instruments, including subsidies, taxes and tax deductions, user fees, certain types of budgetary expenditure; and informational instruments, including advertising campaigns, information booklets, or use of the information technology?)

Evaluation

Policy formulation and its implementation are supposed to improve an identified societal situation beyond the status quo. At least after implementation, policy making should be appraised against its intended objectives and impacts, and this forms the basis for policy evaluation. Evaluation should also be used to identify "best practice" to provide a means of improving future policy initiatives through higher productivity.

Also, with the importance of "knowledge-based" economic activities to economies, it is important to identify how to leverage best-practice policy initiatives.

Hence, evaluation is important to improving the formulating of policy particularly since most governments need to apply budgetary stringency and to better allocate available public resources. Also, evaluation enables the justification of the appropriate role government should play in an economy through accountability, transparency, and the demonstration of a desire to minimize distortions arising from policies.

Evaluation, in the context of policy implementation attempts to quantify "as systematically and objectively as possible the relevance, efficiency and effect of an activity in terms of its objectives, including the analysis of the implementation and administrative management of such activities" (Papaconstantinou & Polt, 1997, p. 10). In this context, evaluation is a systematic and objective process that assesses the relevance, efficiency, and effectiveness of policies or programs in attaining their defined objectives. The evaluation of the outcomes should be able to inform the general policy-making process to contribute to continuous learning of the policy formulation process.

As presented in Figure 2.2, the evaluation process has a direct relation to policy-making and is composed of four steps.

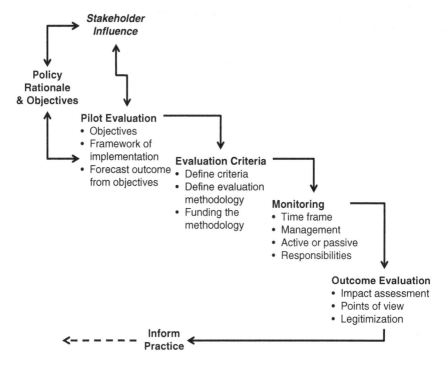

Figure 2.2   The Evaluation Process

In the pilot evaluation phase, the objectives of a policy are confirmed and the framework of implementation is defined. In addition, the potential outcome benefits can be forecast, suggesting the expected efficiency and effectiveness outcomes of the policy. This situation can in turn lead to a timely revision of the policy logic and objectives.

So, although evaluation of policy outcomes would appear to be orderly and rational, in practice, it is subject to considerable bias, subjectivity, and influence from stakeholders. Furthermore, evaluation of administrative management has a tendency to be very subjective (Potter & Storey, 2007), and often overlooked (Storey, 1998). Often, when one side of politics determines that a policy implementation is highly successful, the other side evaluates that same implementation as an unmitigated disaster (e.g., carbon emissions pricing in Australia during 2009–2013).

In attempting to quantify the effectiveness and efficiency of administrative management, it is proposed that a toolkit including Managerial Flow provides a bipartisan approach to determining either a predetermination of the potential issues of management or a post-implementation determination of administrative effectiveness.

MANAGERIAL FLOW

Managerial Assets: Effectiveness and Efficiency Factors

In the 1980s, the success of the Italian public policy initiatives in the development and operation of the collaborative industrial precincts of the Veneto, Emiglio Romano, and Lombardy regions suggested that government should seek to implement policies that have a strong impact on industry development. However, prior to this and subsequently, many similar initiatives a failed in their promise (Guerrieri & Pietrobelli, 2004; Martin & Sunley, 2003; Rolfo & Calabrese, 2003).

Many reasons have been offered to explain the failure of a particular public policy initiative, but most can be interpreted as a failure somewhere in the flow of activities of the implementation process directed through management assets and managerial actions. Many assumptions exist as to the nature of an efficient and effective management process, and some fundamental properties of managers influence a process (Farr-Wharton, 2003).

There are at least three characteristics that relate to a managers ability to achieve flow: These are capacity, competency, and capability that in particular combinations should yield optimum policy implementation outcomes (Argyris & Schön, 1999; Von Krogh, Ichijo, & Nonaka, 2000). However, each of these terms is frequently confused and exchanged when applied to the same issue.

"Capacity" refers to the adequate frequency of resources delivery brought to bear to produce a designed outcome. Capacity is embodied within the **managerial assets** graphic in Figure 2.3.

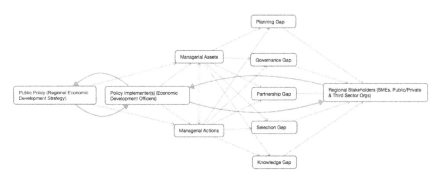

Figure 2.3 The Managerial Flow Process

Capacity directly affects throughput time. Hence, capacity may be viewed as the operational capability of a policy implementation process. The capacity of an implementation flow determines the maximum available operative capability within a particular period. In this sense, the higher the available capacity, the higher the productivity and the shorter the time to implementation. Capacity utilization will have at least three qualitative dimensions:

- Precisional capacity is the amount error (overspend or underspend) or deviation from the particular budget of the process at a particular rate of implementation.
- Dimensional capacity is the load the rate of implementation that the flow can handle in order to maintain a defined level of precisional capacity.
- Variational capacity is the level of operational flexibility remaining for a given rate of implementation and level of precisional capacity.

For management, there are at least two vectors of competency, and three vectors of capability known to improve outcomes. It is assumed that over time, competencies and capabilities are gathered incrementally and assimilated to provide, in the best case, a talented manager or a successful management process. The following are the two components of competency:

- Practitioner Competency: the level of ability to undertake a particular task or related set of tasks
- Methodology Competency: the level of ability to know what to do with the practitioner competency

These two competencies are the result of explicit knowledge transfer from prior learning, can be codified, and reside in user manuals, texts, and standard operating procedures.

Capability refers to the degree of application, using discretion and judgment, of knowledge and skill to produce a standard of required performance; it is the knowledge about doing something and reflecting on its use. The components of capability are an evolving set of knowledge vectors that relate to hunches, feelings, inspiration, and intuition and could be called Managerial Flow–enabling skills, as they are the skills related to successfully undertaking practice and include the following:

- Systematic Capability: the ability to link current work to a strategic output
- Learning Knowledge Capability: the ability to understand a problem, then deploy self-learned solutions reflectively for a successful outcome
- Business-Centered Capability: the ability to consider individual work output to efficiency and effectiveness outcomes

Because these capabilities are gathered over time, at any given time, there will be a certain level of capability that can be deployed dependent on the mental and cognitive processes and are defined in the following:

- Current Potential Capability is the maximum level of capability available by an individual at any given time for a particular task being undertaken.
- Current Applied Capability is the actual level of contribution being applied to a specific activity within a task.
- Future Potential Capability is the predicted level of potential capability of an individual at some time in the future. (Length of service directly relates to quality of output. That is, the longer the term of service, the better the capability and the better the quality of output.)

However, it is unlikely that capability can be quickly transferred if an individual does not have a basic understanding of the explicit skills necessary to undertake a particular type of task and can confidently undertake the task without having to refer to a mentor.

Competency and *capability* have been used interchangeably to describe human operational factors that are important to success. However, competency and capability are separate dimensions of the success factor. Competency is the knowledge about things and the skill of knowing why things are to be done a particular way, when they are to be done and the intended purpose; it is the explicit knowledge gained through training and refers to the level of "know-what" and the "know-when" to apply the what. Thus, competency is embodied in the **knowledge gap** graphic, connected to the **managerial actions** box in the Figure 2.3).

Capability refers to the tacit knowledge gained from experience that can be applied to complete a particular task. Furthermore, when knowledge is applied, competency and capability are mutually dependent on and informed by each other, because competency could not be applied without some capability and in turn, capability would tend to be less effective without some competency.

In this way, capability and competency inform the managerial dimension of agents responsible for developing, managing, and implementing policies. Management in this context is not limited to self-organization but involves the coordination of teams of public servants, SME owner managers, business angels, lobbies, and alliances, among others. In this way, selecting appropriate stakeholders to, for example, pilot development actions or to distribute specific business training, involves a complex interplay between the **managerial assets** (capacity) and **managerial actions** (competency and capability). Under the Managerial Flow framework, this process is conceptualized through the interplay among managerial assets, managerial actions, and **selection gap**, involving regional stakeholders, policy implementers, and policy in the mix (Figure 3.2). Similarly, this same dynamic interplay is present for coordinating partners in development initiatives (**partnership gap**), organizing power structures and feedback loops among stakeholders (**governance gap**), and planning the implementation of policy (**planning gap**).

DISCUSSION

Government decisions to benefit their society have been increasing in complexity since the 1950s, to the extent that a complete new class of problem has been identified—the wicked problem. This type of problem is at best only an optimum solution, never a perfect solution because of continually dynamic conditions. Government policies developed in this type of environment have affect the broad global environment, the country's industry environment, communities, and individuals; attempting to build a policy solution, the government of the day will affect all these levels to differing and evolving degrees.

In such a situation, government officers, who are at best generalists with only some grasp of impact of a particular policy, are relying more and more on specialist expertise to inform policy development and implementation (Page, 2010). Expertise can be technical expertise or policy development or impact. However, it has been observed that such experts derive influence because of their status rather than the content of their expertise (Page, 2010).

Previous research has focused on top-down and bottom-up or mixed models; however, all have been found to be limited in identifying the organizational factors having a negative impact on implementation. The Managerial Flow model provides a means of determining the likely effectiveness of this expertise though conceptualizing the managerial competencies and capabilities involved in implementation management.

REFERENCES

Abramovitz, M. (1956). *Resource and output trends in the United States since 1870.* New York, NY: National Bureau of Economic Research.

Argyris, C., & Schön, D. A. (1999). *On organizational learning.* Boston, MA: Wiley.

Borbás, L. (2009). A critical analysis of the "small business act" for Europe. In *Proceedings—7th International Conference on Management, Enterprise and Benchmarking, Budapest, Hungary* (pp. 373–380). Budapest, Hungary: Óbuda University, Keleti Faculty of Business and Management.

Bridgman, P., & Davis, G. (2003). What Use Is a Policy Cycle? Plenty, if the Aim Is Clear. *Australian Journal of Public Administration, 62*(3), 98–102.

Brunetto, Y., & Farr-Wharton, R. (2005). Implementing business policies within the Australian context: The role of economic development officers within local government. *Journal of Innovation Management, 11*(20), 161–180

Department for Business Innovation & Skills and Her Majesty's Treasury. (2011, March). *The plan for growth.* Retrieved from http://cdn.hm-treasury.gov.uk/2011budget_growth.pdf

Dror, Y. (1968). *Public Policy-Making Reexamined.* Scranton, PA: Chandler.

Farr-Wharton, R. (2003). Multimedia projects and the optimum choice of individuals and teams. *International Journal of Project Management, 21*(4), 271–280.

Hogwood, B., & Peters, G., (1983). *Policy Dynamics.* Wheatsheaf Books, University of Michigan, Mi.

Guerrieri, P., & Pietrobelli, C. (2004). Industrial districts' evolution and technological regimes: Italy and Taiwan. *Technovation, 24*(11), 899–914.

Lasswell, H. (1951). The policy orientation. In D. Lerner & H. Lasswell (Eds.), *The policy sciences* (pp. 3–15). Stanford, CA: Stanford University Press.

Martin, R., & Sunley, P. (2003). Deconstructing clusters: chaotic concept or policy panacea? *Journal of Economic Geography, 3*(1), 5–35.

May, P., Winter, S., (2009). Politicians, Managers, and Street-Level Bureaucrats: Influences on Policy Implementation. *Journal of Public Administration Research and Theory* 19(3), 453-476.

NESTA. (2011, March). *Vital growth: The importance of high growth businesses to recovery* [Research summary]. London: Author.

O'Toole, L. J. (2000). Research on policy implementation. Assessment and prospects. *Journal of Public Administration Research and Theory, 19*(2), 263–288.

Page, E. C. (2010). Bureaucrats and expertise: Elucidating a problematic relationship in three tableaux and six jurisdictions. *Sociologie du travail, 52*(2), 255–273.

Papaconstantinou, G., & Polt, W. (1997). Policy evaluation in innovation and technology: An overview. In *Conference Policy Evaluation in Innovation and Technology, Capítulo* (Vol. 1, pp. 9–14). Paris, France: Science and Technology Policy Division, Organisation for Economic Co-operation and Development.

Potter, J. G., & Storey, D. J. (2007). *OECD framework for the evaluation of SME and entrepreneurship policies and programmes.* Paris, France: Publications de l'OCDE.

Rolfo, S., & Calabrese, G. (2003). Traditional SMEs and innovation: The role of the industrial policy in Italy. *Entrepreneurship & Regional Development, 15*(3), 253–271.

Sabatier, P. (2007). *Theories of Policy Process.* Westview Press, Colorado. Solow R, (1956). A contribution to the theory of economic growth. *Quarterly Journal of Economics, 70*(1), 65–94.

Stewart, J. (2012). Multiple-case study methods in governance related research. *Public Management Review, 14*, 67–82.

Storey, D. (1998). *Six steps to heaven: Evaluating the impact of public policies to support small businesses in developed countries* (Warwick Business School Working Paper 59). Coventry, England: Warwick Business School, University of Warwick.

Von Krogh, G., Ichijo, K., & Nonaka, I. (2000). *Enabling knowledge creation: How to unlock the mystery of tacit knowledge and release the power of innovation.* New York, NY: Oxford University Press.

3 Making Sense of the Complexity of Managerial Flow

The Case of Urban Regeneration in the UK

Alyson Nicholds

INTRODUCTION

The idea of managerial flow incorporates the managerial assets and actions involved in the policy implementation process to highlight the importance of more complex matters of strategy, governance, selection, coordination, and communication (Vecchi and Brusoni, 2012). Part of the value of articulating the decision-making process in this more nuanced way is that it challenges overly rationalist assumptions that the policy decision making process occurs in a *linear and sequential way* and that decision-making process is rooted in *mathematical logic*—that is, that *a* + *b* = *c* (all of which leads to an expectation of *reaching a singular outcome* on grounds that "rational choice drives self-interest"; Stone, 2002).

In keeping with the idea that not only is reality more complex but that there is also a much wider range of actors involved (Arganoff & McGuire, 1998) and that this is based on networks of collaboration (Ansell & Gash, 2007), we argue that by also paying attention to the importance of values in the framing and evaluation of policy, we can consider the human interpretation involved, in addition to the context. By "human interpretation," what Stone (2002) is referring to here, is how "each of the analytic standards that we use to set goals, define problems and judge solutions is politically constructed and there is no gold standard of equity, efficiency, social measurement, causation, effectiveness or anything else" (p. 40). By pointing out the potential for disagreement and lack of consensus involved in any political decision making process, Stone (2002) draws on the work of sensemaking theorists (see Yanow, 1996, 2000 Fischer, 1993; Hajer & Wagenaar, 2003) to ask, "How in terms of goods, services, wealth and income, health and illness, opportunity and disadvantage do we go about deciding who gets what?"

Using the analogy of sharing out a cake with her students, Stone (2002) shows how the goal of equity is rooted in the concept of distribution and as such relies on assumptions of fairness (which are ultimately contested). Hence, it is difficult to divide the cake fairly when opinions differ so widely about what access to opportunity, status, gender, preference, and availability actually mean.

In this chapter, I build on Vecchi and Brusoni's (2012) idea about the need to challenge the "overly rational" tendency of policy by drawing on more complex models of policy decision making, and seek to examine their ideas about managerial flow through this lens of sensemaking in the context of urban regeneration. The chapter begins with an overview of the nature of sensemaking along with some empirical examples of its application in the wider field of policy implementation. Then, after a brief précis of the regeneration case under study, the value of managerial flow is explored through a sense-making lens.

MAKING SENSE OF POLICY

The idea that policy actors make sense of policy decisions differently is well documented in the policy sciences (Fischer & Forrester, 1993; Hajer & Wagenaar, 2003). Writing in a more critical vein, Yanow (1996) echoes the importance of analyzing the human values underpinning policy by stating how "too much of policy analysis, implementation studies and descriptions of the policy process is shaped by the assumption that all human interaction is literal and instrumentally rational" (p. 8). In her book *How Does a Policy Mean?* Yanow (1996) reminds us of the importance of human perception in guiding how agencies state problems and solutions, suggesting that as humans we interpret the world around us using past experience, training, and insight. Consequently, Yanow argues that by exploring the hidden rituals and symbols and understandings expressed through the things actors "say and do," it is possible to surface the implicit "values, beliefs and feelings that a group holds, believes in and practices" (2000, p. 15).

TAKEN-FOR-GRANTED ASSUMPTIONS OF POLICY

One reason for the need for such human interpretation, or "sensemaking," as it is known, is because of the potentially symbolic nature of policy (Mossberger & Stoker, 1997) that fails to produce any "real" outcomes (Atkinson, 2000, p. 230). By way of an example, Colebatch (1995) examines the concept of "programme evaluation," showing how, as an organisational phenomenon, it is rooted in taken-for-granted assumptions about the intentions of organisations. For instance, Colebatch (1995, p. 49) notes the following:

- *Policy is about problem solving*—It is assumed that we have policies because there are problems that need to be solved and these problems are independent of the structures created to deal with them.
- *Policy centres on intentions and choices*—Authorised leaders are seen as confronting these problems by clarifying their intentions about the

preferred outcomes, and making choices about the course of action to be taken in order to get there.

- *Organisations exist to give effect to policy intentions*—Organisations are seen as the instruments of policy makers created to give effect to their intentions . . . in other words, their "raison d'etre."
- *Policy is expressed through programmes*—In order to implement policy, organisational activity is (or ought to be) gathered into programmes, which express more specifically the intentions of the policy makers.
- *Programmes are evaluated in terms of intentions and outcomes*—since programmes are seen as arising from the intentions of policy makers to solve problems, these can be evaluated in terms of the correlation between the problems, the intentions and the outcomes.

STORYLINES AS WAYS OF SEEING POLICY

The idea that policy is filled with such "taken-for-granted assumptions" reminds us of the need to resist the urge to rush to interpretation by listening carefully to the various stories which are invoked by different policies, and to use this as a prelude to becoming aware of the way that theories might serve to focus our attention on some things at the expense of others (Forrester, 1993, p. 187). This brings us to another important facet of symbolism in policy: that of storylines. For example, Forrester (1993, p. 188) talks about the way in which planners and analysts make policy when they "talk and listen to others talk" through the stories they tell one another. Forrester shows how in doing so, we use these stories not only to build moral claims/arguments to support a particular position but also as a means of making sense of injustices and issues and justify a particular course of action. In keeping with Yanow (1996, 2000) and others, this is inherently bound up in the traditional culture and professional background from which these actors emerge, as he describes:

> We can think of listening in on a staff meeting as a way getting inside the organisational mind of the planners, getting to know both how they perceive the situation they're in and how they begin to act on the problems they face.
>
> (Forrester, 1993, p. 192)

The role that such stories play in making sense of policy is that there is much to be gained from seeking views about how actors make sense of the *nature and success* of policy goals. Such approaches are rooted social constructivist epistemology based on the human agency that people have in order to reflect on their situation and make decisions about the nature of cause and effect (Williams & May, 1996) For instance, Kaplan (1993) uses the analogy of the courtroom context to show how legal stories must not only have "beginnings middles and ends" but also coherence and consistency in order for them to make sense and to be believed. Hajer (1993) refers to these different story-lines as "discourses," or ways of talking about a problem. In his exploration of the acid rain debate, he attempts to show how different interpretations of the causes and effects of acid rain can be built around different "discourse coalitions" in terms of "what is" (scientific discourse), "how it can be fixed" (engineering discourse), "what the cost is to society" (economic discourse), and, finally, "whether or not it should be tackled" (political discourse). This reminds us of the need to remain epistemologically reflexive about the under-pinning assumptions that might be driving policy (Nicholds, 2013).

The value of this more discursive approach to policy is confirmed in a study by Linder (1995), whose investigation into the role of electromagnetic frequencies (EMF) in the causation of cancer, showed the presence of five discourses or "communities of meaning," as he called them, each of which framed the debate differently depending on participants' professional back-grounds, technical expertise, and political interests. For instance, critics of the power industry referred to the EMF problem as a "Public Health emer-gency" whereas those within the power industry reserved their judgment that "there was inconclusive scientific research" to raise public concern.

"FRAMING" AS A COURSE OF ACTION

One of the reasons for "making explicit" the otherwise "implicit" language used by practitioners in describing what they do is because it has the capacity to dictate a prescribed course of action. For instance, Yanow (2000) shows how "language shapes perceptions and prescribes actions" (i.e., use of the language of "decay" implies the need for some degree of "treating or preserv-ing" by a "specialist" or a "doctor"). Similarly, in the analogy of "broken homes" lies an assumption that something is in need of physical repair:

> Contending frames entail not just different policy discourses (language, understandings, perceptions) and different courses of action but also different values and meanings.
>
> (Yanow, 2000, p. 12)

MULTIPLE MEANINGS

Taking this seemingly important idea about the power of assumptions fur-ther, Stone (2002, p. 137) shows that by shifting to a more sensemaking focus it is possible to focus on the hidden symbolism in policy and the role it plays in *mediating the meaning* of policy. Such symbolism, she argues, features in the form of four constituents visible in any policy statement:

- *Narrative stories*, which embody taken for granted assumptions of "how the world works"

- *Synecdoches*, or figures of speech in policy in which a small issue is representative of a larger one
- *Metaphors*, or "a likeness between two things"
- *Ambiguity*, or the ability of policy to hold dual meanings

Some empirical studies have attempted to demonstrate exactly how these "figures of speech," "metaphors," or "dual meanings" manifest in practice. One study by Jeanette Hofman (1995, p. 137) shows how assumptions about the nature of competitive relations between universities and the business sector in Germany led to misunderstandings about the role of universities as the "giver of technology":

> According to this construct, termed the "cascade model" by Hack (1988), the cradle of new technologies is situated in the laboratories of basic research institutions and universities. The business community, according to the next assumption, takes up this knowledge—seen as a freely tradable and transferable good—and translates it through applied research and/ or development into innovations i.e. marketable products.
>
> (p. 130)

By exploring the narratives of staff working within universities and small and medium-sized enterprises (SMEs) in the tool and dye industry, Hofman (1995) found that contrary to the idea of universities being at the cutting edge of new technology development, they were actually operating on the periphery, owing to the limited ability of businesses to commission external research to universities and the financial risk involved. As a result, because of the needs of business to continually "road-test" different aspects of production on an ongoing basis, in practice it was often businesses (rather than universities) that emerged as the "technological innovators." Running somewhat counter to the competitive image implied by German government in its stated technology policy, the relationship between universities and business actually operated on more of a mutual exchange.

Instead, what universities were able to offer was a much more cost-effective research proposal to companies over the longer term (i.e., through less risky ventures) because they were not subject to the same degree of market competition that other firms were exposed to. Through the use of sensemaking, what Hofman (1995, pp. 140–142) exposes here is the ultimate paradox where "those whose job it is to develop and sell technology are observed to have a different understanding than those responsible for the administrative promotion of technological change (i.e., governments)." In short, what this valuable study reveals is how the "internal logic" of government serves to conceal the "real" endeavor by universities *not* to act as technological innovators though world-class research but, instead, seek to interact with business on the basis of earned income based on an awareness of their "real" commercial value.

THE CASE OF UK URBAN REGENERATION

In keeping with the findings of Vecchi and Brusoni (2012) and claims that the effectiveness of the implementation process is hampered by managerial gaps, UK urban regeneration saw critics of the last Labour government lamenting the experimental, short-term and spatially targeted nature of regeneration policies (Diamond & Liddle, 2005, both through neighborhood renewal and the more multilevel approach to growth through urban renaissance (Hastings, 2007, p. 85). Despite these ongoing and repeated claims of symbolic policy (Atkinson, 2000; Mossberger & Stoker, 1997), in 2010, the incoming coalition government reaffirmed its pledge to continue with regeneration, noting the value that it can bring in "reversing economic, social and physical decay in areas where it has reached a stage when market forces alone will not suffice" (Communities for Local Government, 2010). Subsequently adopting the term the *3Rs* (regeneration, renewal, and regional development), the emphasis was on "rebalancing the economy" through local growth, privatism (an increasing reliance on the private sector), and localism as laid out in the Local Growth White Paper (Department for Business, Innovation & Skills, 2010).

By making sense of some of the complexity involved in managerial flow, the aim is to seek multiple (rather than singular) views of the importance of strategy, selection, coordination, and communication, allowing the specific *managerial actions* involved (i.e., assessing, reviewing, planning, and reviewing) and the *managerial assets* generated by these actions (i.e., knowledge, leadership, and informal learning) to be identified.

A Sense of Sense in Managerial Flow

Using the data reported here, gathered from interviews with actors working under the previous government, I explore how they made sense of symbolism in their continued efforts to design and deliver "effective" urban policy (Nicholds, 2011, 2012). The study design was based on a selected case study of regeneration within one of the nine (since dissolved) administrative English regions, based on their capacity to provide a sufficiently large and bounded site, covering three major cities and around 10% of the UK population. Each city was, at the time, in receipt of major regeneration funding (Economic and Social Research Council and Neighbourhood Renewal Funding) owing to their past experience of economic and industrial decline. Interviews were conducted with 50 regeneration practitioners who had a wide range of experience (ranging from 1 to 20 years) across a wide range of government-led programs including Neighbourhood Renewal, Economic Development, and Urban Renaissance and operating at a number of different scales at regional, district, and local neighborhood levels. Interviews lasted between 45 and 60 minutes and sought to build a rich picture of the context in which the "situated talk" about their experiences of designing and delivering regeneration could be examined.

Using sensemaking, the analysis of common codes could be further divided into familiar patterns of narrative (Yanow, 1996) to form discourses, each having similar ontology's, beliefs and practices (Dryzek, 1993) and revealing differences in actors interpretations about the way regeneration work was done (see Table 3.1). For instance, out of the 50 actors interviewed, 18 described their work in terms of an "increasing economic opportunity" discourse, 24 described their work in terms of a "narrowing the gap through service improvement" discourse, and 8 described their work in terms of a "building community capacity" discourse. Each discourse was distinguishable by the nature of their assumptions, the beliefs about cause and effect and the ways of framing of solutions. Through use of the concept of managerial flow, it is possible to making sense of why these views might have differed in relation to matters of strategy, governance, resources, coordination, and communication; the managerial actions involved; and the assets generated in terms of knowledge, leadership, and informal learning (Vecchi & Brusoni, 2012).

Discourse 1: Increasing Economic Opportunity Through City Regions

The first discourse to emerge, perceived regeneration as tackling economic disadvantage through attempts to build competitive "city regions" through inward investment. This was premised on assumptions about the need to raise the aspirations of young people whom actors saw as being "trapped in a cycle of poverty" because of generations of unemployment. This produced a storyline about the contribution that training and skills can make to building *entrepreneurial communities*:

> If you make the conditions as such that firms want to relocate there because you have an offer that's acceptable to any, you make the area attractive and you've made the population attractive in terms of skills to "would be" employers.
>> (DS1, Director, Urban Regeneration Company 297)

> What we want to offer is prolonged enterprise training to help people to train to start up their own businesses.
>> (DS14, Manager, Economic Development 46)

> You have to give the opportunity for people to improve their economic prospects in order for them to take advantage of things on offer.
>> (DS72, Director, Economic Development)

However, difficulties arose in the form of a lack of strategy, concerning poor economic growth due to recession, a lack of real jobs because of a

Table 3.1 Making Sense of the Discourses of Managerial Flow in UK Regeneration

The five gaps in managerial flow (Vecchi & Brusoni, 2012)	Sensemaking DISCOURSE 1 (18 actors)	Sensemaking DISCOURSE 2 (24 actors)	Sensemaking DISCOURSE 3 (8 actors)
STRATEGY (i.e., Short-termist, fashion)	"Increasing economic opportunity" by building city regions	"Narrowing the gap" through service improvement	"Building community capacity" through social enterprise
GOVERNANCE (i.e., Confusion over roles/responsibility)	Interference from central government	Failure to demonstrate public accountability, lack of community involvement	Double counting of success
SELECTION (i.e., Resources not allocated appropriately)	Bureaucratic	Lack of strategy leading to the duplication of efforts and the wasting of resources	Lack of sustainable funding
COORDINATION (i.e., Lack of leadership, legitimacy or trust)	Lack of coordination of efforts to improve joint working and reduce silo mentality	Failure to communicate new services coming on stream	Lack of autonomy to respond flexibly to need, lack of trust from statutory sector partners
COMMUNICATION (i.e., players pushed to operate on different wavelengths)	Connecting up the global with the local	Brokering	Raising awareness of the third sector

local skills mismatch, and a failure to generate entrepreneurial communities because of a lack of economic opportunity, as the following narrative demonstrates:

> It's going to take longer than we thought . . . we've got all the plans . . . but it's just that we've got to get some private money to develop it, and that's taking more time . . . if the credit crunch had been a little bit later, we would have been up and running.
>
> (DS19, Manager, Economic Development 286)

> Those who have very little skills . . . are the hardest to reach . . . the lowest levels of skills are the hardest to help and one would say that it's those who . . . have benefitted least on the basis that what is being created in this modern economy are not jobs that require no skills.
>
> (DS1, Executive, Urban Regeneration Company 122)

> [The area] where it didn't work, you had nothing to begin with. You had a very stressed community, a lot of issues around settled travelling communities . . . basically, the community with the greatest need was actually the one that was least able to take [advantage] of the opportunities.
>
> (DS4, Elected Member, Local Authority 105)

Complaints about the bureaucratic nature of public-sector organizations can be linked to gaps in governance where one actor noted a clash of values between the private and public sector in terms of the pace of change and the delays this caused in terms of planning, as a result of waiting to draw down funds. These issues were associated with a lack of coordination of efforts to improve joint working and reduce silo mentality:

> The local authority is such a bureaucratic organisation. I mean for instance, this building has got 24 reception points! The bloke who turns up at the counter—just comes in on a whim and decides he wants to invest 50 million pound in the city—what chance has he got of getting through all that bureaucracy?
>
> (DS3, Planning Manager, Local Authority 155)

Not only were these beliefs fuelled by assumptions about the benefits of wealth creation, but they were also seen to be addressed by better knowledge and leadership about how we might better connect the global with the local:

> The amount of international companies are very limited, even the amount of big companies are very limited, actually the growth tends to

come from a very small area. I'd be very surprised if many companies relocate to [name of city] outside of a 25 mile radius

> (DS1, Executive, Urban Regeneration Company 315)

Discourse 2: Narrowing the Gap Through Service Improvement

In contrast to the first discourse (which talked of the importance of tackling economic inequality), the second discourse placed a high value on the role that public services (or welfare) might play in tackling inequalities in health. Here, in contrast to the first discourse (where assumptions were linked to a lack of aspiration), assumptions about a lack of access to service provision were linked to storyline about the need to tackle health inequalities by "narrowing the gap" in life expectancy and quality of life:

> We talk about regeneration policy, about working with our partners in the local authority, the PCT, the police and others, about how they're delivering their services in the area—in a way that helps to narrow the gap that I've talked about.
>
> (DS11, Manager, Area-Based Initiative 68)

This framed the nature of solutions differently, in that instead of focusing on "training and skills to build capacity" (as in the first discourse), regeneration was seen a means of achieving service improvement by securing resources for public investment through the involvement of communities in service design:

> In terms of new services coming in, that showed a great potential in answering a number of the deprivation indices that are exhibited here.
>
> (DS17, Manager, Area Based Initiative 114)

As the final quote demonstrates, managerial actions involved the detailed analysis of spatial data combined with the process of needs assessment, all with the aim of targeting what were seen as limited public resources:

> It's about making the right interventions in the right way . . . you're never going to get it 100% right but you can through a combination of interpreting data, reading signals on the ground . . . have a strategic overview at a city level.
>
> (DS39, Service Manager, Local Authority 209)

> Most of what we do that works is about sitting down with people and . . . exploring with them what works for them.
>
> (DS 11, Manager, Area Based Initiative)

However gaps, associated with a lack of a strategy, led to actors seeking quick wins for the program (see first quote that follows). This resulted in the duplication of efforts and the subsequent wasting of resources (see second quote):

> There was a pressure to spend money at the beginning and come up with a programme quite quickly and clearly, if it's going to be community led, it takes time to gather the evidence that you need to ensure that what you're going to spend is what the community needs.
>
> (DS11, Manager, Area Based Initiative 253)

> I am surprised by that lack of coordination of those services going in, talking to each other and that lack of overview and strategic plan of how you're going to maximise those training and learning opportunities.

The failure to adopt a strategic approach with the communities generated further problems that resulted in the poor communication of new neighborhood services. Ironically, this lack of communication prevented communities from accessing new services coming on stream such as general practitioners (GP) surgeries, schools and leisure provision, things this discursive community was seeking to achieve!

> Outside of what we're instigating here, there is not a newsletter that goes to every household, there's no level of communication to "joe public" who lives in the surrounding district.
>
> (DS17, Manager, Area Based Initiative 323)

From a governance perspective, there was also a failure to communicate the benefits of improvements to service provision in terms of democratic accountability. This was reflected in talk about the importance of financial probity to government in which actors frequently referred to the importance of "lines of accountability" to central and regional government departments and the local authority as accountable body (all of which seemed to be rooted in assumptions about the importance of demonstrating success to the electorate):

> I couldn't run and hide when [name of car manufacturing company] broke—it would have been a fundamental rejection about what we are about. It's the same with [name of car manufacturing company]—we're mitigating the social impacts of closure through advice and community involvement.
>
> (DS39, Project Manager, Economic Development 39)

In terms of an "effective storyline," actors could frequently be witnessed lamenting their experience of the "pain" of securing highly competitive resources from central government in tandem with the "pleasure" of winning successful bids. Success for this community was seen not in terms of "increasing economic opportunity" (as with the first discourse) but, rather, in terms of "getting large chunks of money onto the estate," even though, in reality, this often only represented a fraction of mainstream spending. In leadership terms, future action was perceived by better brokering between service providers. Here, actors "at the coalface" saw themselves as having the capacity to offer practical help to improve collaboration between partners.

> It's about the connectivity there and neighbourhood management . . .
> we're getting more sophisticated about how we do things.
> (DS39, Project Manager, Economic Development 396)

Discourse 3: Building Community Capacity Through Social Enterprise

The third discourse can be seen in terms of "social enterprise" working in the voluntary and community sector (VCS) where actors placed a high value on adopting a needs-led approach with a view to securing greater resources for communities. Unlike the previous two discursive communities, assumptions here were rooted in the failure of statutory sectors to adequately meet community needs through existing service provision. This invoked a storyline about the need for development work to build community capacity, as these quotes describe:

> We created these networks that cover the whole of the city . . . there
> are 90 membership groups and they can vary from an allotment society
> to social enterprise, and Residential Social Landlords [RSL] or training
> companies
> (DS35, Officer, Local Authority 277)

> There was a hardware store full of pigeons but I needed accommodation myself, admin staff, communities to engage with the workers, so
> we used Single Regeneration Budget funding to renovate the upstairs.
> (DS48, Community Activist 23)

One of the main values underpinning this needs-led approach was the relative autonomy it offered in remaining flexible to community need:

> I guess the services we provide are the services that are needed and they
> aren't mainstream like other providers.
> (DS16, Manager, Voluntary Sector Provider 16)

However, from the perspective of strategy, it was this also this desire for autonomy that created the most difficulties for this group, not only because of the short term funding regimes offered by public bodies (see first quote that follows) but also because of a lack of perceived trust to manage resources adequately (see second and third quote):

> There's no funding for what we do . . . none at all. All our jobs end in March . . . but it's been like that for 19 years.
> (DS42, Director, Voluntary Sector Provider 446)

> Everything had to go through those area managers and then when the NDCs [New Deal for Communities] came that was the same.
> (DS48, Community Activist 494)

> The organisation applied for some SRB [Single Regeneration Budget] monies and put together a comprehensive programme [but] the local authority said "we don't want a VCS [Voluntary and Community Services] group running it."
> (DS48, Community Activist 12)

Also there were governance complaints about the lack of rigor in the government's monitoring of performance related targets. This was typified by frequent reference to national training providers that had been awarded national contracts by government (in preference to VCS providers) to supply job-skills training but who were suspected of gaming. This was alleged to have been done by placing clients in temporary jobs internally on a minimum wage (in order to achieve government targets so that funds could be drawn down; DS42, 909) and by "double counting" the numbers of people involved when their "output" had already been recorded elsewhere (DS42, 919):

> There's so many people [providers] robbing the system and there's so many fiddle[s] going on.
> (DS42, Director, Voluntary Sector Provider 909)

In making sense of this complexity, there was a sense that if long-term sustainability could be built, the sector could be more self-sufficient in tackling inequality, by generating business that would last (DS48):

> We've got to be clear about who are the right people, that can generate businesses that are going to employ our youth and it may be that those are community based things which have got some sustainability in terms of need
> (DS48, Community Activist 624)

In contrast to other discourses, actors in this community perceived that the only way to increase their role in service provision was through educating other sectors about their unique way of operating and inherent value base. This invoked a storyline that the statutory sector did not understand the nature of third-sector business (DS48, 646) or indeed what social enterprise was (DS42, 768):

> Those economic papers [from the Regional Development Agency] don't come down to this level.
>
> (DS48, Community Activist 584)

CONCLUSION

That sensemaking revealed not one but three views of urban regeneration was not, in itself, surprising, given the well-documented nature of past approaches by New Labour, not to mention the current coalition's 3Rs—that is, regeneration, renewal, and regional—development. What was surprising was the highly nuanced nature of the assumptions and beliefs revealed within these three discourses, how they seemingly privilege very different storylines about cause and effect, and how this serves to frame very different understandings of the urban problem.

By looking at the concept of managerial flow through the lens of sensemaking, not only can we examine these different discourses in greater depth, but we can also see the epistemological assumptions driving beliefs about cause and effect (Nicholds, 2013; or "internal logics" as Dryzek, 1993, describes it, in which discourses have similar ontologies, beliefs, and practices). This allows us not only to analyze how each discourse differs in terms of the managerial gaps that arise (i.e., strategy, governance, resources, coordination, and communication) but also to explore the often contradictory nature of the *managerial actions* involved (i.e., what managers actually did to try resolve issues) and what *managerial assets were generated as a result* (i.e., such as knowledge, leadership, and informal learning). For instance, it is easy to see how assumptions about a lack of aspirations concerning entrepreneurial opportunity in Discourse 1 could be tempered by the efforts of Discourse 3 by those who work hard to understand communities, build networks to access communities, and assess their needs (and who, in doing so, subsequently make very different assumptions about the ability of communities to actively take part in economic opportunities that arise).

This is the same in Discourse 2, noted by those whose interventions often failed because of a lack coordination surrounding community involvement. This again could be easily resolved by better working with actors espousing Discourse 3, whose assumptions are founded in the importance of community networks and so already have access to a wide range of local community members from different socioeconomic backgrounds. In this sense, the assumptions of Discourse 3, "that other sectors need educating about the VCS," is probably well founded. This more nuanced, reflexive, and contextualized form of analysis is permitted by using a sensemaking approach applied to managerial flow.

REFERENCES

Ansell, C., & Gash, A. (2007). Collaborative governance in theory and practice. *Journal of Public Administration Research and Theory, 18,* 543–571.

Arganoff, R., & McGuire, M. (1998). Multi-network management: Collaboration and the hollow state in local economic policy. *Journal of Public Administration Research and Theory, 1,* 67–91.

Atkinson, R. (2000) Narratives of policy: The construction of urban problems and regeneration policy in the official discourse of British Government 1968-1998. *Critical Social Policy, 63 (20),* 211–230.

Colebatch, H. (1995). Organisational meanings of program evaluation. *Policy Sciences, 28*(2), 149–164.

Communities for Local Government. (2010). *Valuing the benefits of regeneration* (Economic Paper no. 7). London, England: Her Majesty's Stationery Office.

Department for Business, Innovation & Skills. (2010). *Local growth: Realising every place's potential* (Cm 7961, Local Growth White Paper). London, England: Her Majesty's Government. Retrieved from https://www.gov.uk/government/uploads/system/uploads/attachment_data/file/32076/cm7961-local-growth-white-paper.pdf

Diamond, J. and Liddle, J. (2005) Management of regeneration: Choices, challenges and dilemmas. Abingdon: Routledge

Dryzek, J. (1993). Policy analysis and planning: From science to argument. In F. Fischer & J. Forrester (Eds.), *The argumentative turn in policy analysis and planning* (pp. 213–232). Durham, NC: Duke University Press.

Fischer, F. (1993). Policy discourse and the politics of Washington think tanks. In F. Fischer & J. Forrester (Eds.), *The argumentative turn in policy analysis and planning* (pp. 21–42). Durham, NC: Duke University Press

Forrester, J. (1993). Learning from practice stories. In F. Fischer & J. Forrester (Eds.), *The argumentative turn in policy analysis and planning* (pp. 186–209). Durham, NC: Duke University Press.

Hajer, M. (1993). Discourse coalitions and the institutionalization of practice: The case of acid-rain in Great Britain. In F. Fischer & J. Forrester (Eds.), *The argumentative turn in policy analysis and planning* (pp.43–76). Durham, NC: Duke University Press.

Hajer, M., & Wagenaar, H. (2003). *Deliberative policy analysis: Understanding governance in the network society* (Theories of Institutional Design). Cambridge, England: Cambridge University Press.

Hastings, A. (2007) Territorial justice and environmental services: An exploration of environmental service provision to deprived and better-off neighbourhoods in the UK. *Environment and Planning C, Government and Policy, 25,* 896–917.

Hofman, J. (1995). Implicit theories in policy discourse: An inquiry into the interpretation of reality in German technology policy. *Policy Sciences, 28,* 127–148.

Kaplan, J. (1993) Reading policy narratives: Beginnings, middles, and Ends In: F. Fischer & J. Forrester (Eds.), *The argumentative turn in policy analysis and planning* (pp. 167–185). Durham, NC: Duke University Press.

Linder, S. (1995). Contending discourses in the electric and magnetic fields controversy: The social construction of EMF risk as a public problem. *Policy Sciences, 28*(2), 209–230.

Mossberger, K., & Stoker, G. (1997). Inner city policy in Britain: Why it will not go away. *Urban Affairs Review, 33*(3), 378–402.

Nicholds, A. (2011). Making sense of urban policy in complex times. *Regional Insights, 2*(2), 18-20.

Nicholds, A. (2012). *Building capacity for regeneration: Making sense of ambiguity in urban policy outcomes* (Doctoral thesis). Institute of Local Government Studies, University of Birmingham, Birmingham, England.

Nicholds, A. (2013). 'The way we do things around here': Personal and epistemological reflections of the influence of inter-disciplinary identity on effective knowledge leadership for tackling inequalities. In J. Diamond & J. Liddle (Ed.), *Looking for consensus? Civil society, social movements and crises for public management* (Critical Perspectives on International Public Sector Management, Vol. 2, pp. 141–160). London, England: Emerald Group Publishing Limited.

Stone, D. (2002). *Policy paradox: The art of political decision making.* London, England: W. W. Norton.

Vecchi, V., & Brusoni, M. (2012). The managerial flow of public local development policies: A conceptual framework. *Singapore Management Review, Asia Pacific Journal of Management Theory and Practice, 34*(2), 5–13.

Williams, M., & May, T. (1996). *Introduction to the philosophy of social science.* London, England: UCL Press.

Yanow, D. (1996) *How does a policy mean? Interpreting policy and organizational actions.* Washington, DC: Georgetown University Press.

Yanow, D. (2000). *Conducting interpretive policy analysis* (Qualitative Research Methods Series, 47). London, England: Sage.

Part II

Innovation and Managerial Flow

4 Implementing Innovation Policy
The Function of Strategic Orientation, Networks, and Relationships

Stephen Kelly, Jennifer Scott, Jakob Trischler, and Natalie Wojtarowicz

INTRODUCTION

The Managerial Flow framework (MFF) was designed to facilitate improved implementation of public policies through proactive management of planning, governance, selection, partnership, and knowledge gaps (Vecchi & Brusoni, 2012). As expounded by the framework, this is achieved through undertaking managerial decisions and actions that generate managerial assets. For the purpose of this research, the MFF was used as a lens to analyze a planning gap and the implementation of an innovation policy through an emergent enabling strategy. The enabling strategy formed part of a broader economic development plan developed by a substantive Australian local government authority (LGA).

Historically, planning and strategy were seen as mechanisms that allowed organizations to harness and deploy resources and achieve a competitive advantage over the medium to long term (French 2009a, 2009b). Within the MFF, the planning gap represents a contemporary conceptualization of strategy and strategizing, which foregoes mechanistic planning processes potentially suggested by the categorization. Rather, planning, strategy, and strategizing are recognized as processes that allow organizations to identify and pursue opportunities that fit the organization's mission with demonstrable agility.

Limitations of an historical approach to planning, strategy, and strategizing are accentuated if the planning gap is associated with the implementation of an innovation policy, which is defined by the European Commission on Enterprise and Industry as being focused on helping companies perform better and contribute to wider social objectives such as growth, jobs, and sustainability (Enterprise and Industry, 2013). By its very nature innovation, policy is concerned with responsiveness and agility, is influenced by complex market forces, and is tasked with the conceptualization and commercialization of new ideas, products, and services. As such, it is arguable that a public-sector organization that maintains a traditional approach to planning will be unable to implement effective innovation polices because the opportunity, market, or technology will have matured or been overtaken by newer innovations before an effective response is actioned.

Public policy practitioners who are focused on innovation, therefore, face several challenges. Included in these is the development of innovation policies that are generally cognizant of the MFF and, as a subset, the extant strategic orientation. Organizations must consider how their strategic orientation, and that of relevant actors, may affect the creation and implementation of innovation policies as well as the conceptualization, development, and commercialization of innovations within complex adaptive markets. The strategic orientation is a significant issue, because it will directly influence managerial actions and deployment of managerial assets depicted within the MFF and, specifically, the planning gap. Therefore, consideration of strategic orientation as an inherent factor influencing a planning gap is central to understanding the effectiveness of innovation policy implementation within an LGA.

Likewise, within the context of a LGA, the role of networks and relationships involving private, not-for-profit, and public organizations will influence the effectiveness of innovation policy implementation. By acting as an intermediary, an LGA can facilitate and initiate policy development and enhance implementation effectiveness by leveraging resources evident within the networks. The importance of intermediaries within the innovation system has been highlighted in the Australian context by Howard and Partners (2007) with local governments being potentially substantive intermediaries. Therefore, consideration of how an LGA activates networks and relationships as an intermediary charged with implementing innovation policies would appear to be a component part of understanding issues inherent within the MFF generally and, more specifically, the planning gap.

In this study, we evaluated a substantive Australian LGA tasked with developing an economic development policy that included a specific focus on innovation. This aligned with our research aim, which was to investigate the development and implementation of innovation policy within the context of the MFF. To pursue this aim, we reviewed literature focused on innovation, innovation policy, networks, and relationships.

LITERATURE REVIEW

Innovation has been identified as a driver of economic growth and as a potential solution to pressing societal challenges such as climate change and ageing populations (Organisation for Economic Co-operation and Development, 2011). Thus, a government's decision to foster innovation through respective policies and incentives can be considered a strategic opportunity to promote economic development and growth within its borders. Traditionally, there have been various approaches to designing and implementing innovation policies based on different theoretical frameworks. Although policies targeted at increasing investment in research and development in the private sector are rooted in Schumpeterian endogenous growth theory, the neo-Marshallian approach favors policies directed at promoting the establishment of business clusters (Manjon & Merino, 2012).

As a response to these standard economic frameworks, the concept of national innovation systems (NIS) was developed (Godin, 2009; Lundvall, 2007). Given the intention to set the scene for an economic policy identifying innovation and learning "as important processes behind economic growth and welfare" (Lundvall, 2007, p. 97), the NIS places particular emphasis on networks of institutions whose interaction and cooperation initiate and diffuse knowledge and new technologies (Freeman, 1987; Lundvall, 1992; Nelson, 1993). Even though various nuances of meaning have been attached to this concept, three characteristics are inherent and significant in every definition. These include the involvement of a variety of private- and public-sector actors, the interactions between these actors, and the learning among the actors (Manzini, 2012). That is, innovation can be explained "in terms of technology and knowledge flows mediated by institutions, being initially applied at a national level" (Manjon & Merino, 2012, p. 34). Consequently, innovation policies in a NIS context may affect an enterprise's ability or motivation to innovate (Christensen, Anthony, & Roth, 2004) and are, therefore, directed at fostering collaboration and networking, providing education and training, and creating and changing institutions and organizations (Manjon & Merino, 2012).

The adoption of NISs has changed the way innovation policies are designed and implemented. Not only have innovation policies progressively become more comprehensive and incorporated into domains other than science and technology (e.g., education policy); they have also been extended to other levels of government, such as regional and supranational, as well as beyond government (Couchman, McLoughlin, & Charles, 2008; Laranja, 2012). A relatively new body of literature on regional innovation systems, which highlights the role of regions in innovation processes, has evolved as an extension of the NIS concept (Asheim, Smith, & Oughton, 2011). Similarly, new governance models have emerged, doing justice to the networked nature of innovation policy (Eriksson, 2013; Laranja, 2012) and taking into account that governance is all "about managing networks" (Rhodes, 1996, p. 658).

The central assumption of network theory is that resources, knowledge, and understanding are developed in many different forms resulting from complex interactions, adaptions, and investments within and between actors over time (Hakansson, 1997; Hakansson & Ford, 2002; Hakansson & Snehota, 1995). Hence, actors within a network do not operate in isolation from others or in response to some generalized environment (Hakansson & Ford, 2002), but are embedded in a complex, interrelated, and extensive web of organizations and social structures (Gummesson & Mele, 2010; Hakansson & Johanson, 1993; Turk, 1970). However, this requires a definition of firms, institutions, and even nations as open adaptive systems in which network actors are active resource integrators and value creators rather than passive recipients of value (Gummesson, 2006; Maglio & Spohrer, 2008).

With connections to stakeholder, agency, and social exchange theories (Cook & Emerson, 1978; Rowley, 1997; Shapiro, 2005), network theory captures actor behavior in relationships from a dyadic and network perspectives. Therefore, a central assumption of network theory is that within networks actors are mutually dependent, and it is the interdependency and interactive processes across networks that drive innovation (Freeman, 1991; Lundvall, 1993; Rothwell et al., 1993), the mutual combination and transformation of resources (Ford, 2011), and policy development (Klijn & Koppenjan, 2000). Furthermore, growing interdependence within networks leads to increased information sharing and acts as an important impediment of opportunism because it can damage a member's reputation due to the strong social embeddedness in a network (Provan, 1993). Consequently, interdependency can create collective benefits within the network because it enables members to cooperate with each other and share knowledge and expertise in ways that gain strategic advantages over competitors outside the network (Granovetter, 1985; Powell, 1990; Provan, 1993). Relationships within networks, which are based on trust and information sharing rather than on formal contracts (Granovetter, 1985), become increasingly essential to growth and the competitive performance of firms, industries, and nations (Dittrich & Duysters, 2007; Freeman, 1991; Huizingh, 2011).

Within organizational networks, multiple actors must learn to work together effectively to achieve mutually beneficial and agreed-on outcomes. To do this, interactions and relationships must be managed properly to ensure positive and reciprocal exchanges. At a local government level, this includes the actors working in partnership with key actors in the area as well as other public- and private-sector providers (McGuire, 2012). Moreover, as the role of an organization converges among that of supplier, customer, competitor, and collaborator, the need for an understanding of the relationships within business networks and effective management of such relationships becomes increasing crucial (Laing, 2003). Using organizational behavior and relationship marketing as foundational theories, characteristics such as trust, commitment, and information flow and exchange become a framework for organizations, allowing them to create a basis for partnerships and interactions established on the co-creation of value, relationships, satisfaction, and loyalty, thus reducing barriers to competition (Moore & Bowden-Everson, 2012; Østergaard & Fitchett, 2012; Vauterin, Linnanen, & Marttila, 2011).

The idea of relationships within networks builds on organizational behavior and commitment as well as industrial and services marketing, through which organizations achieve a strategic competitive advantage when positive relational exchanges occur between the organization and the consumer (Kanagal, 2009). By extending the concepts of relationships, networks, and interactions beyond sales into management and social interactions, organizations can understand the need for and best practices of the management of networks better in their key markets and in society as a whole (Gummesson, 2002). Furthermore, when leaders of organizations recognize the need to expand beyond the sales aspects of marketing, they begin to understand the continuity of relationships and how trust, commitment, and the bonds formed between individuals through those relationships provide mutual benefit for the organization and the consumer. Drawing on the understanding that relationship marketing is embedded in the total management of the networks composed of the organization, market, and society, organizations can nurture and develop long-term relationships with multiple stakeholders and can co-create value between all parties (Gummesson, 2002).

In a similar manner to leaders of organizations using relationship techniques to affect consumers' perceptions of the investments the organization is making, leaders within networks can use the same principles to influence the perceptions of key actors regarding the quality of relationships within and between the organizations (Ha & Stoel, 2008). Facilitating such relationships allows organizations to focus on the co-creation of value, build loyalty, improve satisfaction, strengthen its competitive nature, and allow for further development of the principles that drive the parties to continue the exchanges (Ha & Stoel, 2008; McGuire, 2012). A positive relationship in which organizations develop goodwill with current and potential stakeholders will aid the creation of shared benefits for the stakeholders and the organizations (Tadajewski, 2009). However, it should also be noted that because of the intangibility of such relationships, organizations must be cautious of the potential lack of symmetry in information flow and relationships, which could result in failures within the network (McGuire, 2012).

When considered within the context of the research aim, which is to investigate the development and implementation of innovation policy within the context of the MFF, the influence of strategic orientation, networks, and relationships on the effective development and implementation of innovation policy is arguably significant. At the same time, research that specifically examines this proposition set is deficient. As such, we formulated the following research questions (RQs) as a basis for investigating the stated aim:

RQ1: How does strategic orientation influence the implementation of innovation policy and affect the planning gap identified by the MFF?
RQ2: How can networks and relationships foster or hinder innovation policy to minimize, close, or address the gaps identified by the MFF?

RESEARCH DESIGN AND METHODS

Using a single embedded case study with three semistructured, in-depth interviews and document reviews, our qualitative approach to this study allowed the collection of data that were rich in detail based on the personal experiences of executive coordinators and directors of a substantive Australian LGA (Denzin & Lincoln, 2011; Patton, 2001). The case-study design provided a means to conduct a comprehensive exploration of our research questions in a real-life context (Yin, 2009).

We used purposeful sampling to ensure our participants were appropriate for the exploration of what the LGA was doing; their knowledge of the local, state, and federal policies underpinning their actions; and their experiences in implementing innovation policies within the education and the ICT sectors. The three interviewees held the positions of executive coordinator economic development (ECED) and economic development officers of the ICT and education sectors.

Furthermore, in appreciation of the fact that innovation policy development and implementation may vary from sector to sector, we considered both the education and ICT sectors. As such, we were able to examine and compare phenomena of interest across sectors while maintaining a level of focus that supported detailed enquiry within sectors. Our analysis of how the LGA is using strategic orientation, networks, and relationships in their implementation of innovation policy with regard to the MFF follows.

RESULTS AND DISCUSSION

In the absence of a comprehensive and cohesive innovation policy from the state and federal levels of government, the investigated LGA designed their own economic development strategy that incorporated innovation as a major theme. The strategy was developed over an 8-month period and involved extensive consultation to build awareness and ownership among diverse stakeholders. The new economic development strategy supersedes a former focus on nine key industry sectors by identifying six overarching strategic themes, including innovation, culture, infrastructure, competitive business, workforce, and international.

The process for creating the economic development strategy and the planned review and revision mechanism suggest that this LGA has a strategic orientation that incorporates contemporary practices to facilitate agility and alignment in complex markets and, therefore, has the potential to foster innovation. This was evident in the use of multiple stakeholders as part of its conceptualization, development, refinement, and through the inclusion of a preemptive review process that will see ongoing evaluation and formalized semiannual assessments against key performance indicators (KPIs) as well as a full review within the first three years of implementation. As indicated by the most senior interviewee, the LGA's intention is to adjust and, if necessary, abandon and reconfigure strategies if they do not support the achievement of the underlying KPIs. The stated KPIs aligned to the innovation theme include (a) increase of economic value added of innovation, (b) percentage increase in amount of capital raised annually, (c) percentage increase in jobs related to innovation based activity, and (d) reduced creation costs per innovation and knowledge-based job.

With regard to the MFF, our case study revealed that these particular actions helped the LGA address the planning, governance, and selection gaps. The review of the existing program (managerial actions) led to the understanding that the focus on industries was outdated and needed to be superseded by a more strategic innovation policy approach (managerial assets) in order to allocate resources more appropriately (planning and selection gaps). Similarly, the inclusion of business partners and key stakeholders in the policy development process generated legitimacy and leadership (managerial assets) and allowed the LGA to align their mandates and goals from the outset (governance gap). Finally, the preemptive and iterative monitoring and assessment against KPIs leads to experience-based learning (managerial asset) and the revision of future actions (planning gap).

Because it is one of six key themes within the economic development strategy, the LGA has recognized innovation as centrally important across multiple industry sectors. As one respondent explained, "Basically, what we want to achieve for the city is an environment that fosters innovation and grows successful businesses. . . . We went ahead with that [economic development/innovation strategy] ourselves."

Although respondents were aware of state and federal innovation initiatives, they viewed such initiatives as limited in value beyond being additions to the new economic development strategy. This suggests that these policies are not of particular significance to innovation policy design and implementation at the local level, potentially reflecting an oft-maligned lack of alignment among local, state, and federal levels of government in Australia and relatively new state and federal governments that are only now developing and presenting general industry polices and specific innovation policies. Conversely, wherever funding was available, there were partnerships with other levels of government for the implementation of specific projects, such as the Federal Digital Enterprise Programme. Overall we noted that vertical coordination with other levels of government in terms of innovation policy was lacking. As one interviewee noted, "The other two levels of government tend to [have] more motherhood statements, almost a wish list rather than fully funded [programs]."

Nevertheless, the innovation plan evident in the new economic development strategy created by the LGA is broadly aligned with state and federal innovation policy priorities, for example, activities fostering business growth, enabling collaboration, and connecting research with industry. This stems from the focus on these generally accepted innovation policy priorities as well as from the understanding that most problems do not only occur in one area but are also relevant for other regions. Most important, this alignment with general policy priorities provides opportunities for potential future state and federal funding.

It was evident from our research that networks were seen as critical for innovation policy implementation and operationalization. Local networks were recognized as the key drivers for innovation and local government strategy implementation. Given this perspective, the LGA attempted, under its previous economic development strategy, to develop and maintain innovation networks within each of the nine key industry groups by establishing working or steering committee groups in each sector that were funded and administered by designated officers. However, that approach was ineffective because the network management became too complex and the innovation and resource allocation were not focused on the region's key priorities and strategies. As noted by one respondent: "There has been an interesting journey because when we had all the industry sectors, the nine industry groups, and [when] we were focusing on creating industry groups for each of those sectors it just became such a cumbersome vehicle."

Recognizing the challenges of their previous approach, the LGA shifted their focus under the new economic development strategy to manage networks that were established around opportunities, programs, and priorities relevant to the region's economic development strategies. The importance of this shift in focus was noted by one respondent who stated, "If you have not agreed on strategic thinking or project-based thinking in terms of outcomes it is very hard because [network actors] just turn into networking type groups, which is great, but it will not necessarily turn out in any outcomes."

To monitor the outcomes under the new approach, the LGA will regularly evaluate the value added by activities within the region and global benchmarking through the Microsoft Innovation Centre network's Innovation Dashboard.[1] Funding is project based and is directly injected into the networks by the LGA itself, from state or federal levels of government through programs run by agencies such as AusIndustry[2] or from private-sector institutions through programs such as the ANZ Innovyz acceleration program (Innovyz Start, 2013) for start-up firms.

As depicted in the MFF, a disconnect can arise between funding and availability as a result of governance or knowledge gaps within upper level government systems (Vecchi & Brusoni, 2012). For example, in the ICT sector of the LGA, there is significant interest from the private sector for infrastructure developments; however, support is controversial at the federal government level. Such gaps lead to mutual dependency within networks, which, in turn, are an important network and innovation driver, because actors within the network are required to collaborate within and across sectors to achieve their goals (see Granovetter, 1985). To be functional, networks need to be strategically oriented around specific projects rather than being solely based on the industry sector. This was evident where previously the LGA had established networks within the individual industry sectors without focusing on specific opportunities, programs, or priorities that were relevant to the region's economic development. This resulted in a lack of collaboration and competitive behavior of network actors within the networks and subsequently to the dissolution of the network. As noted by the ECED, "I suppose that it is where if something is not working, and that's what we did with a lot of the other industry groups, you just have to let them die a natural death. Or let them, if that is what they want to do, have their networking functions."

The two different approaches to network facilitation illustrate the essential role of well-functioning networks for fostering innovation policy planning and implementation. The LGA activates networks around strategic or project-based goals that are affiliated with regional development strategies. These project-based networks are then aligned with state or federal government–supported funding schemes or private sector–funding programs. Furthermore, the projects are constantly monitored and benchmarked against external networks to determine their progress and outcomes, detect early problem areas, and drive experience-based learning. With respect to the MFF, the facilitation of project-based and strategically oriented networks appears to be effective and proactive approaches to address the managerial gaps.

However, network facilitation also requires the employment of key people to manage the relationships within the networks and intensive resource investment to reinforce the role played by relationships within networks. As the ECED stated, "there is always the level of dysfunction [within the networks] because everyone has their own agenda" and noted that the LGA could only develop the relationships so far without buy-in from each of the key actors. From a political perspective, the LGA worked to streamline the available resources and stay supportive of the key actors and their relationships within the networks; however, the variance of the individuals and their personalities sometimes resulted in ineffective relationships.

To overcome the ineffectiveness and variableness of some relationships within the networks, the ECED highlighted the notion of "throwing all [their] eggs into one basket when [they] see it as a strong opportunity." When the LGA recognized the differences in the individuals such as the comfort level within groups, the amount of input provided, and those individuals who have the drive to take projects to the next level, they managed the relationships most effectively. The LGA could then direct the money, resources, and programs to align with its overall strategies and could foster relationships to support the specific themes or industries identified as those of strategic importance. Furthermore, to determine whether the outcome of the relationship management is effective, the authority can look to their KPIs to assess how the relationships are directly or indirectly adding economic value, helping to increase the amount of raised capital and jobs related to innovation based activity, and reducing creation costs per innovation. When the LGA maximizes the effectiveness of the relationships, and therefore funds and resources, meeting and exceeding their KPIs will follow.

When the LGA brought key actors together, the individuals tended to work informally. However, to ensure the relationships were developed and maintained with a focus on delivering the key outcomes, the LGA needed to ensure people were not simply getting together for a "talk-fest." Rather, by identifying exactly what needed to take place within the group, the gaps, and the goals, the LGA used the individuals strategically to get value from the time spent together as well as the resulting and ensuing relationships. Then, by maintaining the pressure on the key actors within the networks, the

LGA ensured they were delivering on the key measures, thus implementing innovation in their strategy.

Through the discussion in our interviews on relationships within networks, we reviewed the effectiveness of nurturing the relationships as well as the difficulties the LGA faced in maintaining such relationships. When using multiple actors to foster innovation and implement innovation policy, the need for the LGA to work diligently to develop and maintain effective relationships is critical. Without understanding the individuals involved, how they relate to others, and their personalities in the workplace, the relationships that develop may hinder the functioning of the networks rather than support the innovation. That is, simply bringing key people together allows them to work informally, but there needs to be a purpose behind developing the relationships. Through establishing effective relationships, the individuals create a means for co-creation of value and will experience satisfaction and loyalty through their interactions.

As the ECED noted, when convening various key actors, they must "pin down exactly what [they] want to achieve in order to get value and use everyone's time valuably." When the guiding organization or authority does not facilitate the establishment and oversight of the relationships sufficiently, the dysfunction and dichotomy of the goals of each individual arise as each person attends more to their own agenda than that of the authority. Furthermore, when the LGA identifies the gaps in the implementation of the innovation policy, they must consider the individuals required to overcome the gaps and barriers, and facilitate the new relationships required. Understanding the personalities, strengths, and weaknesses of the individuals will aid the LGA in creating networks that will support the relationships required to achieve the overall goals.

When reviewing relationships within networks in the context of the MFF and implementing innovation policy, we can see that managerial assets, including leadership, knowledge, and awareness of the management of the relationships help minimize the selection and partnership gaps. As seen from our case study, when the executive members of the LGA noticed that the relationships became informal or that individuals were attending to their own agendas rather than developing positive relationships to work together, they revised the overall strategy. The purpose of getting key actors together was reviewed, and the working groups were set up only when the LGA could advise the individuals involved what the specific goals were. Furthermore, the managerial actions of continually reviewing the existing actors and programs as well as the planning of projects allow the LGA to improve their managerial flow. The LGA's awareness of the past problems and its understanding of how its projects fit within state and federal agendas have allowed its members to reframe their strategy and find a better means to foster the relationships. The relationships are not only within the LGA only but also between the authority and the state and federal levels of government. When effective relationships develop between the various levels of government, the support the LGA receives from state and federal government aids in the planning and implementation of policies, strategies, and projects.

In the planning phase of establishing new networks, the actions of the LGA's management will continue to minimize the selection and partnership gaps through the combination of the managerial actions and assets. As the selection and partnership gaps arise when there are scarce resources or a lack of leadership (Vecchi & Brusoni, 2012) the LGA can review past problems, increase clear and concise communication about the aims of the projects the authority is overseeing and the reason for including all key actors, and provide leadership and guidance over the information exchange between the LGA and all key actors, to improve the managerial flow of the implementation of innovation policies.

CONCLUSION

The aim of our research was to investigate the development and implementation of innovation policy within the context of the MFF. To achieve that aim, we developed two research questions following a review of extant literature:

RQ1: How does strategic orientation influence the implementation of innovation policy and affect the planning gap identified by the MFF?
RQ2: How can networks and relationships foster or hinder innovation policy to minimize, close, or address the gaps identified by the MFF?

To address the aim and research questions we used a case study involving a substantive Australian LGA that was in the process of implementing a recently developed new economic development strategy, which included innovation as one of its six major themes. Within that context we gave detailed consideration to the education and ICT sectors. Through the development of the economic development strategy, the LGA actioned a range of innovation policies and frameworks developed in-house and that were purposefully aligned to Australian state and federal government innovation initiatives.

In relation to RQ1, we found that a contemporary strategic orientation that was collaborative, responsive, flexible, and outcome orientated provided a sound foundation for the implementation of disparate innovation policies that had been developed by local, state, and federal government authorities. The approach taken by the LGA allowed significant stakeholder involvement in the creation of the new economic development strategy, ensuring ownership by those who would both influence and be influenced by its implementation. The collaborative orientation was demonstrated by the undertaking of an 8-month development process that included expert panels, established industry groups, and commercial and public consultation forums at various stages of the strategies development. The process also allowed extensive opportunities for feedback, refinement, and redirection as the economic development strategy evolved.

It is also notable that the economic development strategy is open to regular and formal review with key stakeholders adhering to the principle that strategies will change if KPIs are not being met. This focus on outcomes is supported by the use of performance metrics generated by the Innovation Dashboard and other data sources, suggesting that ongoing and critical reviews of actions in light of outcomes is a central pillar of the LGA's strategic orientation. Responsiveness and flexibility were demonstrated by the preparedness of the members of the LGA to step away from their previous strategy that was structured around nine industry groups. These groups and associated networks had been initiated and managed by the LGA as part of its previous approach to economic development. However, through reviews and critiques, the LGA determined that an industry orientation did not provide the desired outcomes for a range of reasons, including a lack of cross-sector collaboration and the pursuit of self rather than sector-wide interests.

The new economic development strategy is focused on six major themes, including innovation. In the context of the ICT and education sectors, this has led to a focus on KPIs that have sector-specific and broader economic benefits and that bring disparate groups together in the pursuit of shared objectives. From the perspective of the LGA, this has benefits with education and ICT participants, such as engaging in discussions on how each actor can add value to the other sectors through building formal networks and collaboration rather than relying on informal networks focused on market intelligence with competitive undertones.

Overall it was evident that the strategic orientation the LGA employed moderated the planning gaps effectively. The establishment of measurable KPIs, six major themes, and a preparedness to reconfigure strategy that was not achieving outcomes provided a foundation that ameliorates the negative effects of short-termism, fads, or announcement effects. That is not to say that these gaps will not arise or have a negative impact but, rather, that they are less likely to arise or gain permanency.

In relation to RQ2, there was clear and unambiguous evidence regarding the importance of networks and relationships in the management of the planning, selection, and governance gaps. Additionally, we found partial evidence that the knowledge and partnership gaps characterized under the MFF are influenced by the establishment and management of networks and relationships. While this result is not surprising, it does highlight the importance of network and relationship orientation during the development and implementation of innovation policies. Our case study demonstrated how an LGA could develop a more effective economic development strategy by incorporating a focus on innovation through local and external networks and relationships. These networks and relationships were used in the development of the strategy and facilitated alignment of the strategy with state and federal initiatives that provided primary sources of funding and development aid.

A main limitation of this study was that although the LGA had released the economic development strategy and was in the early stages of implementation, the effectiveness of the strategy in terms of meeting KPIs could not be assessed given timelines. Additionally, we were limited in terms of the understanding of and engagement with the economic development strategy by key stakeholders within the LGA borders. As such, we will return to this case in the fall of 2015 with the purpose of assessing the effectiveness of the strategy and the extent to which the expressed flexibility and responsiveness to outcomes is evident. We will undertake an extensive set of interviews with stakeholders not directly linked to the LGA, with a view to assessing the effectiveness of the implementation from a stakeholder perspective.

Finally, although it is arguable that the issues faced by LGAs seeking to stimulate innovation as part of their economic develop activities are at least in part universal, the evidence provided by a single case study needs to be recognized as contextual. Likewise, the demonstrated generalizability of the MFF and its application within this context suggests that the findings can be applied in other contexts with due consideration given to the political, economic, social, and technological environment.

NOTES

1. The "Innovation Dashboard" is an innovation benchmarking platform used globally between the Microsoft Innovation Center network. Through the collection and global benchmarking of performance data across the city's innovation centers, innovation activities, and businesses, the dashboard assists in assessing the city's presence within the global innovation environment and in identifying new investment opportunities.
2. AusIndustry is an Australian business program delivery division within the Department of Industry, which delivers programs for businesses and individuals worth around AU$2 billion per year, including innovation grants, clean technology, tax incentives, duty concessions, small business development, industry support, and venture capital (see www.ausindustry.gov.au).

REFERENCES

Asheim, B. T., Smith, H. L., & Oughton, C. (2011). Regional innovation systems: Theory, empirics and policy. *Regional Studies, 45*(7), 875–891. doi:10.1080/003 43404.2011.596701

Christensen, C. M., Anthony, S. D., & Roth, E. A. (2004). *Seeing what's next: Using the theories of innocation to predict industry change.* Boston, MA: Harvard Business School Press.

Cook, K. S., & Emerson, R. M. (1978). Power, equity and commitment in exchange networks. *American Sociological Review, 43*(5), 721–739.

Couchman, P. K., McLoughlin, I., & Charles, D. R. (2008). Lost in translation? Building science and innovation city strategies in Australia and the UK. *Innovation: Management, Policy & Practice, 10*(2/3), 211–223.

Denzin, N. K., & Lincoln, Y. S. (2011). *The SAGE handbook of qualitative research* (4th ed.). Thousand Oaks, CA: Sage.

Dittrich, K., & Duysters, G. (2007). Networking as a means to strategy change: the case of open innovation in mobile telephony. *Journal of Product Innovation Management, 24*(6), 510–521. doi:10.1111/j.1540-5885.2007.00268.x

Enterprise and Industry. (2013). Innovation policy. Retrieved November 30, 2013, from http://ec.europa.eu/enterprise/policies/innovation/policy/

Eriksson, K. (2013). Innovation and the vocabulary of governance. *Science & Technology Studies, 26*(1), 73–91.

Ford, D. (2011). IMP and service-dominant logic: Divergence, convergence and development. *Industrial Marketing Management, 40*(2), 231–239.

Freeman, C. (1987). *Technology policy and economic performance.* London, England: Pinter.

Freeman, C. (1991). Networks of innovators: a synthesis of research issues. *Research Policy, 20*(5), 499–514. doi:10.1016/0048-7333(91)90072-x

French, S. (2009a). Critiquing the language of strategic management. *Journal of Management Development, 28*(1), 6–17.

French, S. (2009b). Cogito ergo sum: Exploring epistemological options for strategic management. *Journal of Management Development, 28*(1) 18–37.

Godin, B. (2009). National innovation system: The system approach in historical perspective. *Science, Technology, & Human Values, 34*(4), 476–501. doi: 10.2307/27786171

Granovetter, M. (1985). Economic action and social structure: The problem of embededness. *American Journal of Sociology, 91*(3), 481–501.

Gummesson, E. (2002). Relationship marketing in the new economy. *Journal of Relationship Marketing, 1*(1), 37–57.

Gummesson, E. (Ed.). (2006). *Many-to-many marketing as grand theory: A nordic school contribution.* New York, NY: Sharpe.

Gummesson, E., & Mele, C. (2010). Marketing as value co-creation through network interaction and resource integration. *Journal of Business Market Management, 4*, 181–198.

Ha, S., & Stoel, L. (2008). Promoting customer-retailer relationship building: Influence of customer trustworthiness of customer loyalty programme marketing. *Journal of Customer Behaviour, 7*(3), 215–229.

Hakansson, H. (Ed.). (1997). *Organization networks.* London, England: Thompson Business Press.

Hakansson, H., & Ford, D. (2002). How should companies interact in business networks? *Journal of Business Research, 55*(2), 133–139.

Hakansson, H., & Johanson, J. (Eds.). (1993). *The network as a governance structure: interfirm cooperation beyond markets and hierarchies.* London, England: Routledge.

Hakansson, H., & Snehota, I. (1995). *Developing relationships in business networks.* London, England: Routledge.

Howard and Partners P/L (2007) *Study of the role of intermediaries in support of innovation.* Retrieved from http://www.innovation.gov.au/innovation/report sandstudies/Documents/InnovationIntermediariesReport.pdf

Huizingh, E. K. R. E. (2011). Open innovation: State of the art and future perspectives. *Technovation, 31*(1), 2–9. doi:10.1016/j.technovation.2010.10.002

Innovyz Start. (2013). Accelerator. Retrieved from http://www.innovyzstart.com/the-program

Kanagal, N. (2009). Role of relationship marketing in competitive marketing strategy. *Journal of Management and Marketing Research, 2*(1), 1–17.

Klijn, E. H., & Koppenjan, J. F. M. (2000). Public management and policy networks. *Public Management: An International Journal of Research and Theory, 2*(2), 135–158. doi:10.1080/14719030000000007

Laing, A. (2003). Marketing in the public sector: Towards a typology of public services. *Marketing Theory, 3*(4), 427–445.

Laranja, M. (2012). Network governance of innovation policies: The technological plan in Portugal. *Science & Public Policy, 39*(5), 655–668. doi:10.1093/scipol!scs043

Lundvall, B.-Ã. (1992). *National Systems of Innovation: Towards a theory of innovation and interactive learning*. London, England: Pinter.

Lundvall, B.-Ã. (Ed.). (1993). *Explaining interfirm cooperation and innovation: Limits of the transaction-cost approach*. London, England: Routledge.

Lundvall, B.-Ã. (2007). National innovation systems—analytical concept and development tool. *Industry and Innovation, 14*(1), 95–119.

Maglio, P. P., & Spohrer, J. (2008). Fundamentals of service science. *Journal of the Academy of Marketing Science, 36*(1), 18–20.

Manjon, J. V. G., & Merino, E. R. (2012). Innovation systems and policy design: The European experience. *Innovation: Management, Policy & Practice, 14*(1), 33–42.

Manzini, S. T. (2012). The national system of innovation concept: An ontological review and critique. *South African Journal of Science, 108*(9/10), 50–56. doi:10.4102/sajs.v108i9/10.1038

McGuire, L. (2012). Slippery concepts in context: Relationship marketing and public services. *Public Management Review, 14*(4), 541–555. doi:10.1080/14719037.2011.649975

Moore, D., & Bowden-Everson, J. L.-H. (2012). An appealing connection-the role of relationship marketing in the attraction and retention of students in an Australian tertiary context. *Asian Social Science, 8*(14), 65–80.

Nelson, R. R. (1993). *National Innovation Systems: A comparative analysis*. New York, NY: Oxford University Press.

Organisation for Economic Co-operation and Development. (2011). *The OECD innovation strategy: Getting a head start on tomorrow*. Paris: OECD Publishing.

Østergaard, P., & Fitchett, J. (2012). Relationship marketing and the order of simulation. *Marketing Theory, 12*(3), 233–249.

Patton, M. Q. (2001). *Qualitative research and evaluation methods* (3rd ed.). Thousand Oaks, CA: Sage.

Powell, W. W. (1990). Neither market nor hierarchy: Networks forms of organization. *Research in Organizational Behavior, 12*, 295–336.

Provan, K. G. (1993). Embeddedness, interdependence, and opportunism in organizational supplier-buyer networks. *Journal of Management, 19*(4), 841–856.

Rhodes, R. A. W. (1996). The new governance: Governing without government. *Political Studies, 44*(4), 652–667.

Rothwell, R., Freeman, C., Horsley, A., Jervis, P., T. V., Robertson, A., B., & Townsend, J. (1993). SAPPHO updated—Project SAPPHO phase II. *Research Policy, 22*(2), 110. doi:10.1016/0048-7333(93)90057-o

Rowley, T. J. (1997). Moving beyond dyadic ties: A network theory of stakeholder influences. *Academy of Management Review, 22*(4), 887–910.

Shapiro, S. P. (2005). Agency theory. *Annual Review of Sociology, 31*, 263–284.

Tadajewski, M. (2009). The foundations of relationship marketing: reciprocity and trade relations. *Marketing Theory, 9*(1), 9–38.

Turk, H. (1970). Interorganizational networks in urban society: Initial perspectives and comparative research. *American Sociological Review, 35*, 1–18.

Vauterin, J. J., Linnanen, L., & Marttila, E. (2011). Issues of delivering quality customer service in a higher education environment. *International Journal of Quality and Service Sciences, 3*(2), 181–198.

Vecchi, V., & Brusoni, M. (2012). The managerial flow of public local development policies: A conceptual framework. *Singapore Management Review, 34*(2), 5–13.

Yin, R. K. (2009). *Case study research: Design and methods* (4th ed.). Thousand Oaks, CA: Sage.

5 Transforming Singapore's Innovation System

An Analysis Using the Managerial Flow Model

Pengji Wang and Adrian T. H. Kuah

INTRODUCTION

The national innovation system (NIS) is an evolving and closely embedded system involving private and public firms, universities, and government agencies to develop, diffuse, and exploit knowledge within a national context (Carlsson, 2006; Lundvall, 2003). Sweden and Germany have each created successful innovation systems; the Fraunhofer model in Germany involves 60 research institutes linked to a network of universities. The Fraunhofer system receives some 30% of funding from the state and 70% from industry and government contracts. Sweden is recognized as one of the top European Union (EU) countries in innovation. The Swedish RISE Holding AB is a holding company owned by the state and consists of umbrella research institutes that are externally funded.

Learning from numerous efforts in creating an effective NIS, there are 3 national assets that shape its performance (Organisation for Economic Co-operation and Development [OECD], 1997). The first is strong public–private linkages involving public research infrastructure (research institutes and universities). The second is having labor mobility, which allows the nurturing and mobilization of people with specific knowledge and abilities. The third is industry linkages that facilitate interactions relevant to important technologies, shared knowledge and skills, and producer–supplier relationships.

From the early 1980s to the 1990s, Singapore adopted a multinational corporation (MNC) dependency model that depended on the attraction of, and spillover effect from, MNCs by assimilating and diffusing technology from relevant MNCs (p. Wong, 1995). Singapore conducted and invested in little research and development (R&D) in those days, substantially less than other newly industrialized countries such as South Korea or Taiwan (Amsden, Tschan, & Goto, 2001). More recently, Singapore has adopted an indigenous innovation model, applying its own resources for knowledge creation using their public institutes and domestic private enterprises as the knowledge generator.

Using the Managerial Flow model (Vecchi & Brusoni, 2012) as a guiding framework, this chapter compares the context, goals, and managerial assets and actions in the development of Singapore's innovation system from its origins to the current state. The case study of the Singaporean NIS is "revelatory" (Yin, 1994, p. 41), especially when we can observe transformation management of this NIS and its successes and pitfalls in action. The NIS transformation management, along the utility and promotion of the three important assets, was subjected to some managerial gaps. We argue those managerial gaps in strategy, governance, selection, knowledge and communication, and coordination and integration explain why some measures may be effective in the MNC dependency model but not in the indigenous innovation model, based on the case of Singapore. This chapter further analyzes the government's managerial actions to close these gaps.

THE FIRST ERA (1991–2000)

Initial Strategy and Goals

In 1991, the National Science & Technology Board (NSTB) under the Ministry of Trade and Industry (MTI) and the Economic Development Board (EDB) was formed to enhance Singapore's technology development by promoting industry-driven R&D and by increasing the number of research scientists and engineers (RSEs) to meet the needs of MNCs in technology transfer and diffusion. The NSTB implemented two 5-year plans: the National Technology Plan (S$2 billion, from 1991 to 1995) and the National Science & Technology Plan (S$4 billion, from 1996 to 2000). The plans focused on microelectronics, information technology, electronic system, manufacturing technology, materials technology, energy, environmental and resources, food and agrotechnology, and biotechnology and medical sciences (Loh, 1998).

Managerial Assets and Actions

To support the MNC Dependency Model, the government implemented a strategy of attracting selected industries' to add value into Singapore (p. Wong, 1995). In addition, favorable conditions were made available by the government to attract relevant MNCs, for example, offering tax exemptions and subsidies, helping with building factories or finding suitable land, and training programs for employees (Blomstrom, Kokko, & Sjöholm, 2002). As shown in Table 5.1, Singapore had the second-largest spending for promoting foreign direct investment (FDI) during this era.

Also the government offered key industry MNCs, who located regional operational headquarters in Singapore, a concessionary tax rate of 10% (Loh, 1998). There were additional tax reductions for foreign firms in international trading or oil trading activities (Lee, 1992, p. 39). Furthermore, the emphasis of human capital formation was increasingly shifted from technician to professional training (P. Wong, 2001). Finally, the EDB worked

Table 5.1   Spending on FDI Promotion (1999)

	Annual FDI promotion (US$ million)	Population (million)	Per capita budget (US$)
Ireland	213	3.7	57.6
Singapore	45	3.2	14.1
Costa Rica	11	3.5	3.1
Mauritius (1996)	3.1	1.2	2.6
Dominican Republic	8.8	8.4	1.05
Malaysia	15	22.7	0.66
Philippines	3	76.8	0.04
Indonesia	2.8	207	0.01

Source: Te Velde (2001).

closely with MNCs in order to gain direct information on MNCs' business development obstacles (Blomstrom et al., 2002).

Such an approach enhanced innovation capabilities, as reflected in Singapore's gross expenditure on R&D (GERD) had increased sixfold between 1987 and 1998, reaching S$2.33 billion in 1998, or 1.65% of the gross domestic product. The number of RSEs per a 10,000-person labor force reached 66 in 1998. The total number of patents filed by Singapore-based organizations increased from 142 in 1993 to 639 in 1998. In 1997, revenue derived from commercialized products and processes attributed to R&D performed in Singapore amounted to 9.6%.

THE SECOND ERA (2001–2010)

As Singapore achieved economic growth, the government moved away from an MNC Dependency Model to pursue indigenous innovation competences (from mid-1990s to mid-2000s). Despite early successes, three key gaps emerged during the transition period:

1. *Managerial Gap in Governance.* The principal device that the government had employed was using investment incentives; however, these had not persuaded foreign MNCs to locate their high-level, value-added, knowledge-creation activities in Singapore. For example, there had been 10 major foreign disk-drive manufacturers in Singapore, and the region accounted for as much as 64% of final global assembly and 44% of total global employment, but only received 13 percent of the industry's wages (Amsden et al., 2001).
2. *Managerial Gap in Knowledge and Communication.* R&D activities in Singapore were limited to product development, failure mode analysis, and improvement in manufacturing processes (Kuah, 1998). But

there was a lack of necessary talent and knowledge to capture MNCs' knowledge creation activities into Singapore.

3. *Managerial Gap in Strategy.* As suppliers and contract manufacturers, Singaporean companies only played a minor supporting role to the MNCs. There was little incentive to invest in indigenous capabilities in high-tech innovation (Koh, 2006; p. Wong, 2001). Also, most of the R&D investment was conducted by MNCs, rather than by local firms. In 1997, foreign-controlled firms accounted for more than 61% of private R&D spending (p. Wong, 2001). Indigenous innovation capabilities had much space for improvement in Singapore, and the strategic intent for conducting basic research was not strong in Singapore.

Closing the Managerial Gaps

The reliance on foreign firms to create knowledge did not result in innovation being embedded in Singapore in terms of value-added activities. To deal with the managerial gaps that now emerged, the government took some actions to capture MNCs' knowledge-creation activities.

Closing the Gap in Strategy

The evolving managerial action was to embed knowledge creation through a series of technology development plans. For instance, the second NSTB (1996) plan called for fostering of clusters to attain global leadership of certain key technological areas. The NSTB stressed four strategic directions: (a) meeting demand for manpower, (b) providing a conducive environment for industry-driven R&D, (c) forging infrastructure for more R&D institutions, and (d) providing a climate for entrepreneurship (Loh, 1998). Technology development in Singapore was earlier classified into three tiers. The first tier comprised the development or acquisition of near-term technologies to reinforce the competitive position of its key industry clusters and to foster the growth of emerging high-value-added clusters (Chaturvedi, 2005). The other two tiers (medium and long term) would equip Singapore with a continuous stream of innovative ideas and technologies to support future development. R&D efforts were to be carried out in the research institutes/centers and universities. The government utilized its public research institutes to direct R&D toward long-term, basic research and away from short-term and applied R&D (Lall & Urata, 2003).

Closing the Gap in Governance

The NSTB was renamed the Agency for Science, Technology and Research (A*STAR) to support the creation and exploitation of intellectual capital and the training of research personnel in the transition to a knowledge-based economy. A*STAR controlled some 14 research institutes and 9 research consortia/centers. Both the Biomedical Research Council (BMRC) and the Science and Engineering Research Council (SERC) were formed in 2000 to handle basic discipline research. The research councils coordinated and managed public-sector R&D across the research institutes, research centers, and the public universities. Also a new incentive scheme was formulated to encourage creative work from local researchers by using internationally referred journal publications in evaluating researchers' performance (Wang & Yuan, 2012). More than that, the Science and Technology Plan (2001–2005) formed SPRING, a government agency promoting standards and productivity to provide R&D funds to clusters.

Closing the Gap in Selection

The government substantially increased investment in public research institutes, in pure and strategic basic research in late 1990s, to increase knowledge capability and overcome the low supply of experienced and skilled local RSEs, A*STAR launched the National Science Scholarships in 2001 and the A*STAR Graduate Scholarship in 2003 to send "young talent" abroad. Local universities and research institutes were expected to help create and sustain a diverse and critical mass of skills and talent to meet Singapore's R&D personnel needs.

With these efforts, Singapore built the managerial assets for public research infrastructure; for example, Singapore's publications per capita of population achieved a level similar to that in France and Germany, and exceeded Japan. The annual growth rate of Singapore's scientific publications stands at about 13% (second highest after South Korea), compared with an average of less than 3% for all advanced countries (Koh, 2006), as shown in Figures 5.1a and 5.1b.

Embedding Knowledge Creation via Engagement

Embeddedness is a crucial determinant for anchoring the global into the local context so as to promote sustainable economic development (Coe, Hess, Yeung, Dicken, & Henderson, 2004; Hess, 2004). Two actions have been taken by the Singaporean government to engage the MNCs:

1. In the bid to encourage more foreign firms to engage in R&D activities in Singapore, the government firstly reshaped the structure of engagement. The Science and Technology Plan (2001–2005) required the EDB to work directly with large foreign MNCs. The EDB changed this approach in favor of government-linked companies (GLCs) forming joint ventures with MNCs. One such partnership S*Bio, a joint venture between Chiron Corporation and the EDB, leveraged Chiron's technological platform to develop products for cancer treatment. MerLion Pharmaceuticals, a joint venture between GlaxoSmithKline

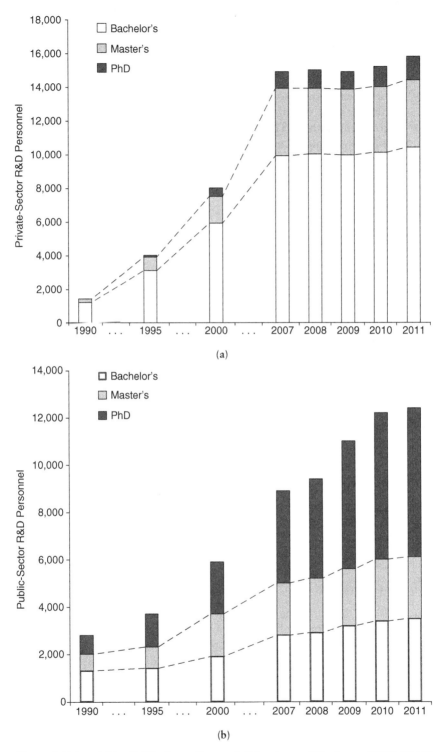

Figure 5.1(a) and (b)   Public-Sector Research Scientists and Engineers (1990–2011)
Source: *National Survey of Research and Development (R&D) in Singapore 2011* (2011).

and the EDB, screened natural samples from Asia for possible drug traces. MerLion was then privatized and collaborated with Merck and NovImmume (Finegold, Wong, & Cheah, 2004).

2. The government also tried to link MNCs with local research institutes for more collaborative projects. For example, Roche signed an agreement with A*STAR, National University of Singapore (NUS), Singapore Health Services (SingHealth), Nanyang Technological University (NTU), and others, to establish a translational medical hub in Singapore and committed a budget of about S$135 million over 3 years to develop improved treatments for cancer and infectious diseases.

Hence, the EDB helped form joint ventures and strategic alliances between Singaporean firms and foreign MNCs in a number of industries, including semiconductor wafer fabrication and chemicals. As such, MNCs' activities were embedded into the knowledge creation activities in Singapore.

THE THIRD AGE (BEYOND 2011)

Emerging Issues

Singapore has now recognized that the linkage between its universities and research institutes is important and governance issues have been less than optimum in achieving commercialization development (Ebner, 2004; Lall & Urata, 2003; W. Wong, 2006). This is because the public agencies and institutions lack the incentive and culture to commercialize R&D outcomes.

Gaps in Strategy

The commercialization of research outcomes has been poor. Other than publications and patents, the measurement of successful basic research contributing toward commercialization is undetermined as impact and consequences are not immediate.

Gaps in Governance

Before 2005, the performance evaluation indicators for the institute and researchers were mainly publications in international academic journals and patents. Commercialization of research and applications into the industry were not part of the performance evaluation index (Wang & Yuan, 2012).

Gaps in Knowledge and Communication

There is a lack of knowledge and skills in the public research institutes to facilitate commercialization. The RSEs in public research institutes tend to lack the necessary connections with others to identify business opportunities, as opportunities for cross-fertilization are not often present.

Gaps in Coordination and Integration

Coordination between research institutes and industry is relatively underdeveloped (Koh, 2006). R&D from research institutes tended to be more fundamental and not ready for, or relevant to, industry. Also, interfirm linkages between local firms are weak and there have been few cases of reported joint R&D (p. Wong, 2011). There have also been few reported cases of industry-wide or multifirm collaboration in technology deployment (p. Wong, 2011). In this regard, there appears to have been inadequate public policy attention to promoting collaboration among local enterprises.

As shown in Tables 5.2 and 5.3, public research institutes received S$877.84 million for R&D from the government but only generated S$1.11 million

Table 5.2   R&D Expenditure by Source of Funding in Singapore, 2010 (S$ million)

Source of funding	Private sector	Government sector	Higher education sector	Public research institutes	Total
Own funds	3,219.27	115.45	107.97	9.54	3,452.24
Private sector	157.51	23.70	40.42	6.30	227.93
Government sector	279.21	526.28	801.73	877.84	2,485.05
Higher education sector	2.10	0.96	4.70	0.04	7.82
Foreign-based companies	275.80	5.48	3.52	3.15	287.95
Foreign government and international organizations	13.73	0.40	9.79	4.12	28.04
Total	3,947.61	672.29	968.12	901.00	6,489.02

Source: *National Survey of Research and Development in Singapore* (2010).

Table 5.3   Research Revenue in Singapore, 2010 (S$ million)

Revenue indicators	Private sector	Government sector	Higher education sector	Public research institutes	Total
Licensing revenue from patents and new technologies Developed in Singapore	32.16	0.57	0.86	1.11	34.69
Sales revenue from commercialized products/processes attributed to R&D performed in Singapore	10,900.29	0.02	0.18	7.99	10,908.47

Source: *National Survey of Research and Development in Singapore* (2010).

in revenue from licensing patents and new technologies, and S$7.99 million by selling commercialized products. Mahmood and Singh (2003) revealed from their study of US patent data, the patenting activity in Singapore, over the past 30 years has consistently been much lower than in South Korea and Taiwan.

Recent Actions

Closing the Gap in Strategy

Since 2008, the Singapore government has recognized that more effort must be put into commercialization and creating indigenous innovative competences. One such move was to restructure the national research institutes and agencies.

Closing the Gap in Governance

To encourage R&D collaboration between public research institutes and industry, the NSTB required public research institutes to gain a proportion of their R&D expenditure from industry (Wang & Yuan, 2012; p. Wong & Singh, 2005). Also, the performance of the public research institutes are monitored for the extent of patenting, licensing of technologies to industry, and joint R&D activities. Partnering with private-sector companies to perform R&D has been embedded as an important component of A*STAR's mission, according *to STEP 2015—Science, Technology & Enterprise Plan 2015* (2013).

Closing the Gap in Selection

Following this incentive scheme for public research institutes, the strategic direction for project decision has also altered. The research projects conducted by public institutes must have the potential to be developed into industrial projects, as determined by A*STAR. Alternatively, the research institutes must create industry-linked projects.

Closing the Gap in Knowledge and Communication

To close the knowledge gap in commercialization, the government has enhanced the role of Exploit Technologies Pte Ltd. (ETPL), established in 2001, as the marketing and commercialization arm of A*STAR. ETPL manages and consolidates all research institutes' intellectual property under one roof as a one-stop center for research institutes, industry, and enterprise. ETPL also promotes promising projects to the private sector, the financial resources, and business insights that facilitate researchers to unlock commercial value (Marshall Cavendish Business Information, 2010). Thus, ETPL bridges the gap between technologies invented in research laboratories and the needs of enterprise.

Closing the Gap in Coordination and Integration

To boost commercialization of innovation, the EDB made changes to the governance structure by shifting innovation from public institutes to local private sector since early 2000. The EDB initiated programs to nurture the growth of local companies. For example, the government pushed some local biomedical sciences BMS firms, such as Rockeby Biomed, Cygenics, and MatrixView to go public. Moreover, the government established venture capital organization Bio*One Capital, which is dedicated to biomedical investment. Local enterprises can also benefit by the secondment of researchers and engineers as well as the provision of technical advice and customized technology roadmaps from the Growing Enterprises with Technology Upgrade (GET-Up) program offered by SERC. The support has led to numerous success stories, for example, Cal-Comp Technology Pte Ltd has successfully developed an environmentally friendly coating technology that will reduce particulate contamination in hard disk drives.

Better coordination between state-owned research institutes and the private sector has been achieved. The managerial assets, gaps, actions in each development stage are presented in Table 5.4.

CONCLUSION

Using the Managerial Flow model and its five key determinants, Singapore's policy management illustrates how a nation may manage a transformation to achieve desirable outcomes. Many countries recognize the importance of the three dimensions of an NIS, there is still lack of a systematic framework guiding the development and management of the dimensions. Our analysis confirms the appropriateness of using the Managerial Flow model in identifying, describing, and analyzing the problems to successfully inform and implement NIS policies.

For a small economy that lacks knowledge capacity, following a dual track, that is, attracting MNCs' knowledge-creation activities and nurturing indigenous innovation capabilities of public and private sectors at the same time, is a feasible approach to enhancing economic growth. Our case also elaborates how the government works on the five determinants, including planning, governance, selection, knowledge, and integration, to build the relevant managerial assets. For example, when attracting MNCs' knowledge-creation activities, it is important to bear in mind that MNCs arrange their global supply chain based on country-specific advantage (Rugman, 2005). Hence, offering the optimum incentive and infrastructure (as

Table 5.4 Analysis Using Managerial Flow Model

	Planning →	Governance	Knowledge & communication	Selection	Coordination & integration →	Outcome
Managerial Assets created in the First Era (1991–2000)	MNC Dependency for utilizing technology and promoting knowledge diffusion	Lead agency EDB, drives incentives to attract MNCs' value added activities	Public institutions on applied research; Education & training to build absorptive capacity	Highly selective on focal areas to develop	Local firms serve as the support to MNCs, supported by cluster approach by SPRING and EDB	Productivity improved
Gaps to make way for new indigenous NIS	Applied research, less fundamental research.	Economic incentive cannot engage MNCs' knowledge creation activities	Less innovative talents in conducting research in local context	Few MNCs locate their knowledge creation activities; Local firms make little R&D investment		Indigenous innovation are underdeveloped; Lack of embededdedness of MNCs innovative acitivities in local context
Managerial Actions to close gaps during Second Divide (2001–2005)	Promote knowledge creation via basic research. Creation of A*STAR as lead agency Engage MNCs through collaborative R&D	Investment in government-led basic research Performance based on patents and publications	Attracting foreign scientists and nurturing local scientists	More basic research selected & allocated to research institutes by government	Promote local–MNC link through joint-venture and cluster approach	

Managerial assets accumulated during Second Divide (2001–2005)	Gaps arising in newly formed indigenous NIS ⇨	Managerial actions to close the gaps (2005–present) ⇨	Managerial assets at present
Long-term basic research is improved MNCs are better embedded into Singapore knowledge economy.	Lack of emphasis on industry link and commercialization	Industry implication, such as collaboration and profit, is highlighted	
Governance promoting basic research established with A*STAR as lead manager	Incentive cannot promote enough industry link	New incentive schemes with industrial project and collaboration highlighted Inviting local private sectors	Intensive and fast public–private link
Stock of foreign and local scientists and engineers	Lack of knowledge and experience on commercialization	Role of ETTL enhanced to facilitate connecting with industry Facilitate local private sectors in taking the lead in innovation	Researchers equipped with business insights
Abundant funding from government in public research institutes	Government and public research center-oriented selection	Industrial projects become the main focus	Quite a few research industry collaboration formed
Solid local-MNC linkage is established.	Lack of link between research institute and private sector	Linkages between state-owned research institute is promoted Link between Private firms is promoted through the cluster approach	
Knowledge creation capabilities improved by Increased international publications & patents	Commercialization rate is still low		Commercialization is facilitated

Source: Based on the results from the authors' research.

the needed country-specific advantage) is important in order to capture their knowledge creation activities. Moreover, knowledge creation and commercialization are equally important in ensuring the sustainability of innovation by also capturing investors' knowledge creation effort. The Singapore case demonstrates how a government, first, invests in knowledge creation competence and, then, equips talent with business insights and facilitates academic–industry linkages.

REFERENCES

Amsden, A. H., Tschang, T., & Goto, A. (2001). *Do foreign companies conduct R&D in developing countries?* (ADB Institute Working Paper No. 14). Tokyo, Japan: ADB Institute.

Blomström, M., Kokko, A., & Sjöholm, F. (2002). *Growth and innovation policies for a knowledge economy: Experiences from Finland, Sweden, and Singapore* (EIJS Working Paper from European Institute of Japanese Studies, No. 156). Retrieved from http://swopec.hhs.se/eijswp/papers/eijswp0156.pdf

Carlsson, B. (2006). Internationalization of innovation systems: A survey of the literature. *Research Policy, 35*, 56–67.

Chaturvedi, S. (2005). Evolving a national system of biotechnology innovation: Some evidence from Singapore. *Science, Technology and Society, 10*(1), 105–127.

Coe, N. M., Hess, M., Yeung, H. W. C., Dicken, P., & Henderson, J. (2004). Globalizing regional development: A global production networks perspective. *Transactions of the Institute of British Geographers, 29*, 468–484.

Ebner, A. (2004). Innovation policies and locational competitiveness: Lessons from Singapore. *Journal of Technology Innovation, 12*(2), 47–66.

Finegold, D., Wong, P. K., & Cheah, T. C. (2004). Adapting a foreign direct investment strategy to the knowledge economy: The case of Singapore's emerging biotechnology cluster. *European Planning Studies, 12*(7), 921–941.

Hess, M. (2004). "Spatial" relationships? Towards a re-conceptualization of embeddedness. *Progress in Human Geography, 28*, 165–186.

Koh, W. T. H. (2006). Singapore's transition to innovation-based economic growth: infrastructure, institutions and government's role. *R&D Management, 36*(2), 143–160.

Kuah, A. T. H. (1998). *Competitive strategies of the disk drive sector in Singapore* (Unpublished MBA thesis). University of Strathclyde, Glasgow, Scotland.

Lall S., & Urata, S. (2003). *Competitiveness, FDI and technological activity in East Asia.* Cheltenham, England: Edward Elgar.

Lee, T. Y. (1992). Economic restructuring policies in the 1980s. In L. Low & T. M. Heng (Eds.), *Public policies in Singapore: Changes in the 1980s and future signposts* (pp. 30–55). Singapore, Times Academic Press.

Loh, L. (1998). Technological policy and national competitiveness. In M. H. Toh & K. Y. Tan (Eds.), *Competitiveness of the Singapore economy: A strategic perspective* (pp. 40–83). Singapore: Singapore University Press.

Lundvall, B.-Å. (2003), Why the new economy is a learning economy. *Economia e Politica Industriale, 117*, 173–185.

Mahmood, I. & Singh, J. (2003). Technological dynamism in Asia. *Research Policy, 32*(6), 1031–1054.

Marshall Cavendish Business Information. (2010). *Singapore biotech guide 2011/2012.* Singapore: Author.

National Survey of Research and Development (R&D) in Singapore 2010. (2010). Singapore: Agency for Science, Technology and Research. Retrieved from http://www.a-star.edu.sg/Portals/0/media/RnD_Survey/RnD_2010.pdf

National Survey of Research and Development (R&D) in Singapore 2011. (2011). Singapore: Agency for Science, Technology and Research. Retrieved from http://www.a-star.edu.sg/Portals/0/media/RnD_Survey/RnD_2011.pdf

National Science & Technology Board. (1996). *National science and technology plan: Towards 2000 and beyond (NSTB plan).* Singapore: Author.

Organisation for Economic Co-operation and Development. (1997). *National innovation systems.* Retrieved from http://www.oecd.org/science/inno/2101733.pdf

Rugman, A. M. (2005). *The regional multinationals.* Cambridge, England: Cambridge University Press.

STEP 2015—Science, technology & enterprise plan 2015: Asia's innovation capital. Singapore: Agency for Science, Technology and Research, Singapore. Retrieved from http://www.a-star.edu.sg/portals/0/media/otherpubs/step2015_1jun.pdf

Te Velde, D. W. (2001). *Policies towards foreign direct investment in developing countries: Emerging best-practices and outstanding issues.* London, England: Overseas Development Institute.

Vecchi, V., & Brusoni, M. (2012). The managerial flow of public local development policy: A conceptual framework. *Singapore Management Review, 34*(Suppl. 2), 26–34.

Wang, P. J., & Yuan, L. (2012). Managerial flow in enhancing research capabilities— One North Singapore and Tianhe China. *Singapore Management Review, 34*(Suppl. 2), 45–51.

Wong, P. K. (1995). *National innovation system: The case of Singapore, ASEAN-ROK cooperation project* (Working Paper). Seoul, Korea: Science and Technology Policy Institute.

Wong, P. K. (2001). Leveraging multinational corporations, fostering technopreneurship: The changing role of S&T policy in Singapore. *International Journal of Technology Management, 22*(5), 539–567.

Wong, P. K. (2011). *Public innovation financing schemes in Singapore* (Final draft report for the Project on Towards Effective Policies for Financing of Innovation in Asia). Retrieved from http://www.academia.edu/2228538/Public_Innovation_Financing_Schemes_in_Singapore

Wong, P. K., & Singh, A. (2005). *Technological specialization and convergence of small countries: The case of the late-industrializing Asian NIEs* (NUS Entrepreneurship Centre Working Papers, WP2005-05). Singapore: National University of Singapore. Retrieved from http://128.118.178.162/eps/dev/papers/0505/0505011.pdf

Wong, W. T. H. (2006). Singapore's transition to innovation-based economic growth: infrastructure, institutions and government's role. *R&D Management, 36*(2), 143–160.

Yin, R. K. (1994). *Case study research: Design and methods* (2nd ed.). Thousand Oaks, CA: Sage.

6 Fostering Innovation in Chinese Industrial Parks

Pengji Wang and Lin Yuan[1]

INTRODUCTION

The last two decades have witnessed a rise in the economic growth of China, with an average annual increase in gross domestic product (GDP) of more than 9% per year. It is now generally accepted that government intervention has, at times, played a positive role in promoting economic growth in China (Linden, 2004). To develop technological competitiveness and catalyse economic growth at the nation, state, and city levels, the Chinese government has enacted a series of national high- and new-technology industrial development programs, namely, the Torch Program, within the context of the country's evolving national innovation system. Within this system, one of the important aims of Chinese government's industrial policy is to establish high-technology industrial parks and development zones.

As a group, China's high-technology industrial parks and development zones have grown dramatically in recent years. The number of science and technology industrial parks and development zones approved by the State Council was 53 in 1991, and this number has increased to 254 in 2013. The total revenue for all zones reached 16,569 billion RMB in 2012. Their export achieved US$376.04 billion, 18.4% of all the foreign trade (News Letter: Torch Centre of Ministry of Science and Technology, 2013).

Although high-technology industrial parks have achieved tremendous economic successes in China, the emphasis of booming high-tech industries has been on hardware rather than software ("Economic Structure," 2012). At the same time, although Chinese firms' manufacturing capabilities are well recognized, their capability for innovation remains relatively weak. This calls into question the Chinese government's ability to nurture the innovation capability of firms within high-technology industrial park.

To examine this issue more precisely, we apply the Managerial Flow framework to analyse the cases of Suzhou Industrial Park (SIP) and Chengdu High-Tech Industrial Park (CIP) in China. These two industrial parks are chosen because they represent different contexts and development models. Through comparison, the potential impact of policy and contextual factors on the fostering of innovation capability can be observed.

The SIP case typifies the nature of technology parks that are located in coastal areas, where the economy is more developed and infrastructure is better equipped. In contrast, CIP operates in an inland environment, not only with a less developed local market but also with a low-cost production advantage. Using a Managerial Flow lens, we analyze and compare managerial considerations that have impact on development of innovation in the SIP and CIP cases. We also identify and suggest some managerial actions to be taken to improve performance in these sites, including recommendations on how indigenous innovation capability can manifest through more targeted policy.

INNOVATION POLICY AND MANAGERIAL FLOW

Supply-side innovation policy tools focus on human resource management, tax reductions, intellectual property (IP) protection, and financing, which can influence decisions on inputs into the innovation system (Department of Business Enterprise & Regulation Reform [BERR], 2008). When applied to the context of technology parks, a focus in policy on these factors is essential in ensuring a base level of capital, within an appropriate legal and policy framework to facilitate production (European Commission, 2013). However, drawing from the experience of Organisation for Economic Co-operation and Development (OECD; 2011) countries, supply-side innovation policies alone cannot bring innovation performance and productivity to desired levels. As part of a greater awareness of the importance of feedback linkages between supply and demand in the innovation process, public policy needs to embrace innovation-friendly market conditions that incentivize demand for innovations (European Commission, 2013).

Demand-side policy instruments that stimulate innovation seek to stimulate demand for and create better conditions for the uptake of innovation, and the diffusion of innovation (Edler & Gerghio, 2007). Policy instruments to enhance demand-side innovation range from public procurement (usually through tenders to private companies who can increase innovation performance of a service), to innovation-related regulations (OECD, 2011). An example of innovation-related regulations includes taxation as a means to create demand for innovations, that is, the government provides energy renewal-target tax incentives for companies who achieve a certain standard in these fields. Accordingly, the companies will be motivated to innovate their production process to enjoy the incentives.

In this chapter we connect the concepts of supply- and demand-side innovation policies to the Managerial Flow Framework. At its most basic level, supply- and demand-side innovation policy instruments align with the managerial competency of *strategy*. Strategy, in the context of Managerial Flow, is concerned with the degree to which a policy program is resourced and supported to achieve long-term, targeted goals

(Vecchi & Brusoni, 2012). While more latent, other Managerial Flow considerations, including *governance, selection, coordination,* and *communication,* are manifested as the outcomes of *strategy* and warrant analysis. For example, government *strategy* can aim to develop industry parks and clusters containing highly competitive firms seeking to achieve a collective innovation target. Such a configuration requires *governance* and *coordination* considerations under the Managerial Flow framework. Furthermore, instruments such as tax incentives for firms that achieve a high level in innovation capacity represent a *selection* consideration. Finally, high-technology firms that develop pipelines of communication with other domestic and global partners receive tacit knowledge. Such pathways can facilitate knowledge and innovation gains and, as a result, competitive advantage. These represent a *knowledge* consideration under the Managerial Flow framework.

METHOD

Using a Managerial Flow lens, we explore the supply- and demand-side policy instruments at play within two high-technology parks in China. Our study is informed by a document analysis of media, economic, and policy material related to CIP and SIP. Our analysis begins with a contextual analysis of CIP and SIP. We move to identify the strengths and weakness of the policy tools in place in these technology parks using the Managerial Flow Framework.

CONTEXTUAL ANALYSIS: CIP

Established in 1988, CIP was one of most successful national high technology development zones in central China. The park is governed by the Chengdu High-Tech Development Zone Party Committee, which is an agency dispatched by the Chengdu Municipal Party Committee and Government to assume all management functions of Party affairs, economic, administration and social affairs.

Since its establishment, CIP has made remarkable achievements in industrial development, product incubation, system innovation, and business attraction. In 2013, CIP achieved an industrial added value of 104 billion RMB, 19% up over the year before. The comprehensive strength ranks the fourth among China's 88 state-level high-tech zones.

As opposed to other large high-tech industrial parks that generally locate in coastal area, CIP resides inland. It is located in Chengdu, the capital of Sichuan province and an important central city in Central and Western China. As compared to coastal area in China, inland areas in China have advantages in manufacturing cost. In terms of human resource cost, the average salary for experienced engineer in foreign firms in Chengdu is from 1,500 to 3,000 RMB per month, while even for senior managers, the average wage is only from 2,300 to 5,000 RMB per month. By comparison, the average wage in Beijing is 4,672 RMB per month, while it is 4,331 RMB per month in Shanghai. This shows that the cost of professional human resource is much lower in Chengdu as compared to other large cities. Chengdu also has advantage in utility cost. For example, in 2013, the power price in Sichuan Province ranks 21st among 31 provinces in China ("Power Price Comparison," 2013).

Although Chengdu has advantage in terms of production cost, the economic development of inland area in China is less advanced compared to coastal area. The inland area also has disadvantages in terms of economic aggregation, transportation and communication network, and technology and education. According to the marketization index (Fan & Wang, 2010), the marketization of western China is also much lower than coastal area, such as Shanghai, Jiangsu, and Guangdong. The western China market has two main characteristics: local government's domination in economic development and the key role of large-scale state-owned enterprises in the market (Hou, 2013). In summary, CIP enjoys both advantages and disadvantages due to its inland location in China.

CONTEXTUAL ANALYSIS: SIP

SIP is a new township located in East Suzhou, a major industrial city approximately 80 kilometers from the commercial center and port facilities at Shanghai. Launched in 1994, SIP now hosts six functioning areas: Jinji Lake-Rim Central Business District, DuShu Lake Innovation District of Science and Technology, Eastern High-Tech Industrial Area, Integrated Free Trade Zone, SIP Ecological Science Hub, and Yangcheng Lake Tourism Resort. According to Peng and Sun (2011), as an effort to clone and adapt Singapore model to China, SIP has been through a series of structural transformation since its initiation.

Before 1999, collaborating with the Singapore government, SIP followed an export-oriented economic strategy dominated by processing trade. At the time, a governance structure typified by a separation between development and administration was established. SIP was developed by China–Singapore Suzhou Industrial Park Development Co. Ltd (CSSD), which was a joint venture between a Singapore consortium and a China consortium,[2] but managed by the local government agency, Suzhou Industrial Park Administrative Committee (SIPAC). From 2000 to 2007, threatened by Asian financial crisis, SIP sought to attract foreign investment and to promote its own manufacturing industry. Since 2008, SIP has set the new target as to highlight technology innovation and manufacturing industry upgrading and to shift toward an industry structure dominated by emerging and high-tech industries, supported by financial industries and modern service industries. To pursue the new strategic direction, in the current stage, SIP formed its own strategic model, that is, to attract foreign investors to remedy the lack of indigenous innovation capability and, at the same time, to depend on international demand as the motive to encourage domestic innovation capability.

To support such a model, SIP has taken series of effective managerial actions to create important managerial assets. In terms of incentive structure, SIP has been improving intellectual property protection, providing support for firms' innovation activities in numerous aspects, such as tax deduction or exemption in the first 5 years for high-tech companies, tax rebate for R&D and training expense, subsidies for patent and copyright application, credit support, discounted leasing rate, and so on (Official Website of Suzhou Industrial Park, 2009). In terms of building knowledge capacity, SIP has worked on attracting high-level talent and personnel in short supply and establishing shared research lab, among other efforts. In terms of coordination and resource sharing, the SIPAC has created more than 10 public sci-tech service platforms (including shared sci-tech literature, Internet resources, commercialization intermediaries) and more than 30 open research labs in several universities (e.g., a water environment lab in University of Science and Technology of China, and a medical materials lab in Dongnan University, among others; *Introduction of the Technology Supporting Policy in SIP*; Official Website of the Suzhou Industrial Park, 2009). The measures were very successful in attracting foreign and domestic firms to locate in SIP.

By the end of June 2008, SIP had attracted around 3,300 foreign enterprises, including 82 *Fortune 500* multinational companies (MNCs) with a cumulative contractual foreign investment of US$34 billion and domestic companies with total contractual investment of 130 billion RMB (US$19 billion; Farole & Akinci, 2011). There has been rapid clustering of industries in information and communications technologies (ICT), thin-film transistor and liquid crystal display screens, and automotive and aeronautical parts and recently, the zone has shown rapid emergence of high-end sectors, including software, outsourcing services, and pharmaceuticals (Farole & Akinci, 2011). In 2009, SIP has been ranked the most competitive industrial parks in China by China Institute of City Competitiveness (Ge, 2011).

At the same time, some other statistics show a different picture, particularly for the performance of high-tech and innovation side. For example, according to SIP 12th Five-year Plan for Technology Development (Suzhou Government, 2011), the sales from new products was only 21.15% in the total sales, far less than those in several other high-tech industrial parks, such as Zhongguancun (54%), Shenzhen (40%), Wuhan (35%), and Shanghai (30%). The profitability in SIP enterprises was 4.97%, lower than those in several other high-tech industrial parks, such as Zhongguancun (7.36%), Tianjin (7.84%), Hefei (6.90%), and Dalian (6.82%). These statistics imply SIP at its takeoff stage, may have some managerial gaps in its public policies in promoting innovation capabilities. In the next section, we identify the gaps following the managerial flow model. Based on our document analysis Table 6.1 profiles the managerial considerations, that is, *strategy*, *governance*, *communication*, *coordination*, and *selection*, in the cases of SIP and CIP.

Table 6.1   Results: Managerial Gaps

	SIP	CIP
Strategy	SIP's policies target both supply- and demand-side innovation. On the supply side, there is a focus on developing foreign investment, local labor training, and tax incentives for domestic firms. On the demand side, there are tax incentives and access to fast finance to encourage domestic companies to meet international software demand.	The CIP focuses on supply-side innovation in its policies, such as developing the human resources, facilitating tax incentives, and ensuring good intellectual property arrangement for foreign investors.
Governance	The governing body of SIP, coined "SIPAC," is a multiparty joint venture with domestic and foreign partners, including the government. It is modeled upon and receives support from Singapore.	CIP is governed by a very large agglomeration of parties, with very strong links to the regional government.
Knowledge	Poor retention of skilled human capital	Poor access to and retention of skilled human capital
Coordination	Foreign companies that locate in SIP do not generally engage with domestic companies and activities, but rather use the site as a platform for further foreign trade. Furthermore, the SIP is dependent on the government to administer operations such as patent licensing.	The CIP has an open access policy and contains firms representing multiple sectors. However, there is very little integration between these firms and sectors, and hence, there is a strong "silo" mentality.
Selection	Selection criteria for high-tech enterprises are too loose to effectively identity the most promising innovators.	CIP targets multiple industries to attain a large scale. CIP allows companies in several listed high-technology industries to enter the park, no matter whether the firm is engaged in R&D.

COMPARISON AND DISCUSSION STRATEGY

On the supply side, to attract foreign investment, SIP has made several efforts. From the very beginning, SIP has made heavy investment in developing physical infrastructure (Han, 2008). Second, by 2009, more than 2,200 Chinese officials has attended the training programs held in Singapore to learn about the "software," including providing investors with a clean and beautiful environment, high-quality infrastructure, and a "lean, unified and efficient" management structure, among other items (Han, 2008). Third, SIP provides numerous tax incentives to attract foreign investment. For example, the imported products by foreign enterprises are free of duties if they are used for R&D activities (Official website of Suzhou Industrial Park, 2009). However, very few, if any, incentives have been effective in targeting foreign investors' knowledge creation activities. In this way, it was expected that incentives will lead MNCs to embed their R&D activities in SIP; the actual situation is that the enterprises dominated by foreign capital are reluctant to apply for patents in China due to that they are subject to the performance evaluation from their headquarters and their home country policy environment. Some foreign invested enterprises even have zero registered patents. Therefore, a large number of foreign enterprises are not embedded in SIP and hesitate to locate their core R&D activities there (Suzhou Government, 2011).

On the demand side, SIP provides incentives to drive domestic high-tech enterprises to better meet international demand, through which to develop their indigenous innovation capability. For example, software exporters in SIP can enjoy tax exemption and subsidy of 0.2 RMB per 1 US dollar. Additionally, fast channel for getting loans and discounted loans are offered for exported software transaction. These demand side policies are helpful in incorporating SIP enterprises into global supply chain. However, because China has been historically advantageous in low value-added activities, foreign demand cannot effectively orient domestic firms to develop their capabilities.

In contrast, CIP emphasizes supply-side incentives for innovation in isolation. According to *Policies to Encourage and Support High-tech Firms' Innovation and Entrepreneur in CIP* (Internet Society of Chengdu, 2005), for example, subsidies of more than RMB 10 million are allocated to those innovative firms with promising market potential. Rewards are given to firms and individuals who contribute significantly in research (getting patents or national-level awards) or make good IP arrangement. Subsidy is given to the high-tech entrepreneurs when they lease or buy the production base. All of these policies work on reducing suppliers' input cost while failing to drive the demand of innovation. This goes some way to explain why the innovation capacity in CIP is underperforming. This issue is revealed by the survey conducted by International Data Corporation (IDC) in 2010 that among six main high-technology industrial parks in China, the level of satisfaction of preferential policies by firms in CIP is far below the average.

GOVERNANCE

SIP in many ways has an advantage in governance structure over CIP. In the first instance, SIP is modeled on already successful technology parks operating in Singapore. At the outset, this modeling facilitates a legitimacy of actions within the park, as well as fosters knowledge sharing with Singapore being the joint-venture partner. In contrast, CIP is located more remotely from the primary trade centers of Asia, which has a domestically oriented governance structure.

KNOWLEDGE

It is generally recognized that professional human resource is one of the most important driving forces in high-technology industries. The steady increase of number and scale of high-technology firms in the park leads to the rise of demand for professional personnel in high-tech sections.

Both SIP and CIP struggle to obtain a supply of professional human resources. The ratio of labor force with postgraduate degree in SIP is far lower than that in other domestic or foreign industrial parks, as shown in Table 6.2. This is mainly due to the intense competition for talent from other industrial parks and coastal cities (Suzhou Government, 2011). Moreover, the high property costs compared to nearby cities further inhibits new talent from setting up bases here (Suzhou Government, 2011).

While CIP has a slightly higher score for ratio of labor force with a master's degree or above, it suffers significantly from a locational disadvantage. The supply of professional human resources in the geographic area of CIP

Table 6.2 Ratio of Labor Force With Master's Degree or Above in Domestic and Foreign Industrial Parks (2011)

	Ratio of labor force with master's degree or above (%)
Suzhou Industrial Park (SIP)	2.52
Chengdu High-Tech Industrial Park (CIP)	5.52
Silicon Valley	43
Hsinchu Science and Industrial Park	25.1
Shenzhen industrial park	13.22
Zhangjiang Hi-Tech Park	10.76
Zhongguancun Science Park	10.22
Wuhan industrial park	6.31
Xi'an High-Tech Industrial Development Zone	6.12

Source: Suzhou Government (2011).

is apparently lower than the coastal area in China, partly because of lack of famous universities in the central area in China. Among the 211 national key universities recognized by the Ministry of Education of China, only five locate in Sichuan province (Official Website of the Ministry of Education of China, 2014). Additionally, the lower salary in central area as compared to coastal area disadvantages CIP in attracting and retaining professional human.

The 2010 IDC survey also demonstrates that firms in the CIP perceived nurturing and attracting talents as very important (rating 3.5 out of 5), while the satisfaction level for the existing talents stock was only 2.5 out of 5. In SIP, nurturing and attracting talent was perceived more important (rating at 4.4 out of 5), while the satisfaction level for existing talent stock was the same as CIP (i.e., 2.5 out of 5).

COORDINATION

Another managerial gap is SIP's insufficient coordination among relevant parties. Several important parties in an innovation system include academic institutions, domestic and foreign high-tech industry players, supporting sectors, and so on. The insufficient coordination in SIP is, first, reflected by most of the foreign enterprises mainly developing specialization and integration in their global network, while making little connection with the domestic private enterprises, owing to lack of pertinent incentive and talent pool (Suzhou Government, 2011). Hence, the spillover effect and clustering synergy are limited.

Additionally, the insufficient coordination is reflected by that high-tech companies depend on government to a great extent in terms of project application and patent application, among others. Hence, the sci-tech intermediary service system is not active at all. In SIP, the proportion of the revenue from the sci-tech intermediary service sector is only 3.81%, much lower than other high-tech district where the proportion is higher than 20% (Suzhou Government, 2011).

However, one positive step that SIP is taking to enhance the access to skilled capital and knowledge spillover in the park is inviting 10 foreign universities to set up research and teaching centers in the park since 2010. Such research and teaching centers include a research and biomedical business center formed by Harvard University and Switzerland-based pharmaceutical giant Roche; a joint PhD program in nanotechnology between University of California, Berkeley and University of Science and Technology of China; and an agreement on long-term cooperation in innovation and commercialization between University of Waterloo and Soochow University, among others. These education and research programs have the potential to add up to some real innovation and creative talents in SIP.

Similarly, CIP suffers from the failure to integrate the several high-technology industries inside the park. Despite that CIP has issued many policies to promote the development of each supporting industries (Chengdu Government, 2012), it lacks of policies to develop a platform for information sharing and cooperation across industries. It results in that the operation of electronic information industry, bio-pharmacy, and precision machinery manufacturing industries are, to certain extent, independent from each other. On the firm level, therefore, it is difficult for firms in the park to materialize the benefits of diversified industry resources.

SELECTION

To promote indigenous innovation capability, SIP provides incentives to domestic high-tech enterprises. The basis to grant any incentive effectively is to identify the right receivers. To identify the high-tech enterprises, SIP has developed criteria, which is much looser compared to the national criteria. Such loose criteria are designed to allow more enterprises to obtain the support for innovation. However, with these loose criteria, receivers are engaging in R&D support in superficial ways (e.g., through only symbolically having R&D department or filing insignificant patents to get a subsidy) without serious commitment (Suzhou Government, 2011). One narrative exemplifying the *selection* gap is SIP comes from those investors from Taiwan who have shifted their production base from Pearl River Delta to SIP when the tax incentive in Pearl River Delta expired. However, they further shifted to Bohai Rim when the SIP period expired to enjoy the tax incentive in there. This implies the incentive is not effective to attract foreign investors to embed their research activities in SIP in the long term.

By the similar token, CIP takes a broad approach for selection. Within the park, three main industries have been emphasized, including electronic information, bio-pharmacy, and precision machinery manufacturing, and several supporting industries (e.g., logistics, finance, and exhibition). With the ambition in multiple industries, CIP is not able to pay enough attention to the development of each, which leads to the imbalance in growth of various industries. In 2010, the increase of electronic information industry almost doubled that of bio-pharmacy industry. Furthermore, CIP allows companies in several listed high-technology industries to enter the park, no matter whether the firm is engaged in R&D. As a result, many firms in the park are assembly platforms doing virtually no research or innovation. The technology is supplied by the headquarters of MNCs or is embodied in the equipment (Chengdu Government, 2012).

DISCUSSION AND CONCLUSION

Our case analysis of CIP and SIP highlights that there are a combination of factors that inhibit the development of innovation capacity within these technology parks. As China becomes a more prominent leader in global production, we argue that there is a need to enhance the domestic innovation capacity, through both supply- and demand-side innovation policy instruments. We conclude with some suggestions, informed by the Managerial Flow framework, that CIP and SIP could take to enhance their respective innovation capacities.

In an effort to stimulate further innovation development within SIP, policies should seek to tighten their selection criteria. By focusing solely on providing support for high-potential domestic firms, the SIP can stimulate domestic innovation leaders. Regarding coordination among relevant sectors, more actions may be needed in developing service intermediaries and promoting the connections between foreign and domestic high-tech firms. With the right incentive scheme provided and the knowledge capacity built, industrial park managers and private firms may be motivated to allocate more resources to innovations rather than simply to low-cost mass production.

For the case of CIP, while the park has achieved high growth in recent years, it has had little effect on the innovation profile of the region. To stimulate innovation, CIP should enhance its strategy by launching effective demand-side policies, such as health and safety regulations, standardization, and public procurement of innovative goods and service, which could stimulate firms to undertake innovation and balance out the supply-side focus. CIP also needs to develop innovation-based performance evaluation criteria for its incentive structure. This may include instruments such as revenue from new product and service, and number of patents.

These cases provide insight into the impact of technology park development policy on the fostering of innovation capacity for regions. Although China has made some very promising developments in this area, new actions are required that target innovation development more directly.

NOTES

1. Both authors contributed equally to this work.
2. From 1994 to December 31, 2000, CSSD was 65% owned by the Singapore consortium and 35% owned by the Chinese consortium. From 1994 to 2003, three of the four chief executive officers of CSSD were Singapore civil servants.

REFERENCES

Chengdu Government. (2012). *12th Five-year plan for Chengdu High-Tech Industry*. Retrieved from http://www.chengdu.gov.cn/uploadfiles/070305020401/20120222132333.pdf

Chengdu High-Tech Industrial Development Zone. (2013). *Chengdu high-tech zone investment guide*. Retrieved from http://www.cdht.gov.cn/cdht/service.do?act=detail&id=00001995

Department of Business Enterprise & Regulation Reform. (2008). *Regulation and innovation: Evidence and policy implications* (BERR Economics Paper No. 4). Retrieved from http://www.berr.gov.uk/files/file49519.pdf

Economic structure and context: Key sectors. (2012, March). *China Country Monitor*, pp. 20–21.

Edler, J., & Georghio, L. (2007). Public procurement and innovation—resurrecting the demand side. *Research Policy, 36*(7), 949–963. doi:10.1016/j.respol.2007.03.003

European Commission. (2013). *Developing an evaluation and progress methodology to underpin the intervention logic for the action plan to boost demand for European innovations.* Retrieved from http://ec.europa.eu/enterprise/policies/innovation/files/action-plan-methodology-final-report_en.pdf

Fan, G., & Wang, X. (2010). *NERI index of marketization of China's provinces:* Beijing, China: National Economic Research Institute.

Farole, T., & Akinci, G. (Eds.). (2011). *Special economic zones: Progress, emerging challenges, and future directions.* Washington, DC: World Bank.

Ge, L. (2011). SIP becomes the most competitive industrial park in China. Retrieved from http://www.subaonet.com/html/24h_news/2011218/11218234812345548125.html

Han, M. (2008). *The China-Singapore Suzhou Industrial Park: Can the Singapore model of development be exported?* Available from ScholarBank@NUS website: http://scholarbank.nus.edu.sg/handle/10635/16090?show=full

Hou, Y. Z. (2013, December 26). No shortcuts to development. *China Daily*, p.8.

International Data Corporation. (2010). *Survey on industrial parks.* Unpublished raw data.

Internet Society of Chengdu. (2005). Policies to encourage and support high-tech firms' innovation and entrepreneur in CIP. Retrieved from http://www.iscd.org.cn/detail/?zhongid=237

Linden, G. (2004). China standard time: A study in strategic industrial policy. *Business & Politics, 6*(3), 1–26. doi:10.2202/1469-3569.1069

News Letter: Torch Centre of Ministry of Science and Technology. (2013). Retrieved from http://isd.arizona.edu/castusa/newsletter/2013NO.19_CN.pdf

Official website of Chengdu High-Tech Industrial Park. (2014). Introduction to Chengdu High-tech Industrial Park. Retrieved from http://www.cdht.gov.cn/cdht/

Official website of Suzhou Industrial Park. (2009). *Introduction of the technology supporting policy in SIP.* Retrieved from http://www.sipac.gov.cn/sipnews/yqzt/bzzcfz/kjfc/kjpdf/200901/P020090123485363248423.pdf

Official website of the Ministry of Education of China. (2014). Introduction to 211 Project. Retrieved from http://www.moe.edu.cn/

Organisation for Economic Co-operation and Development. (2011). *Demand-side innovation policies.* Paris: OECD Publishing.

Peng, W. S., & Sun, M. L. (2011). *Suzhou Industrial Park survey report.* Beijing: China International Capital Corporation Limited. Retrieved from http://wenku.baidu.com/view/d649ba67783e0912a2162a66.html

Power price comparison in China. (2013, August 13). Retrieved from http://money.163.com/13/0813/11/965F14Q300254UOG.html

Suzhou Government. (2011). Suzhou Industrial Park (SIP) 12th five-year plan for talent development. Retrieved from www.zfxxgk.suzhou.gov.cn

Vecchi, V., & Brusoni, M. (2012). The managerial flow of public administration—a conceptual framework. *Singapore Management Review, 34*(Suppl. 2), 26–34.

Part III

Economic Development and Managerial Flow

7 Bottom-Up Local Government Change and Managerial Flow

A Regional Australian Case Study

Grant Cairncross

INTRODUCTION

This chapter investigates the development of a *bottom-up* community and economic development strategy in regional Australia. Using the Managerial Flow framework, we focus on the strategic and coordinative factors associated with the economic development plan, and investigate what factors worked, and what did not. The Managerial Flow framework enables a detailed analysis of the management processes involved in the implementation of public policy (Vecchi & Brusoni, 2012). In addition, the stakeholder issues pertaining to resistance to change associated with the implementation of policy are explored.

The economic development strategy explored in this case formed part of a broader 2030 Economic Development Plan developed by an Australian local government authority, namely, the Coffs Harbour City Council (CHCC). Coffs Harbour is a city of 75,000 situated on the coast in northern New South Wales, which is halfway between Sydney and Brisbane.

The National Centre for Justice Planning (2014, p. 1) defines *bottom-up strategy formulation* as a process whereby

> instead of imposing decisions from above there is a commitment to assisting communities and local governments develop comprehensive strategies to respond to the problems and public safety issues in their neighborhoods.

Bottom-up strategy formulation involves deeper-than-normal community engagement processes and extensive feedback loops. In addition, the breadth of stakeholders involved in community engagement means that bottom-up strategies need to incorporate diverse agendas while also requiring the conceptualization and implementation of new ideas, products, and services that emerge from such an extensive process.

In regional development, local government authorities are the public sector organizations that play a role in facilitating *bottom-up strategy development*. These organizations face significant challenges in operationalizing bottom-up approaches as they have a large number of stakeholders and they operate under a generically legislated approach to strategy formulation. In addition, contextual factors including resistance from local/organizational politics, threats to organizational and/or individual power, challenges to cultural norms and institutionalized practices, bad timing, and a lack of understanding of the principles of bottom-up strategy formulation can also inhibit processes (Dent & Galloway, 1999). Local government authorities who are charged with the task of developing bottom-up policies must therefore consider how their own managerial assets, in the form of organizational strategic direction and planning and that of their stakeholders, may affect any proposed bottom-up strategy development and outcomes (Vecchi & Brusoni, 2012).

This chapter investigates a case of bottom-up Economic Development Strategy (EDS) for regional development using the managerial flow framework. As a foundation for pursuing this aim, literature focusing on public-sector strategy formulation, the history of regional development and local government strategic orientation in Australia, and the management of change are explored.

A History of Regional Development Approaches in Australia

Stimson, Stough, and Nijkamp (2011) argue that in addition to traditional approaches, regional economic development policies need focus on how regions do the following:

(a) Accumulate core competencies;
(b) Develop social capital;
(c) Build strategic leadership;
(d) Manage resources;
(e) Build market intelligence;
(f) Provide strategic infrastructure;
(g) Develop a risk management capability; and
(h) Incorporate principles of sustainability into their regional economic development strategies (pp. 49–50).

What has emerged is an approach where communities and regions are taking greater responsibility for articulating policies and their implementation. These approaches involve communities and other stakeholders having a greater say in the development and implementation of regional economic development plans.

Within the context of this study, that is, the State of New South Wales, Australia, the Local Government Act 1993 (NSW) requires local government authorities to implement extensive community strategic plans (Grant, Dollery, & Kort, 2011). The relevant legislation does not specify that they be done in either a *top-down* or a *bottom-up* way, but in practice, most done in that time have been predominantly top down or in a narrow form of bottom up. The community strategic plans provide the legal and regulatory framework to enable the participation of local communities in the affairs of local government (Department of Local Government [NSW], 2009, 16). As a result all local government authorities need to have the following plans in place prior to implementation:

- A community strategic plan (with a minimum 10-year duration),
- A community engagement strategy that sets out how each council will engage its community when developing its community strategic plan,
- A resourcing strategy that includes a long-term financial plan, a workforce management strategy and an asset management plan,
- A delivery program, and
- An operational plan, including a statement of revenue policy and a detailed annual budget (Department of Local Government [NSW], 2009, p. 4).

Authoring these plans is a process that is largely left up to the local government authorities themselves. Furthermore, often the procedures are influenced by different types of regional economic development strategy theories that have become popular in Australia and elsewhere.

In Australia regional economic development is both a product and a process that Stimson, Stough, and Roberts (2006, p. 6) suggest relate to

> the application of economic processes and resources available to a region that result in the sustainable development of, and the desired outcomes for, a region that meet the values and expectations of business, of residents and of visitors.

Approaches as to how regional economic development should be practiced in Australia have changed over time, often influenced by international trends. For example in the mid-1950s to late 1960s economic development emphasized exogenous factors as the main drivers of economic growth and development as proposed by Harrod (1948) and Domar (1947). This was mostly based on a belief that a comparative advantage/disadvantage analysis was crucial. A region had a comparative advantage if goods and services could be produced at a lower opportunity cost than in other regions. From the early 1970s until the late 1990s there was an emphasis on competitive regional advantage as opposed to comparative regional advantage. This was based on the work of Solow (1994) wherein emphasis was placed on how the goods and services produced by a region with a competitive advantage were hard to replicate (Department of Regional Australia, Local Government, Arts and Sport [DRALGAS], 2013).

Much regional economic development thinking in Australia still reflects these two archetypes, and singly and together they are often euphemistically called "attract and retain." However, over the past 20 years a new regional growth theory has emerged based around endogenous, or internal, growth informed by the work of Romer (1986, 1990, 1994). Endogenous growth theory, sometimes termed "localism," has a greater focus on triple-bottom-line sustainability, as well as an emphasis on the impact of internal factors on regional economic development (Organisation for Economic Co-operation and Development [OECD], 2009). In Europe, for example, it was found that overall the significance of local specificities has ironically intensified against a background of increasing globalization and broader economic assimilation (Storper, 1995). In Australia Stimson et al. (2011) argue that endogenous growth theory supports an integrated approach to regional economic development that pursues a development agenda focused on improving a region's capacity and capability to better develop its own resources by obtaining a collaborative advantage through actively involving the public, private, and community sectors.

This shift in the regional economic development concept has led to a change in focus from top-down approaches with national governments being preeminent in planning and implementation to a more bottom-up, or "place-based," inclusive regional approach. This approach requires decentralized planning and decision making to inform the strategic orientation of local government. The OECD (2009) argues this requires greater intergovernmental coordination of the wide range of networks that contribute to endogenous regional economic development, which has the means to place an extra burden of responsibility on local government authorities and communities (Herbert-Cheshire, 2000).

Nevertheless endogenous growth strategies have started to become more important to local government authorities in Australia as they recognize that by involving multiple stakeholders they have a greater ability to create consensual and effective growth strategies, directly or indirectly (Stimson et al., 2011). This is not to say that exogenous strategic influences have been ignored completely; however, exogenous strategies have been recognized as allowing local government authorities a limited ability to influence outcomes.

Within the Managerial Flow framework, setting up an effective stakeholder governance and coordination framework to facilitate the development of endogenous growth requires significant investment for local government authorities. Noting the diversity of stakeholder groups involved in bottom-up approaches, one of the potential negative influences that may ensue is resistance to community engagement that may be seen by some as "a change too far."

Michaelis, Stegmaier, and Sonntag (2009) argue that local government authorities undertaking community engagement using bottom-up processes need undertake a number of actions for managing resistance to change. Such actions comprise assessing, understanding, and involving those people and stakeholders likely to resist change; empowering resisters and others through offering perspectives as to why the change is happening and why the bottom-up process is pertinent; and through emphasizing that there is no difference between "the greater good" and self-interest (Comte, 1865/2009). In addition, the local government authority in their facilitation role need to communicate to stakeholders that an effective bottom-up approach is also top down under the condition that there is legitimacy in leadership (Vecchi & Brusoni, 2012). In this way, the economic development strategy developed as a result of a bottom-up approach needs an overall commitment by the local government authority to enact/implement.

RESEARCH DESIGN AND METHODS

The chapter moves to explore the managerial assets that comprise the implementation of *bottom-up* economic development through a case study analysis. To achieve this we adopt a single, embedded case study using an action research approach. The case study design provides a means to conduct a comprehensive exploration of the research questions in a real-life context (Yin, 2009). The context of this study concerns the formulation of a *bottom-up* economic development strategy by Coffs Harbour City Council (CHCC; 2013–2017).

This research approach allowed for a rich collection of data provided by several points of interaction between activity within the research context and the research team (Denzin & Lincoln, 2011; Patton, 2001). This took the form of multiple interactions between CHCC, its stakeholders and the researchers. In all, interactions were in the form of (a) a project launch and context analysis activity (Strengths, Weaknesses, Opportunities, Threats [SWOT] analysis and (b) a series of nine industry and sector workshops involving approximately 400 different Coffs Harbour stakeholder participants. The researcher was intimately involved in the process by facilitating the workshops, authoring the final *CHCC Background Report*, and coauthoring the final *CHCC Outcomes Report*. This position aided in the collection of rich thematic data.

The study used stratified purposeful sampling to ensure the workshop participants were appropriate for their industry/sector area. As such, the researcher was able to examine and compare and contrast phenomena of interests across all the industry sectors represented. The results of the analysis of how the CHCC used their managerial assets to inform strategy and coordinate stakeholder in the *bottom-up* process follows.

RESULTS

The aim in the development and implementation of the CHCC economic/community development strategy was to engage the community in creating the future of the City. In line with a *bottom-up* approach, the specific strategic goal of the CHCC was to encourage collaboration between organizations, to build a sense of responsibility within the community, and to unleash the ideas, passions, and expertise of those in the community who wished to make something happen. This is displayed at the beginning of the policy's charter, which was designed to

> encourage and show others that they have permission to create their own projects and it is people with passion that bring them to life.
>
> (CHCC, 2014a, p. 1)

After the community and sector workshops were completed, a *Draft Economic & Community Strategy 2013–2017* was released as part of the CHCC's overall 2030 strategy. The draft economic & community plan had a general "localization" theme running throughout it. A "Love Our City" leitmotif had emerged, and it was supported by six operational strategies, each with a key conceptual title:

- Local is best: Aiming to encourage a strong, sustainable, resilient and culturally and economically diverse local economy.
- Knowledge building: Designed to promote the health and education sectors, encourage research and development and build partnerships.
- Welcoming spaces: highlighting the utilization of already created spaces that are safe, comfortable & encourage interaction between people of all ages and our diverse groups.
- Smart and connected: Designed to ensure the community is connected to each other via new superfast broadband (NBN) to their families and the world.
- Planning for growth: Transport, Logistics, Distribution, Health and Industrial/Commercial Lands are all interlinked with, and supported by, the previous four strategies.
- Invest Coffs: Promote Coffs Harbour as an ideal investment, development, business and new resident destination. Make it attractive so it attracts (CHCC, 2014b, p. 3).

Shortly after this draft was released some degree of resistance emerged. This resistance was not numerically large, but it was represented by some "important local players," of whom most, but not all, believed in the more historical competitive regional advantage approach of "attract and retain" (Solow, 1994). The draft strategy was ultimately presented to a new elected council, which had a number of problems initially working together. For the draft economic/community strategy, these problems were exacerbated by a number of community members who had resisted the bottom-up strategy and the emergent themes that formed around localism. This caused delays in getting final policy approval because the resisters to the bottom-up strategy were acutely aware that the sector groups were, in effect, networks that required to collaborate within and across sectors to achieve their goals and that if they could make that difficult, then they could also make final strategy adoption hard to achieve.

A review of the draft bottom-up economic development strategy program led to the understanding that an initial focus on industry representation, as opposed to broader sector representation, was ineffective. This prompted a change to sectorial representative groups that resulted in a more representative approach. It also included the adoption of a steering committee of sectorial representatives, which allowed for better cross-sectorial communication and, ultimately, a more considered, bottom-up strategy planning approach to the allocation of scarce internal resources.

One problem to emerge with the steering committee was that a lack of a clear framework as to what their role was. This led to some of its members believing that they were a committee of review and it was herein that some of the resistance to change already noted became more overt.

Through the development of the final economic development strategy the local government authority ultimately proscribed a range of innovation policies under a theme of localism, and these were developed in conjunction with relevant stakeholders and were aligned with existing plans all of which were mandated by the NSW state government. The stated revision of actions of the Coffs Harbour economic development strategy included the provision for consistent monitoring. This is noted in the following:

> *Council will host an annual forum of the overall reference group to report on progress, encourage cross industry/sector engagement and action and to also discuss trends, opportunities and issues of relevance to the Coffs Harbour economy . . . These form an independent basis for the monitoring and evaluation process for the Coffs Harbour Economic Strategy. Those actions identified in this strategy that are the responsibility of Council's Enterprise Coffs will be reported to Council as part of Council's six-monthly reviews of its Operational Plan which will be publicly reported.*

(CHCC, 2014b, p. 60)

DISCUSSION AND IMPLICATIONS

Bottom-up change is about empowerment, a possible weakness of which is that the already empowered will resist for differing reasons (Giles & Stokke, 2000) and that it "might be seen as paternalistic in certain cases: an attempt to change people, regardless of their wishes, for their own good" which is something practitioners need to be wary of (Braunack-Mayer & Louise, 2008, p. 6). As discussed earlier, Coffs Harbour was not exempt from such resistance which raised questions as to whether the CHCC had been too innovative, needed to communicate differently, or had not understood that they were, in fact, dealing with a genuine change management initiative. In some respects, this represents a breakdown of Managerial Flow. As depicted in the Managerial Flow framework, a faulty needs-and-expectations analysis can lead to a poor exploration of potential problems, or no such investigation at all, which in turn can lead to planning and knowledge gaps in upper level government structures (Vecchi & Brusoni, 2012). In the selected case there was a belief that community engagement "bottom-up" procedures that had strong majority support from those involved in the process would be adopted as formal policy reasonably easily. However, coordinating and governing the interactions between stakeholders (particularly resistors) proved very challenging. Thus, while the intention to develop a more informed regional development strategy (bottom-up approach) represents a positive strategic step, without significant provision for coordination and governance, this process can be interrupted and slowed down, as in Coffs Harbour, or even fall down.

Through the lens of Managerial Flow, the agreement to include ex post monitoring of the specified goals and, as set out in the final plan, an ongoing appraisal against key performance indicators represent a knowledge asset. Equipped with these reports, the local government authority has the ability to undertake experience-based learning (managerial asset) and to provide informed revision of future strategies (planning gap).

A retrospective analysis of the case study project being analyzed for this chapter would also show that the final economic/community development strategy took far longer to be finally approved than originally anticipated. The main potential impact of this delay is that because political approval took so long the initial enthusiasm for the project and involvement was in decline. As a result much of the momentum and hard work in generating action within sector groups, who have not had an extensive history of collaborative success, may well require future attention and support.

REFERENCES

Braunack-Mayer, A., & Louise, J. (2008). The ethics of community empowerment: Tensions in health promotion theory and practice. *Promotion and Education, 15*(3), 5–8.

Coffs Harbour City Council. (2014a). *Coffs Harbour economic strategy 2014–2017: Growth through localisation and love of our city.* Retrieved from http://www.coffsharbour.nsw.gov.au/learning-and-prospering/projects/Pages/Economic-Strategy.aspx

Coffs Harbour City Council. (2014b). *Coffs Harbour economic strategy: Mobilising the economy through industry groups and their action plans.* Retrieved from http://www.coffsharbour.nsw.gov.au/learning-and-prospering/projects/Documents/CHES_ActionPlan_Dec13_Final_210414_web.pdf

Comte, A. (2009). *A general view of positivism* (J. H. Bridges, Trans.). Cambridge, England: Cambridge University Press. (Original work published 1865)

Dent, E. B., & Galloway, S. (1999). Challenging "resistance to change." *Journal of Applied Behavioral Science, 35*(1), 25–41.

Denzin, N. K., & Lincoln, Y. S. (2011). *The SAGE handbook of qualitative research* (4th ed.). Thousand Oaks, CA: Sage.

Department of Local Government. (2010). *Integrated planning and reporting guidelines for councils*. Retrieved from www.glg.nsw.gov.au/dlg/dlghome/dlg-generalindex. asp

Department of Regional Australia, Local Government, Arts and Sport. (2013). *Regional Economic Development Guide*. Canberra, Australia: Author.

Domar, E. (1947) Expansion and employment. *American Economic Review*, *37*(1), 343–355

Giles, M., & Stokke, K. (2000). Participatory development and empowerment: The dangers of localism. *Third World Quarterly*, *21*(2), 247–268.

Grant, B., Dollery, B., & Kort, M. (2011). *Australian local government and community emgagement:Are all our community plans the same? Does it matter?* (Working Paper, Centre for Local Government). Armidale, Australia: University of New England.

Harrod, R. F. (1948). *Towards a dynamic economics*. London, England: Macmillan.

Herbert-Cheshire, L. (2000). Contemporary strategies for rural community development in Australia: A governmentality perspective. *Journal of Rural Studies*, *16*, 203–215.

Michaelis, B., Stegmaier, R., & Sonntag, K. (2009). Affective commitment to change and innovation implementation behavior: The role of charismatic leadership and employees' trust in top management. *Journal of Change Management*, *9*(4), 399–417.

National Centre for Justice Planning. (2014). *Commitment to bottom-up planning*. Retrieved from http://ncjp.org/strategic-planning/keys-success/bottom-up#sthash. ljAB7mrn.dpuf

Organisation for Economic Co-operation and Developement. (2009), *Regions matter: Economic recovery, innovation and sustainable growth*. Paris, France: OECD Publishing.

Patton, M. Q. (2001). *Qualitative research and evaluation methods* (3rd ed.). Thousand Oaks, CA: Sage.

Romer, P. M. (1986). Increasing returns and long run growth. *Journal of Political Economy*, *94*(5), 1002–1037.

Romer, P. M. (1990). Endogenous technological change. *Journal of Political Economy*, *98*(5, Pt. 2), S71–S102.

Romer, P. M. (1994). The origins of endogenous growth. *Economic Perspectives*, *8*(1), 3–22.

Solow, R. M. (1994). Perspectives on growth theory. *Journal of Economic Perspectives*, *8*(1), 45–54.

Stimson, R., Stough, R. R., & Nijkamp, P. (2011). *Endogenous regional development: Perspectives, measurement and emperical investigation* [Electronic ed.]. Cheltenham, England: Edward Elgar.

Stimson, R., Stough, R. R., & Roberts, B. H. (2006). *Regional economic development: Analysis and planning strategy* (2nd ed.). Berlin, Germany: Springer.

Storper, M. (1995). The resurgence of regional economies, ten years later: The region as a nexus of untraded interdependencies. *European Urban and Regional Studies*, *2*, 191–221.

Vecchi, V., & Brusoni, M. (2012). The managerial flow of public local development policies: A conceptual framework. *Singapore Management Review, 34*(2), 5–13.

Yin, R. K. (2009). *Case study research: Design and methods* (4th ed.). Thousand Oaks, CA: Sage.

8 Evaluating Economic Development Officers Through the Lens of Managerial Flow

Rod Farr-Wharton, Ben Farr-Wharton, and Yvonne Brunetto

INTRODUCTION

Economic development officers (EDOs) are public sector employees that fulfil the role of street-level bureaucrats (SLBs) in the implementation of regional economic development policies. As the importance of regionally embedded organizations for economic output has become more pronounced over the last two decades the managerial pressures placed on EDOs has increased (Markusen, 1996; Porter, 1990). However, the ability of EDOs to provide meaningful outputs for regional business clients has been seriously challenged (Kelly, 2005). This is because there is an extant mismatch between the evaluative framework applied to public-sector employees (such as EDOs), and that of the market in which the business clients operate.

This is an important issue because EDOs are tasked with implementing policies expected to grow business, which is a vital ingredient for achieving regional growth (Brunetto & Farr-Wharton, 2007). However, there is a lack of evidence examining the effectiveness of EDOs to achieve stated policy outcomes. Many top-down policy researchers believe that EDOs are similar to other SLBs in that they implement policies as expected and consequently achieve the desired outcomes, whereas bottom-up policy researchers argue that EDOs are like other SLBs in that they shape policy outcomes by using their expertise and experience to prioritize what is implemented amongst an array of (sometimes conflicting) policies (J. Stewart, 2012). Other researchers use a mixed-model approach using both top-down and bottom-up factors to explain implementation outcomes (Page, 2006). However, the acceptance of different implementation models is a contested terrain with vigorous debate about the advantages and disadvantages. One new framework aimed at addressing many of the previous approaches to policy implementation by taking a more managerial lens for examining where policy implementation fails to achieve policy objectives is Managerial Flow (MF; Vecchi & Brusoni, 2012). The main difference between MF and other implementation frameworks (top-down, bottom-up, and mixed models) is the extent to which managerial organizational factors are captured in analyzing policy outcomes. MF evaluates policy implementation using five dimensions (*strategy, governance, selection, partnership*, and *knowledge*). The new framework provides new insight into the enabling and hindering factors either facilitating or thwarting policy implementation. Although in its infancy of theoretical development, Vecchi and Brusoni's (2012) managerial flow perspective differs from other implementation frameworks by providing a capability growth component that can be used to identify which potential new implementation strategies can be used to improve implementation outcomes. The new paradigm emphasizes responsiveness to the business client while still achieving government accountability/managerialist measures.

Hence, this chapter adopts Vecchi and Brusoni's (2012) MF framework to examine the role of EDOs in implementing policies aimed at facilitating business growth as a strategy of regional entrepreneurial development. To achieve this, the study explores the case of South East Queensland, Australia and observes the managerial gaps present in the implementation of regional economic development policies by EDOs for small to medium-sized enterprises (SMEs) of five local government jurisdictions (encompassing both urban and regional areas). This issue is captured in the following research question:

RQ1: How effective are economic development officers in moderating policy-business relationship to provide meaningful assistant to businesses?

This chapter has four parts. The first part provides a targeted review of the policy frameworks for supporting business growth including policies specifically related to promoting clustering within Australia. This is followed by a review of factors affecting EDO practices and an account of the theoretical framework used to evaluate EDOs. The second part describes the methods used to collect data. The third part reports the results and uses the Discussion section to identify the similarities and differences in perspective of EDOs and businesses in relation to public policies promoting business development in Australia. Finally, the chapter concludes with suggestions for future research.

BACKGROUND

A Policy Framework for Promoting Enterprise Development

In recent years there have been significant changes in the way government has attempted to support and grow business. However, such developments are taking place on top of a chaotic and ineffective platform (Brunetto & Farr-Wharton, 2005; Dean, Holmes, & Smith, 1997). One change has been the integration of all federal-level supporting bodies into one unit titled "Enterprise Connect." To date, the unit has thus far proved resilient, despite an undercurrent of significant ministerial portfolio change in the Australian federal government from 2009 to 2013. Enterprise Connect is charged with the responsibility of implementing business policies in Australia.

However, it cannot be assumed that business policies comprise a coherent set of well-integrated, complementary policies, each supporting the ultimate goal of growing businesses. Instead, business policies in Australia comprise an array of policies across three levels of government: (a) federal (for all Australians), (b) state (for citizens belonging to each state of Australia: New South Wales, Queensland, Victoria, etc.), and (c) local (each state has numerous local government/shire entities), each specifically aimed at growing businesses. Within the three-layered framework, the Australian federal government provides the umbrella policy framework in relation to growing businesses. Policies are developed by the Department of Industry, Innovation, Science, Research and Tertiary Education to promote the growth of small business and/or promoting innovation:

> The Department is a focal point for the development and consideration of small business policy issues within Government. It is responsible for promoting and maintaining links across the Australian Government departments and agencies responsible for implementing elements of the Government's small business policies.
>
> (Department of Industry, Innovation, Science, Research and Tertiary Education, 2011a, p. 126)

One of the main policy documents used to develop strategies for growing businesses is the *Innovation Policy Report* (Australian Government Department of Industry, Innovation, Science, Research and Tertiary Education, 2011a), which states that one of key strategies for promoting business growth and innovation is to "reenergise latent clusters rather than build new ones . . . help remove barriers to collaboration" (p. 15). Such a policy has been informed by the European Commission that states that

> genuinely open innovation requires brokerage, intermediaries and networks in which all players can participate on an equal basis. Internationally competitive clusters play a vital role in bringing together—physically and virtually—large companies and SMEs, universities, research centres and communities . . .
>
> (European Commission, 2010, p. 25)

State governments around Australia use the federal policy umbrella as a basis for making polices specific to their needs, depending on the priorities of the state. For example, the Queensland state government has developed a policy titled *South East Queensland Regional Plan 2009–2035*. The policy objectives include "where business and industry benefiting from high-quality access to regional freight corridors, proximity to workforce, and separation from conflicting uses are expected to cluster" (Queensland Department of Infrastructure and Planning, 2009, p. 113). This means that EDOs are expected to implement policies that promote collaborations amongst businesses (Brunetto & Farr-Wharton 2007).

However, the implementation of policies promoting clustering has not been successful. There are numerous reasons for that. First, Australian businesses have a low take up of government initiatives aimed at growing business (Brunetto & Farr-Wharton, 2005). Further support comes from the *Australian Innovation Systems Report* (Australian Government Department of Industry, Innovation, Science, Research and Tertiary Education, 2011b, pp. 25, 30) in that they argue that compared with other Organisation for Economic Co-operation and Development (OECD) countries; businesses, particularly SMEs in Australia have a poor record of collaborating among themselves. This is not a new problem for Australia; instead, over a decade ago, Hindle and Rusworth (2002) and Enright and Roberts (2001) argued the reason for poor collaboration was that the Australian government provides poor support and direction promoting collaboration. The findings suggest that at a federal level, established clusters are perceived as the mechanism for driving innovation in Australian businesses; however, the method of promoting and funding the policies is limited.

A further complication is the ambiguity surrounding the direction and substance provided to EDOs tasked with implementing business policies promoting clustering. Previous research suggests that in addition to poor policy direction and funding mechanisms, a complicating factor is that many EDOs within different departments across different levels of government can often be working in silos not knowing what agendas and mechanisms are being followed by other EDOs (Brunetto & Farr-Wharton, 2007). Furthermore, all EDOs operate as SLBs, which means that since the implementation of new public management (NPM), they are most likely facing increased accountability—not simply in relation to achieving policy goals, but also in achieving organizational goals—hence they are probably facing increasing levels of bureaucracy (Diefenbach, 2009). Diefenbach (2009) argues that the use of increased accountability measures has been used to increase management's power to get employees "to do with less" (Diefenbach, 2009). Hence, analysis of the implementation outcomes of business growth polices suggests a miss match between policy objectives and policy outcomes, but this does not provide an understanding of how to improve the effectiveness of business growth policies. Hence, the remainder of the chapter uses the MF framework to provide example factors affecting policy outcomes.

Developing an Evaluative Lens Through a Theory Synthesis

Vecchi and Brusoni's (2012) empirically derived managerial flow framework provides a competency based break down of the capabilities and actions mix required to implement policy effectively. Thus, they suggest that managerial assets, including *problem and solution awareness*, *leadership legitimacy*, and *experience-based amativeness*, combined with managerial actions, including *needs and expectations analysis*, *context and stakeholder mapping*, *pilot program implementation*, and *monitoring and assessment*, can combined to

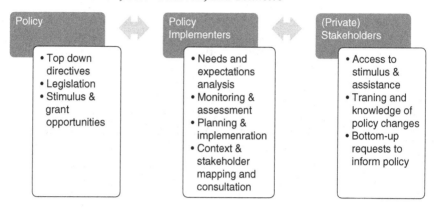

Figure 8.1   Managerial Flow Among Policy, Implementers, and Stakeholders

resolve extant policy implementation gaps including *planning gaps, governance gaps, selection gaps, partnership gaps,* and *knowledge gaps.* The process infers a much more complex and reciprocal relationship among policy, policy implementers, and (private) stakeholders (displayed graphically in Figure 8.1).

The managerial flow model fills a gap in heuristic policy implementation literature (see Ryan, 1996), and provides a balance between top-down and bottom-up policy implementation processes. As with the managerial flow perspective then, Kelly's (2005) client focus implies an enhanced degree of interaction and reciprocity between (private) stakeholder and public body (containing both *policy* and *policy implementation* staff). Owing to this then, we suggest that the presence of *managerial actions* and *managerial assets* (as they are described in the managerial flow framework) are preconditions to developing an effective evaluative framework among policy, policy implementers, and stakeholders.

Background: Managerial Gaps in the Management of Public Policy Implementation

Street-level bureaucrat is a term given to public-sector employees who act in a front line capacity in the implementation of public policies (Lipsky, 1980). Within the context of the policy cycle, EDOs are the key agents responsible for the implementation of federal-, state-, and local-level policies geared toward regional development. Furthermore, Stewart (2012) and Raadschelders and Stillman (2007) suggest that EDOs also have the power to influence the development of policy, and can act as a conduit between government and business in bottom-up and mixed policy development (Ryan, 1996). This position seemingly equips EDOs with considerable powers; however, Kelly (2005) argues that the exponential rise of accountability and administrative performance procedures for public-sector employees has significantly moderated the action of EDOs. Kelly (2005, p. 77) argues that while the goal of EDOs is to create satisfied customer-citizens, the relationship between internal performance and external value creative is not direct. Vecchi and Brusoni (2012) suggest that policy implementation breaks down because of the presence of one or more of the following managerial gaps: *strategy, governance, selection, partnership,* and *knowledge.*

STRATEGY GAP

Vecchi and Brusoni (2012, p. 6) offer the following synopsis of the strategy gap:

> Strategy gaps emerge when public programs are defined on the basis of short-term expectations, current fashions, "announcement effects, or solely to allocate financial resources that otherwise could be diverted towards other policies or programs. Consequently they lack a meaningful definition of performance indicators.

In respect to strategy in the context of a managerial perspective of public policy implementation, Kelly (2005, p. 82), adopting Kaplan and Norton's (1996) approach, suggests that public organizations need to adopt a "balanced" evaluative framework:

> The organization must create value for all stakeholders: customers, employees, financial position, and internal business process. Value creation is translated into action by developing objectives, measures, targets, and strategies in each of these four quadrants of the balanced score card.

Strategy is not only confined to the balance scorecard approach and may be identified in implementation plans affixed to policy documents. However, to date, Kaplan and Norton's (1996) framework provides an advantageous position for strategic planning and evaluation in the context of policy implementation. Finally Hospers, Desrochers, and Sautet (2009) note in relation to regional development policy implementation that industry clusters have become a standard strategy that offers more predictable results than other more selective economic policies. Applied to the context of EDOs, this study poses the following hypothesis:

> H1: *EDOs promote regional networking and industry cluster projects as strategies to enhance economic development.*

Governance Gap

Vecchi and Brusoni (2012, p. 6) offer the following description of the governance gap:

> Governance gaps refer to problems when multiple public agencies and stakeholders work together with different mandates and without a

common goal; resulting in overlapping initiatives and confusion over roles, responsibility, and accountability.

Facilitating governance for regional development initiatives is a complex process involving the management of multiple organizations and organizational types (Keast, 2011; Keast, Mandell, & Brown, 2006). In this context, industry-cluster initiatives and regional networking strategies have proved a popular scaffold around which to structure governance; however, results have been mixed (Dean et al., 1997).

However, the biggest issue for EDOs implementing economic development policies in Australia is that they work within public bureaucracies or hybrid entities and therefore are expected to meet the goals of multiple stakeholders—including the government, business, and the public at large. Brunetto and Farr-Wharton. (2005, p. 305) found that EDOs did not "have a supportive bureaucratic machinery sustaining their efforts," and therefore, their findings were that EDOs found it difficult to negotiate the bureaucratic terrain in which they operated and that this compromised their ability to deliver services effectively to businesses. Drawing from this, the study poses the following hypothesis:

H2: EDOs are inhibited by a governance gap, evidenced by poor hierarchical frameworks to support business growth.

Selection Gap

Vecchi and Brusoni (2012, p. 6) offer the following outline of the selection gap:

Selection emerges when scare resources and efforts are allocated without appropriateness under the fairness illusion. The gap also emerges from the difficulties in designing coherent projects to be supported or funded and monitored. This is particularly true with reference to entrepreneurship programmes.

Mason and Brown (2013) have noted that start-up firms have been typically funded over firms with high growth potential. These authors note that policy has tended to "look in the wrong place" to find firms to support, and as a result, high growth often fails to eventuate. Mason and Brown suggest that indicators of high growth include business internationalization, length of time in business (though this is mediated by proximity to business growth periods), market orientation, and networked innovation. Drawing from this, the study poses the following hypothesis for EDOs in the context of regional development:

H3: EDOs seek to fund start-up firms over firms that may have high growth potential.

Partnership Gap

Vecchi and Brusoni (2012, p. 6) offer the following description of the partnership gap:

> Partnership (coordination and integration) gaps emerge when a lack of leadership, reciprocity, legitimacy, and trust in the Interorganizational activities reduce the integration of public and private financial and human resources.

Coordinative devices in regional economic development programs have been shown to enhance the sharing of tacit knowledge and increase innovation (Mitchell, Waterhouse, McNeil, & Burgess, 2010; OECD, 1999). However, providing a coordinative framework for regionally embedded businesses has proved to be a significant challenge, because organizations need to overcome significant trust issues to realize advantage (Farr-Wharton, 2012; Lorenzen, 2002). Drawing from this, the chapter poses the following hypothesis:

> *H4: EDOs are faced with significant challenges in overcoming trust between firms in regional development initiatives*

Knowledge Gap

Vecchi and Brusoni (2012, p. 6) offer the following synopsis of the knowledge gap:

> Knowledge (and communication) gaps refer to asymmetric information flow and reciprocal knowledge gaps that push players to operate on different wavelengths, focusing only within their own silos.

Brunetto and Farr-Wharton (2005) identified that a number of factors compromised EDOs ability to implement regional development policies. In particular, they found that the tendency of government departments to operate as silos lead to EDOs' having to work in a "minefield" of different departments each containing some information necessary for securing funding for businesses. Drawing from this, the study poses the following hypothesis:

> *H5: EDOs are inhibited by knowledge gaps evidenced by a tendency to promote programs limited to a particular division of government.*

Methods

This study used quantitative (a survey) and qualitative research methods (interviews) to evaluate the ability of EDOs to support business growth. The study focuses on the case of South East Queensland, a largely urban region of Australia that has experienced considerable industrial development over the last few years. The survey was answered by 248 businesses operating across five different local government jurisdictions in the region (the sample size represents 38.7% of the total number of surveys that were administered). An additional 35 interviews with senior managers of businesses were conducted to explore the effectiveness of interactions existing between EDOs and businesses.

Quantitative Variables

The survey sought to profile businesses that were involved in the provision of government support (dependent variable) facilitated by EDOs. As such, the following independent variables were sought from businesses: *Time in business, Number of employees, Industry type, Region, Annual turnover,* and *Network membership.* Using SPSS 20 Statistical Analysis Software, a chi-square test for association was used to determine the relationship between the business profile variables, with the dependent variable being *Government Incentive Recipient.*

Results

The relationship between government incentive and industry type was determined in Table 8.1 and found to be not significant. Table 8.2 examined

Table 8.1   Insignificant Relationships for *Government Incentive Recipient*

Industry type—*government incentive recipient*			
Chi-square test	Value	*df*	Asymp. Sig. (2-sided)
Pearson chi-square	25.678[a]	20	.177
Network membership—*government incentive recipient*			
Chi-square test	Value	*df*	Asymp. Sig. (2-sided)
Pearson chi-square	.196[a]	2	.907
Region—*recipient of government incentive*			
Chi-square test	Value	*df*	Asymp. Sig. (2-sided)
Pearson chi-square	5.039[a]	8	.753

Note: *df* = degrees of freedom.

Table 8.2   Significant Relationships for *Government Support Recipient*

Length in business—*government incentive recipient*			
Chi-square test	Value	*df*	Asymp. Sig. (2-sided)
Pearson chi-square	30.095[a]	8	.000

(*Continued*)

Table 8.2 (Continued)

Number of employees—*government incentive recipient*

Chi-square test	Value	*df*	Asymp. Sig. (2-sided)
Pearson chi-square	74.798	10	.000

Annual turnover—*government incentive recipient*

Chi-square test	Value	*df*	Asymp. Sig. (2-sided)
Pearson chi-square	71.374[a]	10	.000

Note: *df* = degrees of freedom.

the relationship between network membership and obtaining a government incentive. Again this was not significant.

The values of relationships between both *annual turnover—government support recipient* and *number of employees—government support recipient* are larger than *length in business— government support recipient* indicating that turnover and business size (measured by the number of employees) are the most significant predictors of the provision government support to sampled businesses. In summary, we found gaps in as described in Table 8.3 on next page.

The problems identified by the majority of the businesses that have received assistance from EDOs were (a) red tape associated with working with a bureaucracy, (b) the silo mentality of government departments, and (c) the long lead period involved in applying and receiving government support.

Using the MF tool, we found evidence that EDOs were not implementing economic development policies because they did not have the managerial tools required.

DISCUSSION

This study evaluates the effectiveness of EDOs involved in the implementation of regional development policy in South East Queensland, using the managerial flow lens. The first hypothesis sought to gauge the degree to which EDOs promoted networking strategies for supporting business development. While respondents in the qualitative enquiry indicated that EDOs were very active in supporting network membership, results from the quantitative enquiry indicated that network membership was not significantly related to the provision of government support.

The second hypothesis proposed that hierarchical arrangements inhibited the facilitation of meaningful support to businesses. Results from the study support that few EDOs had the ability to effectively communicate the support offered by different departments of government to businesses.

The third hypothesis sought to gauge the degree to which EDOs target high-growth firms for government support; Mason and Brown (2013) suggest that high growth is indicated by business internationalization, length

Table 8.3 Summary of Conclusions

	Strategy	Governance	Selection	Coordination and integration	Communication and knowledge
Hypothesis	*EDOs promote regional networking and industry-cluster projects as strategies to enhance economic development.*	*EDOs are inhibited by a governance gap, evidenced by poor hierarchical frameworks to support business growth.*	*EDOs seek to fund start-up firms over firms that may have high growth potential.*	*EDOs are faced with significant challenges in overcoming trust between firms in regional development initiatives.*	*EDOs are inhibited by knowledge gaps evidenced by a tendency to promote programs limited to a particular division of government.*
Managerial gaps present in the case of EDOs in South East Queensland	While regional development policies target key industries, results from the quantitative findings indicated that neither industry or regions were significantly related to the provision of business support. This indicates that there is a breakdown in the implementation of regional development strategies regarding which business are eligible for support.	A respondent who participated in the qualitative inquiry indicated that they were aware of multiple business support agencies and could identify when EDOs were good, based on their ability to develop a "road map of support." Unfortunately, the respondent also indicated that most EDOs did not have this knowledge.	Businesses that were recipients of government support had a longer length in business, a higher number of employees, and a larger annual turnover than did those that were not. There appeared to be no significant relationship among network membership, region, or industry type. Furthermore, EDOs appeared to support the export development of businesses (as outlined in the qualitative response).	There was a key attempt on the part of EDOs to encourage network membership. Despite this, network membership was not significantly related to being a recipient of government support.	A respondent who participated in the qualitative enquiry suggested that EDOs were not effective in speeding up government processes to match the needs of business. This combined with the unclear documents needed to attain additional support disadvantaged SMEs. Respondents also picked up on the presence of inhibitive red tape, and EDOs that operated in silos were also identified themes by respondents

of time in business, market orientation, and networked innovation. This hypothesis was partially confirmed. Significant indicators of government support were length in business, number of employees, and annual turnover, and this indicates that EDOs in this region were not simply targeting firms that were "start-ups" but had some degree of consideration for growth in their decision making. Furthermore, qualitative results indicate that there was considerable support for business internationalization. Despite this, qualitative results did not indicate significant advantage through networked innovation, suggesting the need to develop further coordinative models to support this aspect of growth.

Support for the fourth hypothesis was inconclusive. Respondents did not indicate that the level of coordination by EDOs had an impact on their trust and innovation. Despite this there was a sense that networking was seen in a positive light, although its net effect on business growth was not effectively gauged in this enquiry, except that network membership did not correlate with the provision of government incentives.

The final hypothesis sought to gauge the degree to which knowledge dissemination administered through EDOs to businesses was clear and considerate of other support opportunities from other wings of government. Results from this line of enquiry conclude that there were knowledge hurdles that businesses needed to overcome to receive support. There was also an inability on the part of EDOs to implement change on the side of the government to support businesses adequately, highlighting a mismatch between the market environment of businesses and the public sector (Kelly, 2005).

CONCLUSION

In conclusion, EDOs face a significant challenge in their intercession role between government and businesses. The results from the study are mixed and indicate that EDOs make a significant attempt to target businesses that are growing and to facilitate network interaction; however, outcomes from these actions, particularly in the case of network facilitation, are limited. Furthermore, EDOs struggled to affect change on the side of the government and to cater programs to adequately support business development. Knowing this, future research, particularly research adopting the Managerial Flow lens, should seek to provide recommendations for EDOs to support their provision of business incentives. Such recommendations could include checklists/indicators for selecting high-growth businesses, frameworks for matching government strategy with the provision of support, governance models to support collaborative arrangements by lateral actors involved in regional development programs, networked innovation frameworks, and the provision of government materials/documents that are accessible by businesses.

REFERENCES

Australian Government Department of Industry, Innovation, Science, Research and Tertiary Education. (2011a). *Innovation policy report.* Commonwealth of Australia.

Australian Government Department of Industry, Innovation, Science, Research and Tertiary Education. (2011b). *Australian innovation systems report.* Canberra: Commonwealth of Australia. Retrieved from http://www.innovation.gov.au/AISReport

Brunetto, Y., & Farr-Wharton, R. (2005). Implementing business policies within the Australian context: The role of economic development officers within local government. *Journal of Innovation Management, 11*(20), 161–180.

Brunetto, Y., & Farr-Wharton, R. (2007). The moderating role of trust in entrepreneurs' decision-making about collaboration. *Journal of Small Business Management, 45*(3), 362–388.

Dean, J., Holmes, S., & Smith, S. (1997). Understanding business networks: Evidence from the manufacturing and services sectors in Australia. *Journal of Small Business Management, 35*(1), 78–84.

Department of Industry Sciences Resources. (1999). *Shaping Australia's future innovation—framework paper.* Canberra: Australian Government Printing Service.

Diefenbach, T. (2009). New public management in public sector organizations: The dark sides of managerialistic "enlightenment." *Public Administration, 87*(4), 892–909.

DITR. (2007). Portfolio overview: The Department of Industry, Tourism and Resources annual report. Chapter 2, pages 16–26. Canberra, Australian Government.

Enright, M., & Roberts, B., (2001). Regional clustering in Australia. *Australian Journal of Management, 26*, 66–85.

European Commission. (2010). *Europe 2020 flagship initiative—innovation union.* Retrieved from http://ec.europa.eu/research/innovation-union/pdf/innovation-union-communication_en.pdf

Farr-Wharton, B. (2012). Southern Gold Coast music hub: Resolving policy gaps through cluster management. *Asia Pacific Journal of Management Theory and Practice, 34*(2), 52–59.

Hindle, K., & Rushworth, S. (2002). Sensis GEM Australia, 2002. Swinburne University of Technology. Available at: http://sites.kauffman.org/pdf/gem_australia_2002.pdf

Hospers, G.-J., Desrochers, P., & Sautet, F. (2009). The next Silicon Valley? On the relationship between geographical clustering and public policy. *International Entrepreneurship Management Journal, 5*, 285–299.

Inkpen., A., & Tsang, E. (2005). Social capital, networks and knowledge transfer. *Academy of Management Review Journal, 30*(1), 146–164.

Kaplan, R., & Norton, D. (1996). *The balanced scorecard: Translating strategy into action.* Boston, MA: Harvard Business School Press.

Keast, R. (2011). Joined-up governance in Australia: How the past can inform the future. *International Journal of Public Administration, 34*(4), 221–231.

Keast, R., Mandell, M., & Brown, K. (2006). Mixing state, market and network governance modes: The role of government in "crowded" policy domains. *International Journal of Organizational Theory and Behavior, 9*(1), 27–50.

Kelly, J. (2005). The dilemma of the unsatisfied customer in a market model of public administration. *Public Administration Review, 65*(1), 76–84.

Lipsky, M. (1980). *Street-level bureaucracy: Dilemmas of the individual in public services.* New York, NY: Russell Sage.

Lorenzen, M. (2002). Ties, trust, and trade: Elements of theory and coordinaton in industrial clusters. *Internation Studies of Management and Organisation, 31*(4), 14–34.

Markusen, A. (1996). Sticky olaces in slippery space: A typology of industrial districts. *Economic Geography, 72*(3), 293–313.

Mason, C., & Brown, R. (2013). Creating good public policy to support high-growth firms. *Small Business Economics, 40,* 211–225.

Mitchell, R., Waterhouse, J., McNeil, K., & Burgess, J. (2010). Proximity and knowledge sharing in clustered firms. In K. Brown, J. Burgess, M. Festing, & S. Royer (Eds.), *Value adding webs and clusters; Concepts and cases* (pp. 62–77). Munich: Rainer Hampp Verlag.

Organisation for Economic Co-operation and Development. (1999). *Boosting innovation: The cluster approach.* Paris, France: OECD proceedings.

Page, E. (2006, July 5). *How policy is really made.* Public Management and Policy Association seminar, London School of Economics, London, England.

Porter, M. (1990). *The competitive advantage of nations.* London, England: Harvard Press.

Queensland Department of Infrastructure and Planning. (2009). South East Queensland Regional Plan 2009–2031. Queensland Government.

Raadschelders, J., & Stillman, R. (2007). Toward a New Conceptual Framework for Studying Administrative Authority. *Administrative Theory & Praxis, 29*(1), 4–40.

Ryan, N. (1996). A comparison of three approaches to programme implementation. *International Journal of Public Sector Management, 9*(4), 34–41.

Scozzi, M., Carvelli, C., & Crowston, K. (2005). Methods for modelling and supporting innovation processes in SMEs. *European Journal of Innovation Management, 8*(1), 120–137.

Stewart, J. (2012). Multiple-case study methods in governance related research. *Public Management Review, 14,* 67–82.

Vecchi, V., & Brusoni, M. (2012). The managerial flow of public local development Policies: A conceptual framework. *Asia Pacific Journal of Management Theory and Practice, 34*(2), 5–13.

9 Managerial Flow and Paradox
Postconflict Development in the Balkans

Eric Martin and Jordi Comas[1]

INTRODUCTION

Policy implementation in development projects does not occur in a vacuum. The process leading to an intended policy or development outcome may produce unexpected results, as may the outcome itself. In this chapter, we conceptualize these unexpected outcomes as "paradoxes" and analyze the case of development officials working in postwar Bosnia to demonstrate how paradoxes emerge within the Managerial Flow framework.

Our protagonists are nation building by forging the institutions they believe would lead Bosnia to develop politically, economically, and socially. These development professionals are employed by a variety of formal organizations across the three sectors: firms, nongovernmental organizations (NGOs), and governments. While mindful of their espoused goals of nation building, the exigencies of this work lead these actors to cross boundaries of national borders, organizations, and professional identities. Managerial Flow (Vecchi & Brusoni, 2012) is an effective practitioner-oriented model to identify the managerial gaps, assets, and actions necessary in such complex development settings.

Obstacles to success in international development center on three sets of tasks (Martin, 2012): *coordination* within the international community, *operations* in the target or host society, and *transfers* between the international actors and host-country actors. In the first, coordination within the international community, relationships abound between different nations regarding the United Nations' quasi-protectorate Office of the High Representative, for example, or the North Atlantic Treaty Organization (NATO), the European Union (EU), and even sectoral task forces. Additionally, complex interorganizational relationships exist within a single country's international development assistance operations. For the United States, for example, the Embassy (State Department), the Department of Defense, the Agency International Development (USAID), the Treasury, the Department of Commerce, and the Bureau of Public Affairs all had interests. We can also consider cross-sectoral (public, private, and NGO) relations within and between each. The international community is a "complex little ecosystem," as one of the participants suggested.

Coordination within the international community, in principle, supports all the activity in the theater of operations. Within the host societies there are typically various sources of weakness to effectiveness, if not outright obstructionist players. Developing competence, efficiency, and effectiveness within the host players, across all three sectors, is the ultimate objective to achieve self-sustainability. Not limited to a state-centric approach, development management also focuses on capacity building to empower locals to take ownership of problems and solutions. This work involves all three sectors through civil society reforms, market development, and public-sector reform.

Third, there are tasks related to the transfer, flow, or exchange between the international community and local partners. The flow does tend to be unidirectional from international to local. However, ideally, flows of need originate within the host country. Then, money, skill, technology, and assistance flow from the international community to the local host recipient in response to that stated need. Finally, feedback flows back to the international players. The ideal of transfer often deviates, however, given international donor agendas.

MANAGERIAL FLOW AND PARADOX

The Managerial Flow framework (Vecchi & Brusoni, 2012) was developed as a practitioner-oriented guide to help managers think through complex development decisions. The original work was based on development efforts in Italy that required cooperation across sectors and at various levels. Vecchi and Brusoni (2012) identified five key gaps in their study of economic development in the Italian Province of Reggio Emilia, and several scholars since have employed the model on a wide variety of development projects including public–private partnerships in the Netherlands (Klijn, Kort, & van Twist, 2012), industrial parks in Singapore and China (Wang & Yuan, 2012), informal markets in Tanzania (Melyoki, 2012), research incubators in New Zealand (Kuah, 2012), and cluster management in the arts (Farr-Wharton, 2012). We extend the framework to include local and international players. In each case, the Managerial Flow model suggested that in a complex, multilevel, multiplayer, multi-sector development activity, managerial assets and actions should be identified and taken with respect to planning, governance, selection, partnering, and knowledge. Our analysis of these five gaps exposed our subjects' understanding of each but went further to identify paradoxes inherent in each gap that limited success.

A paradox is when, in the pursuit of a goal or outcome by particular means, the opposite of the goal is created or the goal becomes harder to accomplish. A common paradox associated with development is encapsulated in this proverb: "Give a man a fish and you feed him for a day. Teach a man to fish and you feed him for a lifetime." The embedded paradox in this folk wisdom is that by solving the immediate problem of hunger, one creates in the recipient dependencies on daily provision of fish, thereby paradoxically making freedom from hunger harder to achieve. This metaphor translates in this case into the paradox between solving immediate, acute problems relating to the war that might prevent the creation of long-term, locally grounded solutions to the chronic and joint problems of economic development and democratic transition.

Paradoxes in management, such as the classic exploration versus exploitation paradox, help explain the unseen difficulties inherent in achieving success (Andriopoulos & Lewis, 2009; March, 1991). Managers or organizations that seek to exploit known opportunities at the cost of exploring more uncertain possibilities can achieve short-term success but forsake longer-term greater opportunities (Lavie, Stettner, & Tushman, 2010). The converse can also occur. Overemphasis on exploring rich but uncertain outcomes can occur at the cost of shorter-term success. There are other well-documented paradoxes. For example, the information technology–productivity paradox occurs when specific technologies increase performance while increased spending overall seems to lower productivity (Brynjolfsson, 1993). The embeddedness paradox suggests managers need economic ties that become embedded in other normative ties that may impede economic action (Uzzi, 1997). The capabilities paradox suggests firms struggle between developing new capabilities and profiting from existing core capabilities (Leonard-Barton, 1992). Disruptive technologies provide another ripe example as firms focus on current customers pleased with safe but limited technologies at the expense of investing in newer technologies focused on future customers (Bower & Christensen, 1995).

Management "gurus" advocate that managers embrace paradox as a way to cope with the turbulence brought on by some combination of digital technologies, globalization, increased competition, or other exogenous factors (Handy, 1994; Harvey, 1988; Peters, 1992). Across these examples, two related meanings of paradox are invoked. One, akin to the older Greek philosophical tradition, is that a paradox is two seemingly incompatible states. The second, rooted more in 19th- and 20th-century social science, is about paradoxical outcomes—the unintended consequences that individuals and managers find themselves. Clegg et al. (2002) describe how key ideas in early management theory including Taylor, Fayol, and Barnard were actually attempting to deal with such paradox.

In general, there are three approaches to addressing managerial paradoxes. First, managers are advised to embrace or accept paradoxes as inevitable (Peters, 1992). There is no actual resolution to them, but success will be the result from ongoing and mindful efforts to understand them (Bouchiki, 1998; Ford & Backoff, 1988). Second, organizations attempt to resolve or tackle paradoxes through combinations of differentiation in two dimensions: organizational structure (Burns & Stalker, 1966) or time. In other words, some "best-fit" combination of organizational structure or sequencing of activities allows managers to successfully resolve or bypass the problems posed by paradoxes. Third, as Clegg et al. (2002) and Seo and Creed (2002) argue, paradoxes can be resolved dialectically through creative or generative action, new organizational structures, actions, cognitive frames, or other solutions. For example, studies of jazz musicians (Berliner, 1994) highlight that the paradox between planning and improvisation. It is resolved through a synthesis of semistructures around which improvisation occurs; improvisation is due to planning, not despite it. Similarly, Shell's use of scenario planning allows for rigid planning and responsive flexibility to co-occur despite the apparent paradox between the two (Wack 1985).

By examining our case through the Managerial Flow model, we expose six inescapable paradoxes in the management of international development work. In the following we report our findings.

METHOD

This chapter stems from research conducted over the course of three 6-week field trips, five shorter trips, and a full academic year based primarily in Sarajevo, Bosnia and Herzegovina, and Belgrade, Serbia. Initial access and preliminary interviews were obtained through USAID contacts working in in Sarajevo, Belgrade, Pristina, Skopje, and Split. The data used in this chapter are based on interviews with 92 development professionals from 30 different organizations and have been used previously for other research questions (Martin, 2007a, 2007b, 2012). Seventeen individuals were interviewed more than once, some several times. Fifty-three respondents were US citizens, 25 were from the EU, and 14 were host-country nationals.

More than 40 hours of interviews were tape-recorded and transcribed; those not recorded were reproduced from detailed notes. For this chapter, we started by analyzing initial codes from previous research on interorganizational relationships to identify all codes representing obstacles to (and opportunities for) success. That initial coding scheme was then analyzed through the lens of Managerial Flow. Interview discussions about obstacles were coded into the five Managerial Flow dimensions. Coding revealed a series of higher order paradoxes, and these are our focal point of analysis in the following section.

FINDINGS

We proceed by describing several types of paradoxes that emerge from the data. The results highlight the way in which policy implementation cannot occur in a vacuum and, instead, produces paradoxical positions, which require future resolution.

Coordination

Coordinating with other organizations can make it harder to achieve development goals. It draws time and resources away from contracted work.

Coordination activities rarely fulfill contractual obligations; they are just intended to make such work flow more smoothly. Our professionals encountered the coordination paradox in many ways. Sometimes it works well. For example, one respondent suggested that "it's one of those relationships where everybody is bringing something to the party. OHR has a lot of political connections as well as the power to impose solutions when faced with problems from the conflict . . . they don't really have a technical knowledge so that is what we bring to the table." The following is another good example: "The Germans had an agriculture program in Republika Srpska and were finding that more people [there] spoke English than German, so they paid for some folks to go to UK and we [British Embassy] put them up and paid for their stay and education, English language . . . so that kind of stuff." Regardless, this apparently obvious solution required intense coordination and additional work as both parties had to explain to their constituents why funds were not used according to plan.

On more sensitive issues, those obstacles could be even more dramatic, as one US Embassy official pointed out: "You know you can't have committees for everything, we are never going to allow US money to be put through a committee where someone else might have veto power. That is virtually impossible to do." The motivation to coordinate often had more to do with preventing negatives than encouraging synergies: "Our biggest concern is that US government money is not duplicated, that is the most important, and the fact that we do not have a coherent plan for all the international community to follow that is a major problem."

Many debated the ability of any one player to serve such a lead role effectively, as noted in the following: "In terms of human capital, I think USAID is the largest not only in terms of the staff on the ground, but also in terms of its contractors and implementers—if there were a moral leader, an objective moral leader, I would say the World Bank, but other people would argue, I can think of people immediately who would laugh at that." Said another chief of party, "This is a business, my shop, my team, my way." Too often, "the word coordination is synonymous with control." In other words, the need for immediate coordination was seen as a threat to local autonomy.

Some reported that technical issues hurt better interorganizational relationships: "Cooperation is often hampered by different funding cycles, various political agendas, it is complex." As noted by another participant, so too did national differences at times: "I will say it is always interesting watching the Americans and the Germans sit at the same table together."

But many were able to look past that to see that coordination is just complex and difficult: "It's very systematic, people don't understand that if you want to coordinate you have to get into the muddle of the detail and that means resources and that means procedures and our procedures for instance every month in every regionalized area of the country there is something called the 'implementers coordination meeting' where we will proactively push and bully the implementer to come in, what are you doing, what projects, etc."

Staffing

The professionals are at times torn between loyalty to the success of the larger project and personal success in their careers. The staffing paradoxes we describe are due to the tensions between, on one hand, the logic of aid that prescribes measurable progress and, on the other, career logics that guide individuals to seek career advancement up hierarchies or laterally to new arenas of conflict or "hotspots." Also, aid needs, like seconding a professional to another organization, or structural issues, resulting in high turnover, can trigger career logics of loyalty.

The first problem many reported was the short-term nature of many assignments that created an environment of constant turnover, limiting organizational and individual learning:

> Turnover in the army breaks the chain of communication, you can't consistently keep the chain of communication open with all the turnover, it takes people too long to learn their job and what they're doing and then to do it and retrain the next guy, there's so many people to learn all the places and what they're supposed to do for you it's just crazy, just for me I came here in January and even though the guy told me that all these people exist, it still took me 2 months 3 months to get out and meet them all and now it will take me, I mean I only get two weeks turnover with the new guy coming in august, I'll walk him around downtown and have him meet people, but I can't bring him around to all the chambers, he's gotta do it himself.

Another suggested, "Your programs are only as good as the people you have implementing them, and before, we could get people easier because this was a hot spot, and now it's not." This refers to the fact that over time, other issues in the Balkans flared up and that "as we fall down in importance, we get less skilled replacements." This resulted in many people getting "chucked into jobs that perhaps they didn't have much experience in, such as the political side of things—how a political party works or how an election works or how you try to get warring parties to negotiate." These lesser skilled replacements closely parallel an overall drop in importance of Bosnia within the international community:

> We all know the money coming to Bosnia will decline and this year was the last main donor conference, so with that in mind there is a need to refocus our attention on what really needs to be done in Bosnia, at a time of diminishing aid, together with the impact of Kosovo and all concerned that money might get taken away from Bosnia to go to Kosovo.

Some suggested this was a bit of a legacy of this type of work and the fact that development agencies do not invest long term in human resources because of this short-term mentality:

I'm talking about working smarter not harder. People here still work till 8 or 11 o'clock at night, take them out put them in IBM, put them in GM. you will find people that do 15 times as much work as those people within a day and leave at 5 o'clock and enjoy their lives. Why? Because their management skills have been invested in. . . . They have had high[-level] management courses. They're taught how to use computers intelligently and they systemize their business. The skills that you have here, lawyers, medics, are not managers and yet their biggest task here is managing resources toward an objective. That skill mix is just not here.

Secondment represents a very special example of this human resource and staffing problem. One informant explained: "We 'second' talented folks from the World Bank (WB) for example, to work for the Office of the High Representative, the protectorate government. But they don't know whose interests they should support—actual Bosnians, the protectorate government, or their home institution." Secondment is a staffing paradox because to create stronger government, organizations import talented professionals; hence, every gain they make is at the expense of creating indigenous talent. To "second" is a manifestation of the logic of aid and of showing results. However, the seconded people do feel torn between a clear idea of progress, on one hand, and a morass of conflicting interests, on the other. This is magnified by the change of working for a single organization, such as the World Bank, to a new and uncertain void or contested space where multiple agendas and actors are in flux:

> The length of time . . . and the extent of choice of individuals seconded I think in some cases may be quite limited, therefore given those two factors, it is very difficult to create organizational entities strong team and corporate spirit also unified system of testing individual performance, accountability.

Flexibility

This paradox is triggered by tension between two perfectly reasonable logics. On one hand is a strong bureaucratic logic that dictates accountability, regulation, and transparency anchored in intergovernmental relationships and long, arduous budgeting; grant making; or contracting efforts, typically with a government player involved in several phases of the process. On the other hand, nonprofits and firms embrace a logic of aid that values measurable short-term goals and the need for extreme flexibility to adjust to changing circumstances on the ground.

One of the great problems in development work is that situations on the ground rarely match the needs assessments written by other firms or agencies months, if not years, prior. As such, field professionals are constantly asking for more flexibility with their programming and project money. As one explained,

> I have to beg embassies or big donors and sometimes it can take months to ask them if OK, can you maybe we have a very urgent project in this area, we think that political authorities are moving we need to show them a good sign, can you give them two computers it's something like $4,000 and it takes months. So this project is blocked because we don't have the few thousands to pay for the rent and things like that.

In a related problem, as noted by another participant, "Donors want to do things, but they pursue an idea, even if not feasible, and just go ahead and do it, they don't get buy in, if they asked the businesses they would have said no, If AID asks, of course, though, they just say, yes." As a result, what development agencies provide can often be viewed as "solutions looking for problems," where development organizations have money and programs earmarked and already detailed and hope to match such solutions to the needs of the recipient country. This is due to their rather chronic inability to be flexible on the ground. Pragmatically, the donor agencies know that they are the ones who will face scrutiny and political repercussions at home when money is seen as poorly spent or spent differently than how originally allocated or donated. The trade-off between being flexible to be responsive and being in control to be accountable remains a difficult one.

Targeting

Here again we can see this paradox as the result of the tension between the aid and development logics. In targeting, the paradox appears in the form of selecting easy-to-solve problems as opposed to the most critical or systematic ones. Development professionals had to think about how best to influence economic growth in a country, for example. While their main task was certainly to help agriculture, for example, this program was housed within economic development. As such, they were forced to choose between widespread approaches that would have an impact on many different farmers, compared to more targeted assistance that would help far fewer but would help the economy more directly. As one suggested, "Individual farms are so small; they don't have a big impact, so we prefer sector approaches." Another agreed, saying, "It is much easier to have an impact with an association to reach a larger amount of farmers, and we can help market what they all produce." As a result, one participant pointed out, "We don't work with the poorest of the poor. We work with big commercial farms." A different example was described by one professional in another sector:

> In auto parts, we could use our network and make connections. We will help a few key firms, hire an auto expert, $500 per day, so 20–30k total,

but we count every dime generated, we can't take full credit of course, but we track it all. By picking strategic firms we can multiply the impact, like the increased sales of suppliers.

The targeting paradox appeared at many levels of decision-making: a thorough capacity study highlighted several target areas for focus, those implementing assistance could choose, and might not choose as strategically, favoring ease and impact over strategy perhaps. "For Bosnia and Herzegovina, what is Bosnia and Herzegovina good at? Textiles, metal and wood—metal is probably the largest, and maybe wood the best, but we chose to start with textiles, it was maybe the easiest and not so capital-intensive." Ultimately, this professional explained how "there was a hole. We said, 'maybe we should maybe fill in this hole and do something especially for these companies,'" which seems a more grounded, client-centered approach.

Paternalism

This paradox has more to do with the attitudes and dispositions of the professionals. On one hand, a logic of development encourages the use and empowerment of local organizations and leaders. On the other, the logic of aid may pressure the professionals to not work through local systems in order to get the job done quickly and "correctly." When faced with the problems of improving governance and civil society from the outside in, very paternalistic mind-sets can develop. This paternalism ultimately makes the logic of development harder to pursue. So much about the nation-building effort in Bosnia lent itself to paternalistic thinking: "For example, last week we had a stupid decision at the Council of Ministers that we're to impose. They were fighting since months, actually more, nearly two years about a border crossing agreement between Croatia and Bosnia and Herzegovina. They all agree on the border crossing, they all agree on everything except for the names of the towns in the written document. Finally we impose a decision and everyone is happy and all the crossing towns are now open."

It seemed the international community felt unable to allow locals to develop due to urgency, and likely the fear of ethnic violence flaring up. Although this was true initially, it lingered for some time after any evidence of such escalation was evident, to the point of "no one in the international community takes what people say, and even at the highest level, at face value. And that's unique because usually there is always one side or another in a conflict or a post-communist system that can be considered to be the good guy. There are different levels of bad guys here. There are the really bad, bad and then there are the recently bad."

This negative view of the locals certainly influenced decisions about the nature of assistance. As one local said, "Development of local institutions is being set back, but it is our own fault." Another summarized the tension as such:

> I think each country needs a kind of state authority and the problem in Bosnia is there is no state authority anymore and in this situation, there is no state authority developed and this is also because of strong international institutions, these institutions are also of course important for the development to bring the money and the expertise, but . . . there will be never in the near future a strong state institution and they will always be dependent on international organizations.

In doing so, like many others, they were "implying that the Bosnians don't feel ownership over the reform agenda, and so they are only the fifth wheel":

> Are you creating a false dependency? Maybe it's always when you distort a market and when it comes to a development piece economic side and if you, like OHR, distort political markets causing the expectation that someone from the outside should be in charge, maybe misused, even some politicians who want to do something in one direction they don't say it in public, if they keep quiet, OHR will do it so this may come to the situation where you don't do institution building, we do the opposite but on the other hand with the mistrust in the country maybe it's the only way to do something.

The worry that short-term need will become long-term dependence to the development professionals is very salient. These concerns can become quite global. Consider this thoughtful account:

> The international community needs to ask itself how much do we need to do ourselves and when do we start to hand over the agenda and the responsibility I mean if you are paternalistic, you are always afraid to give independence to your children to the point that your children are actually going to become mentally handicapped and unable to stand up on their feet and work independently.

Some organizations made this a central feature, or rather a guiding framework, of their work: "I want all the German and other international experts to work with locals so that the locals can take over in a year or two, also with local students who could gain through experience and training and they could make some money and then we could increase local expertise." Some criticized the US for being, perhaps, too ends-oriented without focusing on the process of transferring skills while also delivering aid: "Another weakness of the American program here is that many of the projects which intrinsically should be located insides BiH government institutions are actually situated outside, outside Bosnian institutions, privatization program in my opinion should be inside the privatization agency."

In response, some defended this work as pragmatic and responsible: "We were criticized by USAID over our fly-in, fly-out approach and we had a very interesting, very friendly dialogue, and we said, 'Well, our approach is never to have these expensive consultants on the ground. Why should we have these very costly on the ground if we don't need them to spoon feed people?'"

Local Politics

Three logics are in tension when this paradox is triggered. First, the aid-development logic suggests different actions or strategies for the professionals. Second, the development logic directs professionals to interact with local governments with the aim of creating stronger government. Third, the durability of local governments even in the face of seemingly neutral or technical changes reflects the logic of nationalism, the logic of protecting and advancing the interests of a defined, salient "folk" group. This paradox is also different in that it more directly involves a newer group—the local officials and politicians from municipal to regional and national levels.

First of all, Bosnia is extremely complex with local municipal governments, cantons in the Republika Srpska, then two entity levels designed by the Dayton Peace Accords, and a state- or national-level government. As one local suggested to me, "We have a government of the Federation and the government of Republika Srpska and we have a government of every Canton. We have ministries in the Cantons; they call themselves Minister, Minister for Culture, Minister for Economics. I think every second man is a Minister here [laugh]."

So structurally, government is a problem in that "a huge obstacle is overlapping mandates between, say the Ministry of Agriculture and the Ministry of Health over food safety. So for slaughterhouses, there are two sets of inspectors, sanitary and veterinary, which means excessive costs, actually two times the costs. So we helped draft a law to improve this situation, but there is no political will to give away a portion of revenue or oversight, so the law was accepted, but not voted on yet, not passed, and it will just sit there." Many suggested similar problems: "A lot of these laws have been drafted, and gone through consulting with all the ministries involved, but not acted upon in parliament."

But, the reasons for this often turn to ethnic rationales: "In this country there is more because they made the process very political it allows ethnic problems to be involved," or "In the Federation they haven't got their act together because they can't even sit in the same room together." Another commented, "It is sometimes ticklish to get different entities to work together." Furthermore, these differences are then often interpreted very negatively: "What I know about privatization, the authorities try to delay it as much as they can because they profit from the lack of privatization, because they are on the payroll and they get kickbacks and the whole system is very corrupt."

As a result, some international development officials completely avoid local squabbles: "As a rule of thumb, I stay five miles away from politics; I don't try to influence those with influence." In addition a local commented, "There is not a very good avenue for local staff and expats to suggest changes, at least not one that we would feel comfortable using—we are told repeatedly to never write anything directly to AID, if you have something to say, you say it to your Chief of Party—they have no suggestion box, but if they did, it would have to be some sort of anonymous system of some kind." So the international community is not getting involved in local issues and the locals are not commenting on international issues, which often means really important issues are not addressed because they are too sensitive: "Land reform is a major problem, but we don't deal in that area, it is political, it is emotional and corrupt, so we don't deal with it, doesn't mean it is not important, but we don't focus on policy reform, only real issues."

FROM THEORY TO PRACTICE: MANAGING PARADOX

Paradoxes are not mutually exclusive. Our professionals often faced several of them as they engaged in different task areas. The data also suggest that one paradox becoming enacted can trigger others. Hence, coping with the paradox of coordination can lead to the paradox of paternalism. Once this paradox is triggered, the paradox of local politics may become more severe. By surfacing the prevalence of paradoxes in Managerial Flow, can we better understand the responses and strategies crafted in response to them? Turning from the broader theoretical implications to more pragmatic concerns, we suggest several tactics or approaches for dealing with paradoxes. In fact, we are often merely pointing out that these are in many instances exactly what clever, concerned development professionals actually do to mitigate or avoid triggering paradoxes that left unchecked could thwart the goals of Bosnian recovery and rebuilding. We find two kinds of approaches. First, they use a variety of tactics to create and preserve a certain degree of organizational flexibility. Second, they expend considerable effort in buffering their own zones of flexibility. This work could be seen cynically as providing their various stakeholders with dubious information simply to ape compliance. However, we suggest it can also be seen as a critical act of symbolic management (see Figure 9.1).

But this search for solutions to overcome paradox brings us back to the concept of Managerial Flow. We proposed that international development consists of three fundamental components: (1) the international community responding to needs and providing assistance, (2) the local host community identifying needs and accepting assistance, and (3) the actual transfer of needs and aid through projects, programs, and transfers of knowledge, skill, technology, and funding. Within each of those three domains, gaps occur within the five key Managerial Flow factors of planning, governance, selection, partnering, and knowledge. For each, managers can identify

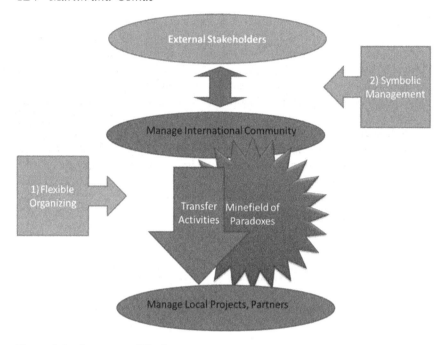

Figure 9.1 Summary of Findings

assets available and actions needed. Consider the paradox of flexibility, as an example. We suggest flexibility, which was created through a variety of means, relates to three dimensions of Managerial Flow: Planning, Partnering and Governance, as shown in Table 9.1.

With respect to *governance*, for example, USAID, who was not formally in a leadership position, would often act informally as the hub of inter-organizational cooperation and coordination. One participant described: "I would say, I don't know what everyone wants to do, but I would say USAID is the informal leader here because they are by far the biggest bulk of the money here, 500 million or I don't know, and also from their expertise." A different professional described how USAID's role emerged: "The main role AID plays is coordination and project management. OHR has a lot of political connections and the power to impose solutions. I don't think it was designed that way, but it emerged that way."

With respect to *partnering*, this flexibility often built on an underlying substrate of trust-based networks. For example, one professional discussed how his prior connections enabled him to bring people together:

We have been very successful in terms of getting the attention of the right people, the reason I was asked to do the secretariat was because I had been working with ever since 1996 directly with the top level

Table 9.1 Mapping Paradoxes on to Managerial Flow

	The six paradoxes	Managerial Flow dimension	Example
International community	**COORDINATION** *(Time and money spent coordinating is not time and money spent on assistance.)*	PLANNING PARTNERING GOVERNANCE	"You know you can't have committees for everything, we are never going to allow US money to be put through a committee where someone else might have veto power."
International community	**STAFFING** *(Bringing in short-term international experts disrupts long-term staff development.)*	KNOWLEDGE	"You can't consistently keep the chain of communication open with all the turnover, it takes people too long to learn their job"
Transfers between international & local	**FLEXIBILITY** *(Flexibility allows progress, grounded solutions, and innovation, but control is lost.)*	PLANNING PARTNERING GOVERNANCE	"Donors want to do things, but they pursue an idea, even if not feasible, and just go ahead and do it, they don't get buy in."
Transfers between international & local	**TARGETING** *(Successful assistance often helps those who need help the least.)*	SELECTION	"Individual farms are so small; they don't have a big impact, so we prefer sector approaches."
Transfers between international & local	**PATERNALISM** *(The more the international community does, the less the host community is empowered.)*	GOVERNAN CEPARTNERING	"The international community needs to ask itself how much do we need to do ourselves and when do we start to hand over the agenda and the responsibility."
Local/host community	**LOCAL POLITICS** *(The more local control, the less macro vision.)*	GOVERNANCE	"It is sometimes ticklish to get different entities to work together."

government officials the prime ministers so I had a rapport with them and they had some trust in me, and this has proved to be very useful, it has given us the ability that when we come to a problem, I can sit down with the PM and say this is the problem . . .

Buffering, or symbolic management, involved providing information or other forms of compliance to outside stakeholders such as donor agencies or national government agencies. Those stakeholders, often because of the institutional pressures they faced, would expect or require certain information or tactics from the development professionals. These demands would often surface some of the inherent paradoxes in the development work in Bosnia.

And, finally, with respect to *planning*, we see how the work on the ground had to be massaged to fit into reporting requirements of a donor. It was difficult to get information about programmatic spending in Bosnia. First, many NGOs and contractors had separate programs for the two entities—yet budgets reflected total figures spent, as many programs cut across entities. Here is one informant explaining this:

> [I said] How would you like the figures expressed where the money has been spent in two [different entities] . . . split in half? They said well ahhh, not quite sure, you give us the figures and we'll [decide] . . . I said, "what about our projects that cut across entities? I can't actually say how much was spent within the Federation. I can make a guess, but, you know, these figures are worthless."

Aside from massaging information to fit expectations, there were also times when specific requirements of projects or activities needed to be set aside or altered to actually get work done. In this example, a member of the international community is describing how their adoption (through an informal meeting) of a project that the World Bank needed done in health care was already underway when suddenly the World Bank found that the timeline of the project did not conform to its needs. The resolution came from some after-the-fact negotiation to keep the paradoxical demands of solving the problem with unrealistic timelines at bay:

> We started our program we discussed it with the World Bank and it was complementary to what they were doing, they were delighted with it, but we didn't or the World Bank didn't draw particular attention to particular appendices, and a year into our program, the world bank, somebody in the World Bank did a review of the world bank program and realized that the World Bank wasn't achieving its target as set out in those particular documents, we looked at the reasons why and one of the reasons why was that our program wasn't achieving our objectives

to their timeframe, and it caused a little bit of difficulty initially because after it was done we never decided to continue the World Bank timetable . . . we both have our own deadlines, but it's unrealistic for the World Bank to expect us to just, because they've woken up to the fact they have this appendix . . . so it took negotiations with staff at quite senior level to take the process forward and now we're back on track, and everybody's happy. It's all in the process of dialogue . . .

CONCLUSION

To summarize, the Managerial Flow model identifies key factors for partnering. Our understanding of the three components of development (the international community, the local community, and the transfers between) contextualizes this complex setting within which flow must take place. The paradoxes then highlight obstacles and possible opportunities for successful flow within each. This is the challenge to effective development work. Tensions inherent in many required activities can trigger paradoxes of action. We hope this work may better explain or uncover pragmatic solutions to persistent paradoxes. Embracing the Managerial Flow model can provide one such pragmatic solution.

The three components of the delivery of international aid each could each be viewed through the Managerial Flow model. International development practitioners need to view planning, governance, selection, partnering, and knowledge first within the international community. The same exercise could also be projected on and modeled within the host community. And, finally, the very same exercise needs to be done with respect to the transfer of needs and assistance between the two. In each cell, the paradoxes, as well as how they cut across action steps, can be explored and addressed in isolation.

A thorough understanding of the assets available to the collective with respect to each gap and the actions necessary would, if nothing else, improve transparency and understanding among all involved. It may, however, indeed improve the Managerial Flow in an environment where gaps, actions, and assets blur constantly and prove very difficult to understand, let alone implement, measure, and evaluate. Finally, and perhaps most important, different perspectives on gaps, assets, and actions emerging from cross-sectoral and international partnerships may mitigate the paradoxes that prevent success.

NOTE

1. We would like to thank this book's reviewers, as well as panels at ARNOVA 2012 in Indianapolis and 2013 in Hartford and the Academy of Management Public and Nonprofit Division 2013 in Orlando for feedback on earlier versions of this work. We especially thank Ben Farr-Wharton for his helpful comments.

REFERENCES

Andriopoulos, C. & Lewis, M. W. (2009). Exploitation-exploration tensions and organizational ambidexterity: Managing paradoxes of innovation. *Organization Science, 20*(4), 696–717.

Berliner, P. F. (1994). *Thinking in Jazz: The Infinite Art of Improvisation.* Chicago, IL: University of Chicago Press.

Bouchikhi, H. (1998). Living with and building on complexity: A constructivist perspective on organizations. *Organization, 5*(2), 217–232.

Bower, J. L., & Christensen, C. M. (1995, January–February). Disruptive technologies: Catching the wave. *Harvard Business Review, 73*(1), 43–43

Brynjolfsson, E. (1993). The productivity paradox of information technology. *CACM— Communications of the ACM, 36*(12), 66–77. doi:10.1145/163298.163309

Burns, T., & Stalker, G. M. (1966). *The management of innovation.* London, England: Tavistock.

Clegg, S. R., Pitsis, T. S., Rura-Polley, T., & Marosszeky, M. (2002). Governmentality Matters: Designing an Alliance Culture of Inter-organizational Collaboration for Managing Projects. *Organization Studies, 23*(3), 317–337.

Farr-Wharton, B. (2012). Southern Gold Coast music hub: Resolving policy gaps through cluster management. *Singapore Management Review, 32*(Suppl. 2), 52–59.

Ford, J. D., & Backoff, R. W. (1988). Organizational change in and out of dualities and paradox. In R. E. Quinn & K. S. Cameron (Eds.), *Paradox and transformation: Toward a theory of change in organization and management* (pp. 81–121). Cambridge, MA: Ballinger.

Handy, C. B. (1994). *The age of paradox.* Boston, MA: Harvard Business School Press.

Harvey, J. B. (1988). *The Abilene paradox and other meditations on management.* Lexington, MA: Lexington Books; San Diego, CA: University Associates.

Klijn, E. H., Kort, M., & van Twist, M. (2012). Effective public–private partnerships: Managerial flow or organizational form? *Singapore Management Review, 32*(Suppl. 2), 23–28.

Kuah, A. (2012). Managerial assets and actions: What can we learn from New Zealand's research and innovation landscape? *Singapore Management Review, 32*(Suppl. 2), 45–51.

Lavie, D., Stettner, U., & Tushman, M. L. (2010). Exploration and exploitation within and across organizations. *The Academy of Management Annals, 4*(1), 109–155.

Leonard-Barton, D. (1992). Core capabilities and core rigidities: A paradox in managing new product development. *Strategic Management Journal, 13*(Suppl. 1), 111–125. doi:10.1002/smj.4250131009

March, J. G. (1991). Exploration and exploitation in organizational learning. *Organization Science, 2*(1), 71–87.

Martin, E. (2007a). Nation building in Bosnia and Herzegovina: Cooperation, coordination and collaboration. *South East European Journal of Economics and Business, 2*(2), 7–22.

Martin, E. (2007b). The co-evolution of development needs and IOR forms: Development by committee in bosnia. *International Public Management Journal, 10*(1), 59–77.

Martin, E. (2012). The interorganizational flow of international development. *Singapore Management Review, 32*(Suppl. 2), 14–22.

Melyoki, L. L. (2012). Informal economy development policy in Tanzania: Implications and relevance. *Singapore Management Review, 32*(Suppl. 2), 38–44.

Peters, T. J. (1992). *Liberation management: necessary disorganization for the nano-second nineties.* New York, NY: A. A. Knopf.

Seo, M. G., & Creed, W. E. D. (2002). Institutional contradictions, praxis, and institutional change: A dialectical perspective. *Academy of Management Review*, 27(2), 222–247.

Uzzi, B. (1997). Social structure and competition in interfirm networks: The paradox of embeddedness. *Administrative Science Quarterly*, 42, 35–67.

Vecchi, V., & Brusoni, M. (2012). The managerial flow of public local development policies: A conceptual framework. *Singapore Management Review*, 32(Suppl. 2), 5–13.

Wack, P. (1985). The gentle art of reperceiving. Scenarios, uncharted waters ahead. *Harvard Business Review 63*(9), 73–89.

Wang, P., & Yuan, L. (2012). Enhancing research capabilities in industrial parks: One North Singapore and Tianhe China. *Singapore Management Review, 32*(Suppl. 2), 29–39.

Part IV

Clusters, Entrepreneurship, and Managerial Flow

10 Managing Complexities Through Flow in Industry Clusters

An Emergent Framework and Case-Study Evidence From Australia

Ben Farr-Wharton and Kerry Brown

INTRODUCTION

Although definitions vary, it is generally accepted that industry clusters are made up of geographical agglomerations of organizations and associated institutions that are relevant to a particular industry (Delgado, Porter, & Stern, 2010; Porter, 2000). Research has established that industry clusters can provide a mechanism whereby participating firms benefit as a result of enhanced competitiveness, regional branding and innovation spillovers. However, although some particularly famous clusters, such as California's Silicon Valley or the Sports Systems Cluster in the Veneto, Italy, significantly contribute to regional economic and firm-level prosperity, clusters are rarely a panacea for success. In reality, in the event that a clustered firm fails to achieve a competitive position, the act of clustering can catalyze firm failure (Brown, Burgess, Festing, Royer, & Keast, 2010; Organisation for Economic Co-ordination and Development [OECD], 2007). In spite of this, industry clusters have proved to be one of the most popular and frequently applied regional development strategies of governments over the last two decades.

In academic research, industry clusters are contenious. This is largely due to disagreements regarding how clusters should be defined, measured, and analyzed (Martin & Sunley, 2003). One of the most common mechanims for deriving an understanding of the impact of clusters is to measure the degree to which firms collocate within a region and the degree to which regional employment is facilitated through clusters (Boix, Lazzeretti, Hervas, & De Miguel, 2011; European Cluster Observatory, 2011). However, this analytical frame lacks the ability to facilitate an understanding of the impact of clustering for firms and/or the managerial configurations required to make clusters successful. Furthermore, the complex considerations, such as cluster-network management, required to faciliate a platform of success for clusters is frequently ignored by governments seeking to promote linear, "one-size-fits-all" solutions for regional development (He, Rayman-Bacchus, & Wu, 2011).

In an effort to more aptly capture and analyse the complex dynamics that occur within industry clusters a group of researchers have developed the *value-adding web* (VAW) conceptualization of clusters (Brown et al., 2010; Royer et al., 2009). In contrast to an economic geography, top-down, or region interpretation of clusters, the VAW conceptualization emphasizes the web of networks that connect single firms within a cluster. In this way the VAW captures the impact of clustering at the firm, network, and region levels.

In this chapter we fuse the VAW and the Managerial Flow framework to establish a theoretical platform to conceptualize the complex management process occuring within clusters at the firm, network, and regional levels.

CLUSTER GOVERNANCE AND MANAGEMENT

Here we discuss two separate, but related, aspects of cluster governance. The first is an internal investigation into cluster governance and concerns the mechanisms and systems by which cluster members coordinate and/or compete with each other. The VAW synthesis, with its focus on network-based interactivity, is used as a frame to examine the coordination and competition that occurs within clusters. The second aspect of cluster governance explored in this section concerns an external examination, focusing on the interaction among regional government, regional development policy instruments, and industry clusters. Typically, this activity occurs through a conduit, often in the form of a cluster coordination organization (CCOs), that mediates the relationship between the government and cluster members (Nishimura & Okamuro, 2011).

Cluster Governance

Eisingerich, Bell, and Tracey (2010) argue that the analysis of governance within clusters has been generally limited to a single design exploring a relational model of governance based on implicit rules and understandings. In this way, industry clusters are composed of networks of firms that compete and cooperate (Porter, 1998). Through competition and cooperating, relationships and norms (ways of operating) between clustered firms are developed, and sometimes this is coordinated through a CCO, with connections to public institutions (Zaheer & George, 2004).

Within the VAW framework clusters are said to involve networks between three firm types: horizontal, vertical, and lateral firms. Horizontal firms produce the core products or services of the clusters. Vertical firms are the distribution points for products or services. Lateral firms, such as cluster coordination bodies, economic development officers, and so on, provide the infrastructure, funding, and education for the cluster (Royer et al., 2009). These relationships are modeled in Figure 10.1.

Brown et al. (2010) suggest that horizontal, vertical, and lateral actors form relationships that vary regarding collaborative integration. When actors begin to work together they are said to cooperate. Cooperation

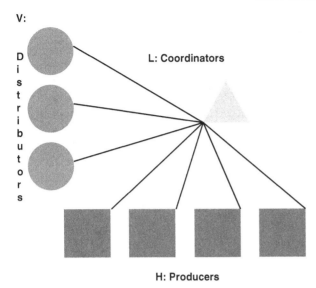

Figure 10.1   Horizontal, Vertical, and Lateral Firms in Clusters

involves firms sharing information, space, or referrals voluntarily. The next level of integration occurs when clustered firms begin to coordinate activity. Coordination encompasses open joint planning and strategy formation between organizations. The final integration configuration on the integration spectrum is collaboration. Collaboration connotes strong links between groups of clustered firms. Through this, comprehensive planning activities, underpinned by well-defined communication channels, occur through networks of firms. The paradigm of cooperation, coordination, and collaboration is referred to as the 3Cs, as is believed to represent a linear flow that can be enhanced over time (Brown et al., 2010; Polenske, 2004).

While clustered firms must ensure that competitive advantage is not diminished as a result of integration, collaboration provides the greatest mechanism for firms to receive network resources (Brown et al., 2010; Zaheer & George, 2004). Finding the balance between collaboration and competition poses one of the most significant challenges for clustered firms, as well as for CCOs and public policy (Lima & Carpinetti, 2012; Newlands, 2003). Furthermore, a reliance on the forces of the market, and the network, to achieve this balance is a reactive and risk-heavy option, particularly for regional governments that seek to invest in, and bank on, the success of clusters.

Industry Clusters and Governments

Governments intervene in clusters in targeted ways. Interventions can focus on stimulating clusters in specific, often depressed regions, or in a high-growth potential sector (OECD, 2007). Governments also seek to intervene with specific firms in clusters that are significant for the employment profile of a region (Farr-Wharton, Farr-Wharton, & Brunetto, 2014).

Nishimura and Okamuro (2011) delineate between the types of interventions that governments inflict on clusters. *Soft Interventions* involve governments coordinating meetings for cluster members, as well as representative, advisory and consultancy services. *Hard Interventions* are characterized by direct research-and-development (R&D) support, subsidy, and incubation services. Of these kinds of support programs, Nishimura and Okamuro (2011) find that Soft Interventions have a strong impact on firm and cluster output, whereas Hard Interventions have a weak effect. On the surface this result appears counterintuitive. Nishimura and Okamuro note that Soft Interventions strengthen network integration within clusters, and this helps to remove obstacles and relax constraints within the cluster, thereby mitigating knowledge-specific failures.

Although Soft Interventions appear to be significantly more cost effective for governments seeking to stimulate cluster performance, they are not necessarily a more popular option. In this regard an Australian study conducted by Farr-Wharton, Farr-Wharton, and Brunetto (2014) found that large, financial support to big companies (i.e., Hard Interventions) operating in hub-and-spoke clusters were more consistently applied. This configuration inhibited the support of innovative products developed by smaller firms within clusters and was rather seen as a mechanism to retain companies that were significant for the regional employment profile. In this way Hard Interventions can destabilize the competition–collaboration balance, particularly between small and large clustered firms.

Furthermore, although Soft Interventions cost less in terms of upfront resources, they can require governments to make long-term commitments. Such commitments do not typically fit well with election cycles and federal and state tax-distribution regimes. With these considerations in mind, we move to apply the Managerial Flow framework to the sphere of cluster governance and cluster-government relationships.

CLUSTERS FOR REGIONAL DEVELOPMENT: A MANAGERIAL FLOW PERSPECTIVE

Regional development management has traditionally been aligned with the field of public policy implementation (Ryan, 1996). One of the key weaknesses of a public policy approach to regional development is its reliance on unstructured processes, with little managerial control, and diminished opportunity to adequately predict outcomes. However, particularly at the local level, regional governments have developed mechanisms to help manage a continuity of policy processes, particularly those involving industry clusters (Bresolin, 2013).

The Managerial Flow framework offers a more comprehensive platform for governments to guide regional development. This is because it distinguishes between the *assets* and the *actions* involved in implementing policy, as well as accounting for the *selection gap* considerations that are required for a specific policy program to realize success (*planning, governance, partnership, selection,* and *knowledge management*). Whether specific cluster interventions are either hard or soft, governments seeking to stimulate regional productivity through industry clusters should give consideration to each of the selection gap considerations. Table 10.1 synthesizes these selection gap considerations.

We apply these to these selection gap considerations to context of industry clusters.

Planning and Strategy in Clusters

Planning and strategy gaps exist in industry clusters when Hard or Soft Interventions for cluster members have poor take-up are irrelevant or are absent (Farr-Wharton, Farr-Wharton, & Brunetto, 2014). Thus, from a public policy/external perspective, cluster interventions should be integrated regional strategic planning. However, cluster members should have the ability to contribute to this plan. Furthermore, a realistic appraisal of the cluster's growth potential, with respect to the context/region should be considered. Such an appraisal entails mapping of public policy relevant to the cluster and its members, mapping of stakeholders connected to the cluster.

Table 10.1 Selection Gap Considerations

Selection gap	Description (Vecchi & Brusoni, 2012)
Planning & strategy	Strategy gaps arise when programs are short term and poorly resourced, with a poor connection to a specific context or problem.
Governance	Governance involves collaboration between multiple parties to achieve a common goal. When mandates are not adequate, collaboration breaks down resulting in confusion and breakdowns in responsibility and accountability.
Selection	Selection refers to the degree to which targeting certain firms for intervention has been effective. Selection gaps emerge when firms feel unfairly treated.
Coordination and integration	When a lack of leadership, trust and reciprocity is present in a regional development intervention there is a gaps in coordination.
Communication and knowledge	When feedback loops are incomplete modifications to correct systems errors in regional development projects can ensue.

The needs of local stakeholders, such as the community, require consideration for expansion efforts to be successful.

At the cluster level, policies and programs formed by cluster representatives and/or CCOs need to ensure that the competition–collaboration nexus is not undermined through targeted enhancement programs (Newlands, 2003). This process can be aided through mapping the current level of firm and interfirm activity within the cluster (Royer et al., 2009).

Governance in Clusters

At its highest form, governance in clusters can occur through lateral actors, typically by CCOs (Brown et al., 2010). Alternatives to this model involve a representative team made up of cluster actors or through a top-down government actor. In its most balanced form, cluster governance allows for internal cluster management and external cluster advocacy.

External cluster advocacy involves lobbying to ensure that the cluster or clusters are considered in regional development plans. It also can act to increase the visibility of the cluster, thereby enhancing its potential market. Internal cluster management involves boosting overall cluster productivity without violating the competition–collaboration nexus that exists between firms. In this way, informed cluster governance is strongly linked to the *selection* of firms within programs, the *coordination* of programs and *knowledge management* within the cluster.

Selection

Hard or Soft Interventions to stimulate cluster performance can target specific groups of actors simultaneously, or focus on single actors. Again, consideration is required to ensure that the competition-collaboration nexus is not undermined.

Different cluster typologies warrant different approaches, and this is particularly so for Hard Interventions. For example, while on the surface it may seem unfair to economic stimulus or R&D funds to the largest firms within a cluster, in hub-and-spoke clusters (i.e., clusters that are centered on one or a small few very large horizontal firms) such stimulus is likely to trickle upward to vertically integrated firms (suppliers and distributors; Markusen, 1996). In more evenly distributed clusters by contrast, targeting small firms in Hard Interventions may promote innovation spillovers to larger firms through outsourced work, as smaller firms struggle contain increased productivity.

Soft Interventions, as noted earlier, seek to boost overall cluster productivity through enhancing collaboration between firms (Nishimura & Okamuro, 2011). In this way Soft Interventions, by definition, should not be exclusive but by contrast, seek to instigate whole-of-cluster development.

The link between *selection* and *coordination and integration* is thus more apparent in the case of Soft Interventions.

Coordination and Integration

When appropriate, collaboration between cluster members should be encouraged, however, not at the expense of competition. In this way, consideration needs to directed to anticipating future challenges. For example, a clustered horizontal firm that collaborates with another horizontal firm to win a large production contract may inadvertently share seemingly insignificant firm-specific or tacit knowledge that is exploited by the competition in the future to diminish its market (Brown et al., 2010). To avoid this firms and CCOs should ensure that the sharing of intellectual property is done so with consideration for the future and in a trusting environment. Boosting the social capital that exists between clustered firms can enhance the ability for joint activity to lead to long-term advantage (Brunetto & Farr-Wharton, 2007).

Knowledge Management

Clusters benefit from a degree of interconnectivity between firms. These connections provide a mechanism for knowledge to be exchanged and opportunities to be recognized (Farr-Wharton, Farr-Wharton, Brunetto, & Bresolin, 2014). Thus, CCOs should ensure that (a) they are connected with all firms within the cluster and (b) clustered forms are aware of each other. CCOs need to also establish appropriate communication channels so that single firms have a voice in cluster-level decisions, and potentially context level decisions (such as in public policy). In this way CCOs need to be constantly evaluating cluster activities and responding to the needs of cluster members.

Drawing from this synthesis of Managerial Flow and industry clusters, we graphically conceptualize these actions in Figure 10.2—the Managerial Flow Model of Cluster Management.

Context analysis, encompassing public policy mapping, stakeholder mapping, and cluster-activity mapping, is concerned with the *planning* and *strategy* components of cluster management. The intersection among cluster policy development, external cluster advocacy, and internal cluster management is concerned with cluster *governance*. Actions involved in cluster development represent *selection* and *coordination* considerations for clusters. Finally, evaluating the degree to which clusters members remain connected with each other and the performance of cluster initiatives is concerned with *knowledge* considerations for the cluster.

We move to apply the Managerial Flow model of Cluster Management to the case of a creative industries cluster operating in Australia's South East Queensland region.

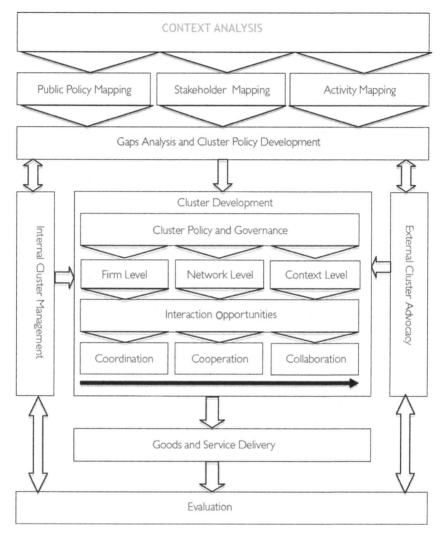

Figure 10.2   Managerial Flow Model of Cluster Management

METHOD

To test the ability of the Managerial Flow Model of Cluster Management framework to capture cluster management dynamics we adopt an embedded case study design to examine a small creative-industries cluster operating in Australia.

The cluster under examination in this case study developed in the 1950s as a set of entertainment venues and festival (vertical firms) and musical groups (horizontal firms) with strong connections to the local tourist destination. A high level of cluster activity was maintained until the 1980s; however, as neighboring regions experienced a tourism boom and other entertainment opportunities, creative production in the region began to diminish. Activity was further diminished in the 1990s and 2000s when successive local, state, and federal governments introduced legislation packages that heavily taxed venues that served alcohol and had live music. Throughout the period the region retained and attracted a high proportion of musicians; however, there were very few performance opportunities at local venues and festivals.

In 2009 the region's economic development agency approached *us* (the authors of this chapter) to develop a mechanism to revitalize creative production within the cluster. We developed a three-phase research project. The first phase gathered context and network- and firm-level data from musicians and venues operating in the region. The second phase involved an 18-month Soft intervention that sought to stimulate collaboration among musicians, venues, and festivals. This was facilitated through the development of a CCO that coordinated a performance opportunity involving multiple cluster members. The final phase involved an evaluation of the impact of the intervention.

In all 25 individual firms (musicians, venues, and festivals) were involved in the project. Of these, five were solo performers, six were musical groups/bands, four were disc jockeys, two were annual festival bodies, four were bars, and the remainder included a café, a weekly market, a recording studio, and a musician management company. Data were collected in the form of policy document, field notes, and social network mapping. Analysis took the form of qualitative textual analysis and social network analysis using the UCINET software.

RESULTS

Planning and Strategy in Clusters

A meeting was held in 2009 involving local cluster members and local government representatives. The meeting collected information from attendees regarding the inhibitors of creative production and ideas and suggestions to enable a revitalization of the cluster. Inhibiting factors identified by horizontal actors included (a) a lack of opportunity for local musicians to play at local venues and locations and (b) a lack of awareness of other musicians and venues in the region. Inhibiting factors identified by the vertical actors included (a) the high cost of employing an unknown a musician and (b) the high cost of paying alcohol and APRA (copyright) licensing fees. Suggestions included activating funding by third parties in the form of arts grants and government donations to facilitate performance of original music (to avoid APRA fees) in local venues and at local festival. These suggestions were synthesized with an audit of local creative activity and public policy mapping to inform the developed of a cluster intervention strategy.

Governance in Clusters

The cluster intervention strategy facilitated the development of CCO (named the Music Hub) made up of representatives from the research team and local economic development office. The CCO received government funds to coordinate local performances and network activity involving clustered venues and musicians. In all, 25 activities were held over the 18-month period. These events included seven networking meetings involving cluster members, nine performance events involving local musicians in local venues, four musicians' workshops, and the establishment of a busking showcase component as part of a local festival. In addition the Music Hub developed regular newsletter and social media presence to connect actors with each other. Members of the CCO also engaged with local government members on more than three occasions to report on the project's development and to explore possibilities for expansion.

Selection

Prior to the intervention, networked activity in the region was very low. Figure 10.3 shows a map of the social network activity occurring between firms (blue boxes) and musicians (red circle) prior to the intervention (2009).

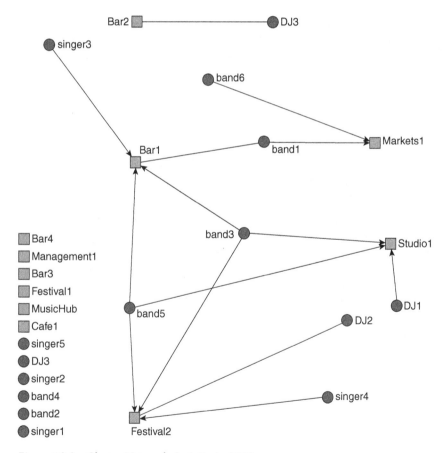

Figure 10.3 Cluster Network Activity in 2009

Many of the clustered musicians, festivals, and venues had no connection with each other at all.

In 2012 the network activity between cluster members had significantly expanded, leaving no cluster member disconnected from the next (Figure 10.4). The central connecting role of the CCO Music Hub is apparent, because it is embedded in relationship with the majority of musicians.

The growth in network connections from 2009 to 2012 is displayed in graph form in Figure 10.5. Network connection is measured with respect to degree centrality, betweenness centrality and Eigenvector centrality. Degree centrality is the number of links per node, betweenness centrality is the degree to which a node acts as a link for other nodes, and Eigenvector centrality measures the connection of one node to other, highly connected nodes (Borgatti et al., 2002). As can be noted, the network of cluster members underwent exponential growth over the 18-month period. Degree centrality was up on an average of 16% for all network members, except for one festival who had a focus on employing nonlocal musicians. The graph and network map also exhibit the connection power of the Music Hub CCO. The CCO had centrality scores nearly 60% above the average for each measure.

In all, the network data displayed in the network maps and chart shows (a) the growth of network connectivity within the cluster, (b) the central governance role of the CCO, and (c) the pattern of selection for Soft Interventions (network development activity).

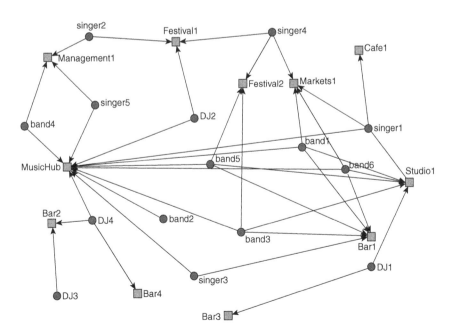

Figure 10.4   Cluster Network Activity in 2012

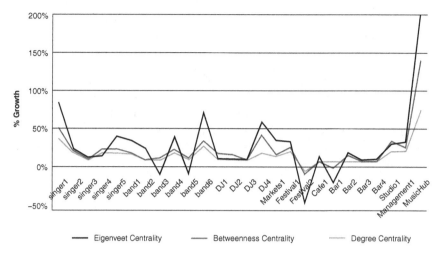

Figure 10.5   Centrality Difference, 2009–2012

Coordination and Integration

Figure 10.4 shows the way in which the CCO operated as a conduit between members. It achieved this distributed, but connected, network profile through a balanced targeting of specific cluster members in particular performance opportunities. Although the allocation for performance funds given to respective musicians in coordinated performances varied in line with the standard market pricing, all musicians receive an opportunity to engage with at least one venue during the intervention. This strategy of using government funds to pay standard rates to bands to perform in local venues was used to ensure that the collaboration–competition nexus was not violated, and to meet the needs of the venues whom had expressed a concern about paying for a local act with whom they were not familiar with.

Knowledge Management

The CCO Music Hub, in its centralized network position, was well placed to collect knowledge directly from most cluster members or through a communication chain that was no more than one or two degrees of separation at any point. This greatly facilitated the diffusion of opportunities throughout the network. Furthermore, the CCO was able to facilitate connections between local musicians and the recording studio. The recording studio grew its degree centrality by 20% over the course of the intervention and greatly increased the amount of business it conducted with local musicians.

However, the high centrality score of the CCO Music Hub was in some ways a liability. As when government funds for the development projects were removed, the efficacy of the CCO to continue to stimulate activity was significantly reduced. However, while the continual growth of activity was not sustained when government support was drawn to a close, many of the newly formed linkages, and subsequent activity among venues, festivals, and musicians continued.

IMPLICATIONS AND CONCLUSION

Despite being a single case study, our analysis using the *Managerial Flow Model for Cluster Management* is effective in capturing internal and external cluster dynamics from a network and policy implementation management perspective. The results highlight the central role of CCOs in a) acting as a conduit between government and cluster members, (b) connecting cluster members, and (c) guiding and stimulating cluster activity. In this way, the development of the CCO, an implantation plan and resourcing from local government grants and donations was a very important external consideration that greatly enhanced internal activity within the cluster.

Although the case study did not contain a Hard Intervention, the Soft Intervention activities undertaken appeared to be particularly effective in forging network connections between firms, as well as increasing overall cluster activity. This is consistent with the findings of (Nishimura & Okamura, 2011, p. 814).

The limitation of this research is that the overall impact on firm performance, bought about through the CCO cannot be adequately gauged. To this end, while it is known that the amount of local venues and festivals employing local musicians increased as a result of the Soft Intervention (a positive outcome in itself), the long-term impact on firms has not been measured here. It is known that some firms were able to establish long-term financial arrangements that extended far beyond the data collection of this research, for example, between Singer 1 and Café 1. However, in the case of the music industry, venues require a diversity of performance to maintain competitiveness. Thus, certainly in the case of the bars, although they become more aware of local musicians as a result of the research project, it is likely that they may only employ local musicians sparingly. Furthermore, as time goes on the liability of disconnection enhanced by this kind of irregular contact will mean that some bands will leave the area, and new ones will come in.

From a practical perspective however, the *Managerial Flow Model for Cluster Management* coupled with this analysis, provides a useful guide for CCOs in understanding the importance of Soft Interventions, connectivity and relationships with public policy. Similarly, a key recommendation for policy makers stemming from this case is to facilitate adequate and effective CCO relationships. Furthermore, policy makers should provide funding mechanisms that target network development for firms and enable CCOs to measure the impact of such interventions.

For CCOs this case highlights the managerial considerations that must be maintained within cluster operations, including *strategy, governance, selection, coordination, and knowledge management*. CCOs are essentially responsible for ensuring the collaboration-competition nexus is not violated, and key to achieving this is developing effective Soft Interventions that enhance network connection.

REFERENCES

Boix, R., Lazzeretti, L., Hervas, J. L., & De Miguel, B. (2011, August–September). *Creative clusters in Europe: A microdata approach*. Paper presented at European Regional Science Association: New Challenges for European Regions and Urban Areas in a Globalised World, Barcelona, Spain.

Bresolin, F. (2013). Evolution of cluster policies and Europe and some possible new scenarios and strategies. In K. Brown, J. Burgess, & S. Royer (Eds.), *Resources for competitive advantage in clusters* (pp. 12–29). Munich, Germany: Rainer Hampp Verlag.

Brown, K., Burgess, J., Festing, M., Royer, S., & Keast, R. (2010). *Value adding webs and clusters—concepts and cases*. Munich, Germany: Rainer Hampp Verlag.

Brunetto, Y., & Farr-Wharton, R. (2007). The moderating role of trust in SME owner/managers' decision-making about collaboration. *Journal of Small Business Management, 45,* 362–387.

Delgado, M., Porter, M. E., & Stern, S. (2010). Clusters and entrepreneurship. *Journal of Economic Geography, 10,* 495–518.

Eisingerich, A. B., Bell, S. J., & Tracey, P. (2010). How can clusters sustain performance? The role of network strength, network openness, and environmental uncertainty. *Research Policy, 39,* 239–253.

European Cluster Observatory. (2011). *Strong clusters in innovative regions*. Stockholm, Sweden: European Cluster Observatory Centre for Strategy and Competitiveness.

Farr-Wharton, R., Farr-Wharton, B., & Brunetto, Y. (2014). Regional development: The importance of a relationship with government. *Journal of Social and Economic Policy, 16,* Article 7.

Farr-Wharton, R., Farr-Wharton, B., Brunetto, Y., & Bresolin, F. (2014). The role of generational cohorts: Comparing approaches to innovation using internal networks. *International Journal of Innovation Management, 18,* 1450028.

He, Z., Rayman-Bacchus, L., & Wu, Y. (2011). Self-organization of industrial clustering in a transition economy: A proposed framework and case study evidence from China. *Research Policy, 40,* 1280–1294.

Lima, R., & Carpinetti, L. 2012. Analysis of the interplay between knowledge and performance management in industrial clusters. *Knowledge Management Research & Practice, 10,* 368–379.

Markusen, A. (1996). Sticky places in slippery space: A typology of industrial districts. *Economic Geography, 72,* 293–313.

Martin, R., & Sunley, P. (2003). Deconstructing clusters: Chaotic concept or policy panacea. *Journal of Economic Geography, 3,* 5–35.

Newlands, D. (2003). Competition and cooperation in industrial clusters: The implication for public policy. *European Planning Studies, 11,* 521–532.

Nishimura, J., & Okamuro, H. (2011). Subsidy and networking: The effects of direct and indirect support programs of the cluster policy. *Research Policy, 40,* 714–727.

Organisation for Economic Co-operation and Development. (2007). *Competitive regional clusters: National policy approaches* (Reviews of Regional Innovation). Paris, France: Author.

Polenske, K. (2004). Competition, collaboration and cooperation: An uneasy triangle in networks of firms and regions. *Regional Studies, 38*, 1029–1043.

Porter, M. E. (1998, November–December). Clusters and the new economics of competition. *Harvard Business Review*, pp. 77–90.

Porter, M. E. (2000). Location, competition, and economic development: Local clusters in a global economy. *Economic Development Quarterly, 14*, 15–34.

Royer, S., Festing, M., Steffen, C., Brown, K., Burgess, J., & Waterhouse, J. (2009). *The value adding web at work: Developing a toolbox to analyse cluster firms* (Danish–German Research Paper No. 1). Flensburg, Germany: International Institute of Management, University of Flensburg; Sønderborg, Denmark: Department of Border Regional Studies, University of Southern Denmark.

Ryan, N. 1996. A comparison of three approaches to programme implementation. *International Journal of Public Sector Management, 9*, 34–41.

Vecchi, V., & Brusoni, M. (2012). The managerial flow of public local development policies: A conceptual framework. *Asia Pacific Journal of Management Theory and Practice*, 34(Suppl. 2), 5–13.

Zaheer, A., & George, V. (2004). Reach out or reach within? Performance implication of alliances and location in biotechnology. *Managerial and Decision Economics, 25*, 437–452.

11 Small to Medium-Sized Enterprise Innovation
Using Collaborative Networks to Bridge Policy and Praxis

Christina Donnelly O'Connor

INTRODUCTION

It is acknowledged that small to medium-sized enterprises (SMEs) require support as they are limited by their financial and internal resource capacity. Ultimately this "smallness" is distinctive, but "this distinctiveness of SMEs affects their support needs and how such support is delivered if it is to be effective" (North, Smallbone, & Vickers, 2001, p. 311).

BACKGROUND

Collaborative Innovation

Various sources provide SMEs with access to external information including suppliers and customers; university, government, and private laboratories; competitors; and other nations (von Hippel, 1988). Typically SMEs rely on suppliers and customers to provide external market information informally through day-to-day interactions with access to formalized market intelligence viewed as a luxury and/or too expensive (Donnelly, Simmons, Armstrong, & Fearne, 2012). In many cases, SMEs may seek free assistance from knowledge providers such as universities and/or funding from governments or trade bodies.

This ability to network and to work with others serves SMEs well, as extant literature suggests that by operating in multi-organizational arrangements, problems can be solved or done much easier than alone (McGuire, 2006, p. 33). Typically within "collaborative public management," emphasis is ultimately on government being held responsible for the satisfactory delivery of the services. However, according to McGuire (2006, p. 33) action can be commanded by others, other than that of public managers. In this research the SME plays a central role in commanding action.

Regional SME Marketing

Despite SMEs being more flexible, entrepreneurial, and responsive to change than larger firms, there are obvious limitations restricting their business development. It is therefore not surprising that SMEs may not be able to develop sufficient absorptive capacity themselves, but seek to utilise strategic alliances or complementary resources to exploit that knowledge (Gulati, 1998, Therefore the need for collaboration is recognized as beneficial, with firms "opting for an integrative approach that invites and includes different stakeholders in a collaborative network" (Volpentesta & Ammirato, 2013, p. 55). This need may be heightened further in the context of location and regionally.

The Public Policy Initiative

In Northern Ireland (NI), "the agrifood industry has made a significant contribution to the development of the NI economy" (Food Strategy Group, 2004, p. 2). The sector is estimated to be worth more than £800 million (Goldblatt McGuigan, 2010, pp. 1–2) and is dominated by SMEs accounting for 98% of the businesses and providing employment for more than half a million people (Mitchell, 2009). Given the value of the agrifood sector and the role of SMEs with the NI economy, this provides an important setting for research considering the significance of agriculture to many economies.

The need for a public policy initiative was driven by the NI government's focus on food, which highlighted the increasing difficulties facing agrifood SME growth and the need for innovative support (Agri Vision 2015 Committee; Department for Environment, Food and Rural Affairs, 2010; Food Strategy Group, 2004). This was recognized in Recommendation 6 of the *Fit for Market Report* (Food Strategy Group, 2004, p. 41), which highlighted the lack of market information available for access and analysis by businesses in the NI region in comparison to other competing economies, stating that "the flow of information on Market Developments . . . should be provided proactively and systematically to producers as well as processors in order to promote a common understanding of market trends and opportunities." Simmins (2008) cited two main barriers to SME continued success as the substantial costs of formalized market information and the lack of analytical capacity within the SME to disseminate and to utilize the data.

Due to an evolving market, increasingly demanding consumers, coupled with the restricted nature of the SME in terms of marketing resources, skills, time and market knowledge (Henchion & McIntyre, 2000), the need for a solution was acknowledged and a policy instrument was developed. In light of the demand for free flow of market information for SMEs, a collaborative network was established in 2006 between the government's Department of Agriculture and Rural Development (DARD), the regional trade agency body Invest NI, a marketing consultant, the University of Ulster, and agrifood and drink SMEs across NI. The purpose of this public policy initiative was to address the existing "failure" of regional small business to compete, through the provision of highly formalized market information as a "one-stop solution" to increasing business competitiveness through innovation.

All stakeholders were consulted in the phase of policy design, the implementation, and, most important, the actual management of the policy instrument, and series of meetings were arranged between all parties over an 18-month period to discuss the value and potential role of this policy instrument in supporting SMEs, and ultimately the NI economy. The policy instrument focused on addressing the following objectives:

1. Provide a detailed understanding of consumer/market for primary and processed food products produced in NI.
2. Provide evidence to support the DARD for NI and Invest NI in their efforts to encourage farmers and small producers to differentiate, add value, and adopt a more market-oriented approach to their businesses.
3. Provide evidence to support individual businesses (farming and food processing) in their pursuit of sustainable competitive advantage through enhanced marketing and (new) product development

In order to address these objectives, the stakeholders created a collaborative network, in which formalized market information would be provided free of charge, disseminated, and analyzed for SMEs.

This chapter focuses on one form of formalized market intelligence, real-time shopper purchasing data from Tesco's loyalty-club card data.[1] Shoppers use this card to collect points when products are purchased at the point of sale in all Tesco retail outlets. Simultaneously the product information was captured by marketing consultancy firm into a database called "The Shop." This database captured and stored shopper's real-time purchasing behavior and provided access to data from more than 1.7 million transactions every 2 weeks (Anstead, Samuel, & Crofton, 2008).

Once firms are in possession of loyalty card data, they used this source of useful data to design effective marketing strategies (Cortiñas, Elorz, & Mugica, 2008). Through the policy initiative SMEs gained free access to the club-card data, providing the SMEs with access to transactional history of millions of customers and bridging the gap between what customers say they do and what they actually purchase (Humby, Hunt, & Phillips, 2007). Reports were provided that consisted of information detailing what shoppers bought weekly, monthly, and yearly; what the best performing products in a category were; what the best-selling stores were; a profile of shoppers in terms of their lifestyle and life stage were purchasing; and what other products are purchased by the shoppers.

METHODOLOGY

Research Design

Despite multiple stakeholders being involved in the network, key representatives of the agribusinesses (owner/managers) had been chosen in order to reflect multiple realities. An interpretivist perspective was adopted in order to fully appreciate the challenges and to uncover any facts that were unknown about the day-to-day agrifood SME marketing practices (Blumberg, Cooper and Schindler, 2005). Seven agrifood case firms were selected based on predetermined criteria (see Table 11.1).

An action research approach was adopted alongside case based research, in order to facilitate hands on field research and unique insight into the real world problems existent within an agrifood SME on a daily basis. The research was carried out over a 3-year period (2008–2011) and utilized seven agrifood SME case studies (see Table 11.2) in order to illuminate a set of decisions made arising from exposure to loyalty card data (Yin, 1994).

The research was broken into three stages as follows:

Stage 1: Fourteen face-to-face interviews were completed exploring the SMEs current marketing activity prior to the collaborative innovation network to provide exposure to loyalty card data. Exploratory questions were used based on the market-orientation study by Pelham and Wilson (1996) in order to assess the current level of marketing activity.

Stage 2: Over a period of 6 months, SME agrifood owner/managers were exposed to monthly interaction with the researcher and the loyalty card data. It was up to the SME respondents to initiate any further contact in between the standard once a month meeting.

Stage 3: After the regular collaborative network's exposure to loyalty card data, 11 face-to-face interviews took place with seven of the agrifood firm respondents, adopting the previous questions used in Stage 1 to assess whether change had occurred as result of the collaborative network and exposure to the data.

The action research approach adopted was based on the conceived notion of action research: "as a way in which researchers could bridge the gap between practice and theory" (Blichfeldt & Anderson, 2006, p. 2). In

Table 11.1   Research Sampling Criteria

1. The agrifood firms are independent firms.
2. The agrifood firms fulfill the definition of SME in accordance with the EU definition 2005.
3. The agrifood firms supply premium-niche food or drink products.
4. The agrifood firms represent different sizes within the SME definition utilized in this research.
5. The agrifood firms represent various stages in a business life cycle.
6. The agrifood firms operate within varying sectors of the agrifood industry.
7. The agrifood firms operate within varying markets (national, domestic, local).
8. The agrifood firms represent various channels (supermarkets, Tesco, non-Tesco, local independents, farmers' markets).

Table 11.2 Summary of the seven SME agrifood firms involved in this research

SME	Participant	Focus/issues	Size	Start up	Years old	Sector	Current market	Family	Supply Tesco	Current channels
C1	C1P1 C1P2	Launching new flavors into supermarkets to create larger consumer base	5	2008	2 years	Dairy—Yogurt	NI/ROI/ENG	No	Yes	Supermarkets, farm shops, Independents Service sector
C2	C2P1 C2P2	Trying to establish brand as home-made artisan soup and to build business	3	2009	10 months	Vegetable—Fresh Soup	NI	No	No	Independents
C3	C3P1 C3P2	Creating a new category with innovative health foods in multiples	13	2002	8 years	Pulses/Cereals—Wholesome health foods	NI/GB/ROI	Yes	No	Supermarkets
C4	C4P1 C4P2	Launching new indulgent products & strengthening brand image	40	1955	55 years	Bakery	NI/ROI/GB/USA	Yes	No	Supervalu, Centra, Sainsbury, Dunnes
C5	C5P1 C5P2	Expansion of business through stuffed prepared mushrooms but also looking for new opportunities	20	1998	12 years	Vegetables—Mushrooms	NI/ROI	No	No	Superquinn, Dunnes Independent Cafes and Delis, Restaurants, Food Service
C6	C6P1 C6P2	Aiming to get into supermarkets	6	2005	5 years	Drinks—Teas	NI/ROI/GB/International	No	No	Food service, Retail, Farmers' Markets Online
C7	C7P1 C7P2	Strengthen their hold on the market	55	1988	22 years	Ready meals, soups & desserts	NI/ROI	Yes	No	Independents, Butchers

Note: ENG = England; GB = Great Britain; NI = Northern Ireland; ROI = Republic of Ireland addition to this, is the more recent description of action research by Coghlan and Shani (2005) as "undertaking action and studying action as it takes place" (p. 533). In particular, a participatory action research (PAR) was adopted because of the collaborative nature of the study, in which the researcher involved was able to engage directly with the multiple organizations and, in particular, the small-business case studies on a daily basis. Communication was two-way, with the diagnosis of the problems presented and discussed by the SME owner and the researcher at the very first stage of the longitudinal study, aligning with the action research process with that of Sussman and Evered (1978). The research approach adopted allowed for in-depth and insightful findings both on a managerial and an SME level.

FINDINGS

The implementation and management of this regional policy initiative was not without its gaps when presented in the context of managerial flow (Martin, Vecchi, Brusoni, Borgoniovi, & Kuah, 2012). The strategy gap highlighted the overall success of the initiative in the short-term 3-year period, between 2008 and 2011 with the government being recognized for proactively addressing a "failure" of regional small business to compete through a "one-stop solution." However, the sustained roll out of this project waivered as the government sought to place funding elsewhere post 2011 as the key personnel within the stakeholders had moved and/or had failed to agree on the next stage of the initiative.

Strategically the engagement of all stakeholders was valuable, with all parties benefiting with increased uptake of SMEs using the data, therefore developing their products and their businesses, respectively, which had a knock-on effect on all parties engaged. Despite training provided by the university to a small number of government (DARD) executives, it was not sufficient to aid in the delivery of bespoke data to small businesses throughout the region. In fact the SMEs acknowledged that

> all of this [policy initiative] is only as good as the people that are delivering it.
>
> (Case Study 4)

Interestingly the governance of this project flowed extremely well, despite stakeholders having different agendas, they were largely focused on the same goal of supporting small businesses. The accountability and risk analysis at the implementation stage rested on the university's keeping adequate recordings of the initiative in terms of workshops delivered, attendees, the number of small-business bespoke reports completed, the value or return on each complete bespoke report, and analysis. This was not as comprehensive as it could have been, but given the nature of the initiative, positive change or new products or listings were not always guaranteed within a short time frame, requiring a period for the process to take place. For example, in some cases, it took considerable time for new products to be created, for retail buyer meetings to be secured, and for successful delivery of the pitch to buyers before a decision would or could be made on a listing within the retailer and before being in a position to quantify his or her actions. The actual implementation of the project took place gradually, with the first-year targets realistic in terms of the businesses engaged in the initiative and the actual reports delivered. Years 2 and 3 saw an increase in the targets to be reached and for a more efficient and effective delivery of the initiative. Essentially Year 1 was spent generating "awareness" of the initiative by stakeholders to small businesses, informing and educating small businesses on the power of these formalized data and for the need to remain competitive in an evolving and competitive marketplace.

The selection, development, and implementation of the initiative in September 2008 served to highlight the clearly defined and defendable objectives by (a) providing a detailed understanding of consumer/market for primary and processed food products produced in NI. For example, at Stage 1 (prior to the implementation of this initiative) all firms relied predominately on their own knowledge to extract market information. This was done informally to a large extent:

> Market information [on the consumer] is usually based on ourselves, seeing what is out there, seeing the products, tasting the products.
>
> (Case Study 2)

Although some firms had access to information such as Mintel, Data Monitor, TNS data, and Tesco Link, the agrifood SMEs failed to see the relevance of this data for their business:

> It is interesting to see [Mintel data], but it's not a very useful and easily used type of information
>
> (Case Study 1)

To a large extent, SMEs had become reliant on the retail customer such as larger multiples to dictate what products to put on their shelves:

> In between us and the end user is the actual customer. And if we can't convince them of it (product), there is no hope that the end actual consumer is going to change the way they use it.
>
> (Case Study 5)

So despite firms perceiving themselves as innovative, the majority of SMEs responded to retailers' demands on what to produce, or innovate through imitation of leading products. At Stage 2 (during the implementation of the initiative) all stakeholders involved facilitated support through funding, analysis, and their time to ensure the maximization of the exposure and the utilization of the loyalty card data. The SME food firms, in turn, continued to keep their informal networks open and were utilizing this access and were understanding the data to open further networking opportunities, with supermarket buyers and other suppliers.

At Stage 3, the majority of agrifood SMEs reported a positive increase in market and consumer understanding through the exposure and utilization of the data. The greatest impact on the SMEs was the realization that they *did not know* who their consumer was. On the exposure and analysis of the data, agrifood SMEs received a real-time picture of their consumers for the first time:

> Before it was our own personal opinion . . . But now we know who our target consumer is.
>
> (Case Study 2)

With this newfound awareness, the firms instantly acknowledged the need for this type of information:

> That is why we need this information . . . Knowledge is power.
>
> (Case Study 1)

The other two objectives to be met and addressed required evidence to be provided to *support individual businesses (farming and food processing) in their pursuit of sustainable competitive advantage through enhanced marketing and (new) product development* and *to support the Department of Agriculture and Rural Development for Northern Ireland and Invest Northern Ireland in their efforts to encourage farmers and small producers to differentiate, add value, and adopt a more market-oriented approach to their businesses.*

The drive by the government for SMEs to become innovative was being addressed for the majority of firms:

> We see innovation coming through the data . . . it is not just about recipe, it is about product shape, size. . . .
>
> (Case Study 3)

However, having access to this high level of data highlighted the need for other forms of support required by the small firm to innovate:

> I know when you are a small producer like we are, if you don't have the capabilities and the efficiencies within your factory you can't compete with the bigger players no matter how innovative you are.
>
> (Case Study 3)

The overall impact of the exposure and utilization of the data was captured through the utilization of the data through the collaborative innovation network. This took three forms: conceptual, instrumental, and symbolic (Moorman, 1995; see Table 11.3).

Table 11.3 Agrifood Case Firms' Utilization of Supermarket Loyalty Card Data

Case study/ utilization	C1	C2	C3	C4	C5	C6	C7
Conceptual	Better understanding of products' performance against other competitors. Clearer idea of end consumer. Broadened understanding of the poorer performing areas of sales.	Better understanding of the end consumer and the gap in the Soup market for the new offering.	Better insight into the consumer. Reinforced existing understanding of market leaders.	Reinforced ideas and decisions already undertaken- e.g., Indulgent brand line. Highlighted the limited nature of the retail bakery market.	Heightened awareness of their potential consumer. Insight into the top-line view of loose and packed mushrooms.	Better understanding of key flavors in retail. Reinforced belief on the need to improve packaging.	Better understanding of top performing products in the ready meal category.
Instrumental	Utilized information to inform the in-store taste-testing demonstrator. Provided data to the researcher to inform the strategic business plan.	Utilized the data to create the Tesco pitch, successfully getting five new lines listed.	Utilized data to assist development of new seed product.	Utilized data to support pricing strategy.	Utilize data to replicate what's already on the shelves. Developed products and flavors, e.g., roasting trays.	Developed website based on segmentation deriving from data. Reconsidered pack size.	Developed two new dessert lines and three ready-meal lines from the data.
Symbolic	To aid discussions with buyers at the Balmoral Show, Taste of Ulster, and Tesco events.	Used to engage with Tesco buyers to set up a meeting.	Stated data use to engage with government bodies on funding.	Utilized networking opportunities to engage with Tesco.	Discussion at local events.	No use.	No use.

Overall the SMEs regarded this initiative as an important source of support:

> You do need something to support you and give you confidence that the product is going to work in the market place and I suppose that is where the loyalty card data comes in.
>
> (Case Study 5)

The findings suggest that the overall coordination and integration of stakeholders within the network appeared to work collaboratively and effectively to implement and develop the initiative. To a large extent, this initiative was "trial by error" because it was the first time the government had engaged with stakeholders in this fashion and with the delivery of real-time marketing intelligence data deriving from the Tesco club card. All stakeholders engaged in this project were appropriate and showed evidence of considerable trust in one another, but not all stakeholders were fully engaged; that is, not all staff at various levels of the organization were fully aware of this initiative and of their role within the implementation and delivery of this initiative. There was an obvious communication and knowledge gap within various stakeholder organizations, which disadvantaged the awareness generation and the value of this initiative for all businesses.

In general there was an effective marketing approach with government letters sent to all small businesses in relation to the delivery of sector workshops, as well as website promotion and regular coverage in local and regional *Farmer Journal* or magazines and government newsletters. However, the best form of marketing for this initiative was that of "word of mouth," by which SMEs who benefited from the initiative would inform a fellow businesses and, ultimately, an informal marketing network.

DISCUSSION

The findings provided insights into how formalized market intelligence from digital loyalty card data can enhance business development and innovation through a collaborative network. Nambisan's (2008, p. 11) definition on collaborative innovation as "an approach to innovation and problem solving in the public sector that relies on harnessing the resources and the creativity of external networks and communities to amplify, or enhance the innovation speed as well as the range of and quality of innovation outcomes" was supported with each stakeholder harnessing its own resources and skills, which complemented others in the delivery and analysis of the digital loyalty-card market intelligence for the advancement of business knowledge, development and innovation opportunities.

The marketing consultancy firm facilitated the reduced cost of access to the digital loyalty-card data. The University of Ulster provided the expertise of the action researcher to disseminate and analyze the market intelligence on behalf of the network to the SMEs. The DARD provided the funding for the data, as well as the expert support and access to the small businesses availing of the data. The SMEs involved benefited from the free access, analysis, and bespoke reports and the support of the government, regional agency body, and academia (see Figure 11.1).

Research findings demonstrated that exposure to the data facilitated innovation within the SME agrifood firm as it successfully utilized the data to depart from old ways of thinking, merging its production orientation toward a more market-oriented outlook (Harmsen, Grunert, & Declerck, 2000).

Exposure to digital loyalty-card data did aid risk management, encouraging agrifood firms to take risks supported by the information deriving from the digital data. Therefore, an enhanced market-oriented culture aided firms' ability to adapt to the food promotions environment.

Those firms with a higher level of proactiveness actively engaged with the data to advance their products. However, the digital loyalty-card data also enhanced proactiveness. Where there was a low level of proactiveness prior to exposure, the data increased the firm's ability to be more proactive, by engaging in new lines or by speaking to retail customers whom they had not before.

The capacity to innovate (Baker & Sinkula, 2009) was evident within the research with the SME agrifood firms combining their innovativeness with the new formalized digital data resource to implement new ideas or processes successfully. The findings illustrate that the digital data did not provide new insights but contributed to existing ideas already established (Naidoo, 2010).

The role of trust and information sharing (Granovetter, 1985) appeared to emerge at quite an early stage in the project in place of any formal contracts, which facilitated a stronger basis of mutual understanding and respect between each party within the network. Traditionally, agrifood SMEs are distrustful and suspicious of the government and perceive many government initiatives as irrelevant.

CONCLUSION

The findings demonstrate the role of a collaborative network for the maximization of knowledge. The nature of the collaborative network stakeholders serves to support and build on public policy and management literature, which highlights the success and challenges faced by a new form of support instrument to small businesses within a regional setting.

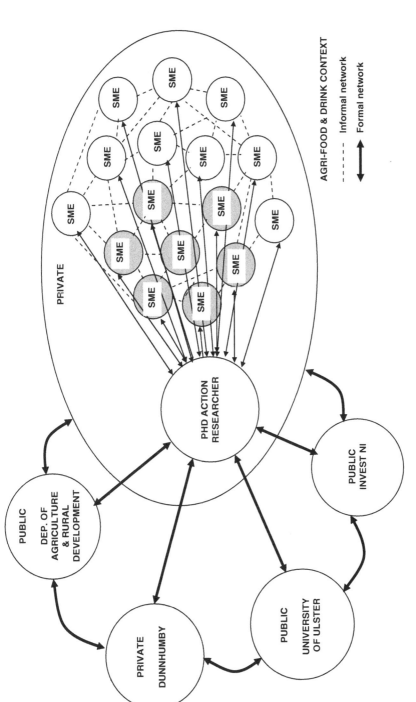

Figure 11.1 Collaborative Network

NOTE

1. The Tesco loyalty-club card data referred to hereafter as the digital loyalty-card data.

REFERENCES

Agri Vision 2015 Committee. (2004). *Report on the Agri Vision 2015 Committee.* Cambera City, Ireland: Department of Agriculture, Forestry and Fisheries, Cambera City.

Anstead, J., Samuel, J., & Crofton, A. (2008). Dunnhumby—a retailer's secret weapon. *Citi-group Global Market, Feeder's Digest, 60,* 1–25.

Baker, W. E., & Sinkula, J. M. (2009). The complementary effects of market orientation and entrepreneurial orientation on profitability in small businesses." *Journal of Small Business Management, 47*(4), 443–464.

Blichfeldt, B. S., & Anderson, J. R. (2006). Creating a wider audience for action research: Learning from case-study research. *Journal of Research Practice, 2*(1), 1–12.

Blumberg, B., Cooper, D. R., & Schindler, P. S. (2005). *Business research methods.* London, England: McGraw-Hill Higher Education.

Coghlan, D., & Shani, A. (2005). Roles, politics and ethics in action research design. *Systematic Practice and Action Research, 18*(6), 533–546.

Cortiñas, M., Elorz, M., & Mugica, J. M. (2008). The use of loyalty-cards databases: Differences in regular price and discount sensitivity in the brand choice decision between card and non-card holders. *Journal of Retailing & Consumer Services, 15,* 52–62.

Department for Environment, Food and Rural Affairs. (2010). Food 2030. HM Government, available at: http://archive.defra.gov.uk/foodfarm/food/pdf/food2030strategy.pdf

Donnelly, C., Simmons, G., Armstrong, G., & Fearne, A. (2012). Marketing planning and digital customer loyalty data in small business. *Marketing Intelligence and Planning, 30*(5), 515–534.

Food Strategy Group. (2004). *Fit for market report.* Belfast, Northern Ireland: DARD/ DETI.

Goldblatt McGuigan. (2010). *Value of food & drink industry to Northern Ireland.* Belfast: Northern Ireland Food & Drink Association.

Granovetter, M. (1985) Economic action and social structure: The problem of embeddedness. *American Journal of Sociology, 91*(3), 481–510.

Gulati, R. (1998). Alliances and networks. *Strategic Management Journal, 19,* 293–317.

Harmsen, H., Grunert, K. G., & Declerck, K. (2000). Why did we make that cheese? An empirically based framework for understanding what drives innovation activity. *R&D Management, 30*(2), 151–166.

Henchion, M., & McIntyre, P. (2000). Regional imagery and quality products: The Irish experience. *British Food Journal, 102,* 630–644.

Humby, C., Hunt, T., & Phillips, T. (2007) *Scoring points: How Tesco continues to win customer loyalty* (2nd ed.). London, England: Kogan.

Martin, E. C., Vecchi, V., Brusoni, M., Borgonovi, E., & Kuah, A. T. H. (2012). Perspectives on managerial flow. *Singapore Management Review, 34* (Suppl. 2), 60–71.

McGuire, M. (2006). Collaborative public management: Assessing what we know and how we know it. *Public Administration Review, 66,* 33–43.

Mitchell, W. (2009). *Budget must recognise the importance of small businesses.* Retrieved from http:www.fsb.org.uk/News.aspx?loc=ni&rec=5357

Moorman, C. (1995). Organisational market information processes: Cultural antecedents and new product outcomes. *Journal of Marketing Research, 32,* 318–335.

Naidoo, V. (2010). Firm survival through a crisis: The influence of market orientation, marketing innovation and business strategy. *Industrial Marketing Management, 39,* 1311–1320.

Nambisan, S. (2008). *Transforming government through collaborative innovation* (Innovation Series). Washington, DC: IBM Centre for the Business of Government Research.

North, D., Smallbone, D., & Vickers, I. (2001). Public sector support for innovating SMEs. *Small Business Economics, 16,* 303–317.

Pelham, A. M., & Wilson, D. T. (1996). Longitudinal study of the impact of market structure, firm structure, strategy, and market orientation culture on dimensions of small-firm performance. *Journal of the Academy of Marketing Science, 24,* 27–43.

Simmins, G. J. (2008). *An exploration of the determinants of SME website optimization: A study of the food industry* (Doctoral dissertation). University of Ulster, Jordanstown, Belfast, Northern Ireland.

Sussman, G., & Evered, R. (1978). An assessment of the scientific merits of action research. *Administrative Science Quarterly, 23,* 582–603.

von Hippel, E. (1988). *Sources of innovation.* Oxford, England: Oxford University Press.

Yin, R. K. (1994) *Case study research: Design & methods.* London, England: Sage.

12 Souk At-Tanmia

An Integrated Approach to Entrepreneurship Development in Postrevolution Tunisia

Emanuele Santi and Federica Ricaldi

INTRODUCTION

Micro, small, and medium-sized enterprises (MSMEs) are a vehicle to create jobs and drive economic growth (Haltiwanger, Jarmin, & Miranda 2010). In developing countries, MSMEs have considerable difficulties obtaining the necessary financial resources to effectively start and then grow their businesses. Access to traditional growth capital, including debt and equity, is often prohibitively costly, and MSMEs' main sources of capital are their retained earnings and informal savings, more rarely loan associations that nevertheless are unpredictable and not very secure.

Many MSMEs in Africa get caught in the so-called valley of death—the financing gap between an entrepreneur's immediate resources and the investment floor of many venture capitalists and banks, whereby starting a company has a net negative cash flow for a certain period of time (at the beginning of its activities) before generating sufficient revenues and running out of liquidity. Given the limited access to finance, MSMEs' main sources of capital are their retained earnings and informal savings, more rarely loan associations—that are unpredictable and not very secure (African Development Bank [AfDB], 2011; Boss, 2013).

With high levels of unemployment and limited opportunity, government policy that supports self-employment represents an appealing prospect for many countries today (European Commission, 2013). Social enterprises could play a powerful role in the overall growth and prosperity of African countries, offering a more accountable and sustainable business model. However, starting a new venture is risky, and securing external finance, along with basic business knowhow is a major issue (Dasgupta & Serageldin 1999).

Tunisia has one of Africa's best performing economies in terms of macroeconomic and social policies, yet it has experienced increasing social and developmental challenges. After the turmoil that engulfed the country in January 2011, the economy partly recovered in 2012, with gross domestic product (GDP) growing by 3.3%, but this has been insufficient to social unrest. (Grossi, Van Beers, Doranova, Markianidou, & Miedzinski, 2012; Kauffmann 2005; Stevenson & Theus 2014)

Using the managerial flow model (Vecchi & Brusoni, 2012), this chapter demonstrates how Souk At-tanmia, or "Market for Development," a partnership initiated by the African Development Bank in Tunisia encouraged enterprise development.

ADDRESSING MANAGERIAL GAPS IN TUNISIA: THE CONTEXT

The potential to develop entrepreneurship in Tunisia after the 2011 revolution was constrained by a set of challenges that can be captured around the gaps analysis framework (Martin, Vecchi, Brusoni, Borgonovi, & Kuah, 2012), namely, (1) strategy/planning gap, (2) governance gap, (3) selection, (4) coordination, and (5) communication and knowledge gap. These gaps are illustrated in the Table 12.1.

Table 12.1 Gap Analysis

Type of gap	Definition	Description
Strategy/ planning	Strategy gaps emerge when public programs are not defined on the basis of long-term goals but on short-term expectations with the result of allocating financial resources in a noneffective way.	Shortcoming of existing support programs, focusing on limited aspects (equity financing or training or debt financing or coaching). Lack of comprehensive approach and coordination between various activities
Governance	Multiple actors, multiple stakeholders with different mandates and objectives, resulting in overlapping of initiatives, lack of coordination and confusion in roles and responsibilities	Poor coordination between actors in the entrepreneurship ecosystem, namely, among the public sector, banks, local entrepreneurship centers, incubators, business associations
Selection	Difficulties in designing coherent programs (especially entrepreneurship programs) and scarcity of resources allocated	Multiple start-up programs lead to scarce resources being spread across multiple programs.
Coordination and integration	Lack of coordination and lack of trust, resulting in noncooperation especially between public and private sector	A general lack of coordination of government bodies supporting entrepreneurship and a lack of tradition of dialogue between public sector and private sector
Communication and knowledge	Asymmetric information flow and reciprocal knowledge gaps that push players to operate on different wavelengths, focusing only within their own silos	Lack of information on financing opportunities. Capacity constraint on business planning, particularly in the poorer rural areas

The strategy/planning gap: Programs were often successful in providing some support to private-sector development, yet they rarely created an effective entrepreneurship ecosystem, because they were relatively limited in their target, financial resources, and type of intervention.

The governance gap: The work of the public ministerial bodies (labor, professional education, industry) and local entities (municipal entrepreneurship centers, local incubators) were very much uncoordinated and characterized by a silos culture, with the institutions often lacking leadership and clear direction.

The selection gap: Rather than concentrating financial resources in comprehensive programs, multiple actors operated separate programs, addressing only parts of issues.

Coordination and integration gap: A general lack of coordination of government bodies supporting entrepreneurship and a lack of dialogue between public sector and private sector hampered the creation of an environment that nurtures and sustains business start-ups.

Communication and knowledge gap: Asymmetric information and lack of knowledge on the specific context of the country and of its needs limited the effectiveness of various private-sector development initiatives.

CLOSING THE GAPS

To address these challenges, the AfDB and its partners developed Souk At-tanmia, a nationwide initiative aimed at fostering job creation through entrepreneurship development.

Approach

A feature of the intervention was its broad partnership of 20 international and national partners, chosen according to their expertise, their commitment to social values, and their leadership position in their respective fields. While some were providing solely a financial support or technical support, others are providing both financial and technical support (AfDB, 2012).

The pilot initiative Souk At-tanmia provided €1 million in seed financing to entrepreneurs, with grants between about €5,000 and €15,000, while encouraging them to obtain cofinancing loans from local banks. It also provided a tailor-made mentoring/coaching program supplied by various private/public partners, through which a potential entrepreneur was matched by knowhow to a partner; for example, Microsoft provided mentoring and coaching to entrepreneurs undertaking information communication technology (ICT) projects, while the Food and Agriculture Organization provided coaching to entrepreneurs in the areas of agriculture (AfDB, 2012).

In a first phase, the support to candidates included an outreach program that assisted potential candidates in disadvantaged regions. A network of civil organizations delivered this and it aimed at achieving a strong participation rate irrespective of their education and access to ICT and remoteness. More than 2,000 proposals from candidates were received for the first round, of which 300 were shortlisted by the selection committee (formed by representatives of the partners). In the second round, these 300 candidates were given a 3-day capacity-building seminar by one of the partners. A second and more detailed call for proposals from these 300 candidates led to a further refinement of proposals and there were 71 finalists (British Council 2012; Hannachi & Chabaud, 2013).

Successful beneficiaries received both mentoring and seed money and were granted preferential access to additional lending from the local banks. This differentiates Souk from many other entrepreneurship schemes in Tunisia and elsewhere, which are often limited to providing either mentoring or other nonfinancial assistance or finance, but not both. While the grant helped strengthen an entrepreneur's financial position, the coaching helped build the necessary capability. The program was managed and funded through a steering committee with members from each partner that monitored results, oversight, and transparency throughout the lifetime of the program. Souk At-Tanmia was being implemented over 2 years, starting July 2012.

Key Managerial Actions

There were four main managerial actions, shown in Table 12.2, (1) needs assessment, (2) review of existing programs, (3) piloting, and (4) monitoring and learning (Grossi et al., 2012):

1. Needs and expectations analysis: This action included a mapping of the Tunisian entrepreneurial ecosystem, was conducted to gain an understanding of the overall situation. The analysis determined that access to the finance was an important obstacle to private enterprise development, particularly for the vulnerable sections of the population who either lacked funds to start activities or lacked the personal contribution or guarantees required by banks to raise funds in initiating a project. A review of in-country instruments and programs enabled the initiative to establish possible linkages with other initiatives and to provide some flexible start-up capital for entrepreneurial assets vis-à-vis the banks and/or to pay off initial unforeseen or recurrent costs during the initial stages of a business venture.
2. A review of existing programs: A review of institutional players and best (and worst) practice was able to help the program managers to gain an understanding of the local situation before. One of the reviewed programs was the World Bank's Development Marketplace (DM) Program; founded and administered by the World Bank since its inception in 1998, the program has been supporting social innovation and entrepreneurship for decades, by awarding more than

Table 12.2   Managerial Actions

Partners' actions	Milestones achieved	Gap
Analysis of the local enterprises needs with the support of local stakeholders Analysis of public policy plans Literary review (GeoPoll) Research through the main experiences in Tunisia (mapping exercise)	Knowledge about the main problems regarding the entrepreneurship ecosystem in Tunisia Setting up of a pilot which seeks to address unemployment and regional disparities in an innovative way	Planning/strategy
Design of a pilot program, which involves public and private sectors, international, national and local levels, academic and civil society organizations	No overlaps with other actions or similar initiatives planned by other development actors in Tunisia Coordination and effectiveness in order to reach the planned outcomes	Governance and partnership
Preselection of proposals and basic training	Assessment of about 2,000 proposals by the Evaluation Committee and based on a combination of socioeconomic criteria. Selection of enterprises with high potential carried out by a mix of bankers, existing entrepreneurs, and development agencies	Selection
Involvement of potential investors (local banks) and business angels, other entrepreneurs, and business services associations	Capacity building through training and bridging demand and supply of investments, market opportunities and market needs	Partnership and coordination and knowledge
Continuous monitoring of enterprise needs and learning assessment. Midterm evaluation (quantitative and qualitative assessment)	Evaluation of feedback to (a) reshape the coaching and training aspects during the implementation phase, (b) make possible amendments and improve the future of the partnership.	Knowledge

US$60 million in grants to more than 1,200 innovative projects. Using DM funding, many projects have gone on to secure additional funding support from other donors, foundations, governments, and corporate social responsibility (CSR) investors. The program has evolved over time from being a simple challenge fund for innovative projects with a strong focus on social impact to becoming increasingly business oriented, including an advisory service provided by the International Finance Corporation, the private-sector arm of the World Bank Group. Thus, while taking stock of the emerging trends by the DM, the Souk At-tanmia delivered a wider spectrum of partners and engaged them throughout all stages, from financial contributions to mentoring/coaching, of projects financed.

The United Nations Industrial Development Organization (UNIDO) has been successfully conducting a similar initiative in West Africa for over three years. UNIDO's initiative has helped finance some 100 projects and generated more than 1,000 full-time and 500 part-time jobs. In addition to the innovative nature of projects to be financed, one of the common features of the partnership with the UNIDO initiative was the emphasis on providing mentoring to projects, beyond simply financing them. However, the partnership's main innovation compared to the UNIDO initiative was the engagement of and the integration of additional financing in the form of loans from local banks. This allowed the funds mobilized to have a strong multiplier effect. The partnership also drew inspiration from various entrepreneurship support programs in Tunisia, such as the national Start-up Program (Program Essaimage) that encourages private businesses of a certain size to foster entrepreneurship in the same sector of activity. Independent entrepreneurs from this program can benefit from access to the commercial networks of the large businesses in which they were employed. Building on this this experience, the partnership enabled successful private sector enterprises to be involved in the coaching of projects in their areas of expertise (British Council 2012).

Existing collaborations between the BFPME (Banque de Financement des Petites et Moyennes Entreprises—Bank for Financing Small and Medium Enterprises) and other institutions to fund personal equity contributions. This helped demonstrate the "leverage effect" (an important component of the partnership) that such financing could have; for example, in January 2011, BFPME approved the financing of more than 1,000 projects with an investment cost of 802 million TND, which required personal contributions of 94 million TND. The mobilization of such personal contributions from venture capital investment companies enabled developers to obtain the 802 million TND required for their projects. This represents a multiplier effect of more than eightfold. The Swiss Confederation's grant to BFPME to provide "participatory loans" to serve as the personal contributions of developers wishing to mobilize more funds from BFPME also created a significant leverage effect of more than 10 times the grant amount (Grossi et al., 2012).

Other experiences of challenge funds or private entrepreneurial initiatives (e.g., the international Reseaux Entreprendre) inspired the partnership in its provision of ensuring the dual provision of financing as well as coaching.

All these initiatives depended to some extent on external financing (mainly from the same institutions that promote them) to be sustained over time. If these initiatives were successful in terms of resources mobilized and enterprises funded, they often lack a self-sustaining capacity, thus depending on external and constant financing. Such initiatives often fail to form a critical mass to support a long-term and sustained competitiveness and to have a real and long-term impact.

3. Pilot Program: The notion of pilot program proved useful to initiate the program. While in the long term, the initiative would require a local institution of excellence (not-for-profit, private, or public) that would host the platform. The pilot aimed at creating a demonstration effect and required an "external" institution to play the role of honest broker and convener to help foster entrepreneurial spirit in the country and to help create jobs for the most disadvantaged. The AfDB, a multilateral development institution with a long history of support in Tunisia, played that role.

   The notion of a pilot program also helped "sell" the initiative within the AfDB, an organization accustomed to much larger operations and with limited experience in engaging directly with small entrepreneurs, yet with a solid credibility and reputation in the country. The pilot was also useful in avoiding possible intrusion by the government. Apart from the participation of the state-owned bank and an assigned role of observer in the steering committee, the government has no direct role and no influence in the decision making, particularly in the selection of the award recipients. The planning and the execution of pilot actions were also useful because, while achieving small wins, it tested the reliability of the designed initiative. Indeed, while the access to financing was largely known to be critical, the pilot program enabled a determination of the amount and type of support needed. The financial support certainly helped entrepreneurs to fill the gap between being a start-up at an early stage and a small enterprise accessing the market.

   The pilot revealed that entrepreneurs' financial commitment could be enhanced by making the grant size proportional to project cost, and requiring entrepreneurs to use personal resources for an equity contribution. Furthermore, several beneficiaries would have been willing to consider equity funding instead of a grant, while others needed additional funding once they started growing but were not ready yet to attract funding from existing financial sources.

4. Evaluation: A midterm evaluation (MTE) was carried out after the first year of implementation to determine the relevance, efficiency, effectiveness, and sustainability of the Souk At-tanmia program, by assessing the achievements against its stated outcomes. The learning dimension was paramount, in order to gather the lessons learned and recommendations to prepare the ground for the future edition of the program.

   The midterm evaluation pointed out that the initiative managed to reach the intended beneficiaries (vulnerable people, youth, and underserved regions). Souk At-tanmia was deemed highly relevant by surveyed and interviewed entrepreneurs. The most valued aspects of the program were grant funding to support design, improvement, and growth of projects; coaching on product and management issues; and facilitation of networking and exposure. The MTE thus confirmed the assumption that the difficulty in accessing financial resources was one the major obstacles MSMEs' faced in Tunisia, often hampering the growth of small private-sector players who were foregoing opportunities that had the potential to create employment.

The monitoring and assessment framework, of which the MTE constituted an important part, enabled a managerial process that started to close certain gaps and paved the way for effective development policy execution. Preliminary results showed early signs of effectiveness of the partnership, although achievements were mostly in the form of outputs rather than outcomes. The MTE revealed that the intervention (financial and nonfinancial support) achieved satisfactory results in relation to the program objective: the partnership mobilized slightly more funding than originally intended (€1 million). There was a significant leveraging effect through other sources of finance, particularly loans and additional contributions by entrepreneurs, which amounted to two times the grant value.

A significant number of beneficiaries came from poorer regions (63%) and created a significant number of direct and indirect jobs (437 for 2013, with 600 expected by the end of 2014). Beneficiaries also expressed satisfaction with coaching services provided during the pilot program.

Beneficiaries valued the administrative and technical support and evidence suggests that the quality and involvement of the coach, and level of interaction, could hinder or enhance the business success especially for greenfield projects. Some of the projects that received the grant have already started to expand their sales, and from the 23 projects visited, they all reported either a sustained level of growth in their jobs and sales. At the institutional level, the MTE highlighted the need to develop a more financially sustainable model for the future as the current business model relies on constant replenishment of the fund (as it was grant financed) and in-kind contributions by partners (British Council, 2013).

Managerial Assets

The preceding managerial actions led the program to be able to produce three fundamental managerial assets: (1) knowledge about problems and awareness of possible solutions, (2) legitimacy and leadership, and (3) experience-based learning and revisions of future actions.

1. Knowledge about the problem: The initiative enabled the AfDB and its partners to gather great insight on entrepreneurship and employment

generation in Tunisia. The various partners gained hands-on experience on the challenges posed by the lack of a strong entrepreneurship spirit, the lack of skills and supporting institutions, and the urgent need to promote an entrepreneurial culture among youth. The initiative, however, also pointed out the need to change the mind-set of the development partners, who should be encouraged to complement each other and establish a synergic cooperation, with the key role to be played by the local banks, which are at the core of the problem of limited access to finance, and they can be part of the solution if engaged with from the very beginning.

2. Legitimacy of entrepreneurship programs and leadership: The Souk At-tanmia initiative produced a new legitimacy for entrepreneurship programs centered on people and their ideas, as well as the creation of an entrepreneurship ecosystem. Against a backdrop of a fragmented environment, where multiple development partners and public policy managers act uncoordinatedly, Souk At-tanmia demonstrated that engaging such partners is possible. A factor in the success of this program was the building of transparency, accessibility, and trust, which helped address governance, the style of the selection process, and communication between partners. Transparency occurred at all stages of the initiative through continuous involvement of the media and full coverage of all steps of the selection process, particularly during selection where the key national media outlets were invited.

3. Experience-based learning and revisions: From the need assessment and through the MTE, the program gave insight on future versions of the program and the development of similar programs to be carried out elsewhere. The lessons learned during the pilot program suggested a number of improvements, including (a) more emphasis on communication and sourcing efforts, (b) a review of selection criteria and process to improve quality at entry, (c) the strengthening of the mentoring and coaching activities to better adapt them to the needs of beneficiary projects, and (d) more differentiated financial support to greenfield (grant) and brownfield (equity) projects.

   Among the frequent recommendations made by beneficiaries to improve the quality of the coaching program are to use coaches with hands-on business experience and to offer support to access potential market opportunities and facilitate access to other stakeholders. Indeed, a number of beneficiaries interviewed pointed to the importance of receiving support to commercialize their products and to benefit from partners' networks. The pilot program included success stories in linking entrepreneurs to their markets through the various partners. However, future versions and similar programs may leverage the partners' networks more explicitly and capacity to facilitate greater access to markets.

CONCLUSION

By supporting the creation of MSMEs nationwide, Souk At-tanmia contributed to improving the momentum of economic growth and generated
productive employment while helping to reduce social and regional disparities. The primary beneficiaries were youth, women, and the underprivileged.

Support for entrepreneurs within the Souk At-tanmia program was
tailored to the entrepreneur's needs along the implementation phase. The
coaching was a service provided by partners with specific expertise (e.g.,
Microsoft for ICT projects, Food and Agriculture Organization for agri-
cultural projects, etc.). Furthermore, the support included the transfer of
knowledge and technical knowhow from the partner organization to the
recipient.

Souk At-tanmia contributed to strengthening the ecosystem, ensuring
linkages, synergies and knowhow transfer to increase tangible results. It
also accomplished a great degree of visibility within the Tunisian entrepreneurial ecosystem. The grant financing not only helped the entrepreneurs in
pursuing their projects but also created a significant leveraging effect. The
institutional structure proved highly efficient albeit with a hefty administrative burden on the secretariat.

The pilot program demonstrated its relevance and value in supporting
entrepreneurs by providing financial and nonfinancial assistance. The program, going beyond the expectations of the program managers, displayed
the latent value of nonfinancial support, apart from the coaching and the
skills developed.

REFERENCES

African Development Bank. (2011). *Supporting the transformation of the private
    sector in Africa. Private sector development strategy, 2013–2017.* Tunis, Tunisia:
    Strategy Department of the African Development Bank.
African Development Bank. (2012), *Souk At-tanmia operational manual* [Internal
    project document].
Boss, S. (2013). An Arab Spring for entrepreneurs? *Stanford Social Innovation
    Review, 3,* 56–58.
British Council. (2012). *Growing enterprise—Souk At-tanmia, business develop-
    ment initiative scoping report. Skills for employability program.* Retrieved from
    http://www.britishcouncil.org/
British Council (2013). *Growing enterprise—Souk At-Tanmia, business develop-
    ment initiative scoping report. Skills for employability program—consultancy
    report.* Retrieved from http://www.britishcouncil.org/
Dasgupta, P., & Serageldin, I. (1999). *Social capital: A multifaceted perspective.*
    Washington, DC: World Bank.
European Commission, (2013). *The observatory of European SMEs.* Retrieved from
    http://ec.europa.eu/enterprise/policies/sme/facts-figures-analysis/performance-
    review/index_en.htm
Grossi, F., Van Beers, D., Doranova, A., Markianidou, P., & Miedzinski, M. (2012).
    Eco-innovation practices and business opportunities for European SMEs in the

emerging markets of Asia, Latin America and Africa (EIO Thematic Report). Retrieved from http://www.scp-centre.org/

Haltiwanger, J., Jarmin, R., & Miranda, J. (2010). *Who creates jobs? Small vs. large vs. young* (NBER Working Paper No. 16300). Cambridge, MA: National Bureau of Economic Research.

Hannachi, M., & Chabaud, D. (2013). L'écosystème entrepreneurial de la Tunisie postrévolution: le cas de l'initiative pilote "Souk At-tanmia" [The entrepreneurship ecosystem of post-revolution Tunisia: The Souk At-tanmia pilot initiative]. Paper presented at Académie de l'Entrepreneuriat et de l'Innovation, Fribourg, Suisse, 22nd October.

Kauffmann, C. (2005). *Financing SMEs in Africa* (Policy Insights No. 7). Retrieved from http://www.oecd.org/dev/aeo

Martin, E., Vecchi, V., Brusoni, M., Borgonovi, E., & Kuah, A. (2012). Perspectives on managerial flow. *Singapore Management Review, 34*, 60–71.

Stevenson, L., & Theus, F. (2014). *Accélérer la création d'emplois et la croissance à travers le développement et des MPME dans les pays du Partenariat de Deauville* [Accelerate employment creation and growth through the development of MSME in the countries of teh Deuville partnership]. Tunis, Tunisia: African Development Bank.

Vecchi V., & Brusoni, M. (2012). The managerial flow of public administration. *Singapore Management Review, 34* (Suppl. 2), 5–13.

Part V

Investments, Public–Private Partnerships, and Managerial Flow

13 Urban Regeneration in the Netherlands

Managerial Flow and Organizational Form

Michiel Kort

PUBLIC–PRIVATE PARTNERSHIP AS EMERGING POLICY INSTRUMENT

Globally, public–private partnerships (PPPs) have become prominent policy instruments. PPPs exist when there is a "sustainable cooperation between public and private actors in which joint products and/or services are developed and in which risks, costs and profits are shared" (Klijn & Teisman 2003, 138). Within PPPs, private parties are involved in the decision-making process and are said to contribute more intensively than in more traditional client–supplier or principal–agent partnerships. In theory, this results in a bundling of expertise, knowledge and interests, and the sharing of risks and responsibilities, which in turn produces better and more efficient results and *value* (Ghobadian, Gallear, O'Regan, & Viney, 2004; Hodge & Greve 2010). Value encompasses better and more efficient policy outcomes, and can take on different shapes, such as more timely delivery, higher cost-efficiency, risk-sharing opportunities, synergetic and/or integrated development, and the introduction of new product and services (Ghobadian, et al., 2004; Huxham, 2000).

Despite a prominent belief that PPPs are a universally good way of undertaking development projects, research from the Netherlands indicates that PPP projects have in the past, resulted in poor project outcomes, such as time delays and budget overruns (Algemene Rekenkamer, 2002, 2013; National Audit Organization [NAO], 2001, 2009; Flyvbjerg, Bruzelius, & Rothengatter, 2003). In this view on PPPs, the expected *value* is not often realized; however, this has not affected the popularity of the concept. Instead, there seems to be a call for better models, more transparent arrangements, and more effective governance of PPPs.

This chapter uses the Managerial Flow framework to provide a more robust conceptualization of complex actions, which have an impact on the performance of PPPs. The chapter beings by proposing an analytical framework that incorporates Managerial Flow and the network management concepts aligned with PPPs. This analytical framework is applied to three cases of urban-renewal companies (URCs) that operate through PPPs in the Netherlands. I conclude with a discussion of the results and highlight the impact of coordinative network management assets on the performance outcomes of PPPs.

PPPS: ORGANIZATIONAL FORM, GOVERNANCE, AND MANAGERIAL FLOW

In an effort to improve project outcomes, much of the attention in research concerning PPPs has focused on tracing the organizational forms that facilitate success (Klijn & Teisman, 2003). In this context, organizational forms refer to the network that forms between PPP actors, which occurs within a contractual and institutional framework. In general, organizational forms within PPPs typically take on structures such as partnerships, consortium forms, or institutional PPPs (Cruz and Marques, 2013; Klijn & Teisman, 2003; Marra, 2007).

The implicit assumption in much of the literature on PPPs is that organizational form is a determiner for the added *value* realized by a project and, hence, its success. In various national policy documents in the Netherlands, the dominant argument is that the best project results are produced when the organizational form exists as a contractual arrangement with arm's-length distance between individual organizations within the partnership (Kenniscentrum, 2002; NAO, 2002). However, there is no definitive statement about which organizational form is best.

Counter to the organizational form proposition, there is some PPP research that suggests that project success is related, at least in part, to the managerial efforts that are made in respective PPP networks (Hodge & Greve, 2010; Klijn & Teisman, 2003). These networks are complex and involve many actors (even actors who may be connected to a project, but are outside of the organizational form). Decision-making processes in these partnerships have to be actively managed, and these management-related activities are frequently referred to as network management activities (Mandell, 2001; Meier & O'Toole, 2007; O'Toole, 1988).

Within the Managerial Flow framework, the functions of PPP-network management that occur through organizational form relates primarily to the *governance* managerial consideration. *Governance* is *the degree to which multi-actors are working for a common goal* (Vecchi & Brusoni, 2012). PPP networks, as opposed to more traditionalist, bureaucratic and top-down network hierarchies, contain a *flatter* network structure, and one that devolves some degree of power from a central agency (government) to other public, private, and not-for-profit actors. Governance in PPPs is thus very complex and dynamic, and may evolve throughout the lifecycle of a project (Agranoff & McGuire, 2001; Mandell 2001; Meier and O'Toole 2007). This also means that setting up a workable design for a PPP (i.e., *strategy and selection considerations*) is highly important. However, we argue here, in line with the position of Meier and O'Toole (2007), that no one organizational form is sustainable without ongoing managerial attention. This attention comes in the form of ongoing and effective *communication* and *coordination* between PPP actors (Vecchi & Brusoni, 2012).

Communication and coordination within PPPs requires the perpetual implementation of different strategies to achieve the desired results. In general, network management research suggests that four different strategies are at play in PPP networks, these are connecting actors, exploring content (creating more variety, organizing research, etc.), arranging the structure of the interaction, and establishing process rules (Agranoff & McGuire, 2001; Klijn, Steijn, & Edelenbos, 2010). Some scholars approach managers as individuals with the explicit role of managing the network (Meier & O'Toole, 2007). However, management in PPPs is not necessary the action of one actor exclusively. Many actors in the network may be performing management activities, and different people may have an impact on the interrelations between actors and the development of collaborations (Klijn et al., 2010).

URBAN REGENERATION COMPANIES AS PPPS

In various countries, new PPPs are being created where public and private actors are working together to stimulate, guide, and implement processes of urban regeneration (Geddes 2008; Pierre 1997). An urban regeneration PPP can be defined as an organizational form, at arm's length from the government, owned by local partners, which leads and coordinates redevelopment and investment in declining urban areas (Ministerie van VROM, 2002; Office of the Deputy Prime Minister, 2004).

Urban-regeneration PPPs are often referred to as URCs and can be found in many countries such as the UK and the Netherlands. In these countries, URCs raise financials means for urban redevelopment and undertake project development.

The actors in URCs create and manage an intensified partnership. URCs in different countries show similarities but also differences in terms of the organizational form of the partnership. In the UK, URCs are established by the relevant local authority, the regional development agency, and the homes and communities agency, as well as in the private sector. In the Netherlands, important partners include the local authority, housing associations, and private parties such as developers and financers. However, within the Dutch landscape there is no prerequisite organizational form or network governance structure for URCs (Kort & Klijn, 2011).

METHODOLOGICAL FRAMEWORK

We explore the management processes and organizational forms of three Dutch URCs through a qualitative comparative case analysis. The URCs were selected on the basis that they represented a true PPP and were activate in the urban regeneration sphere. The data collection for these cases was performed in the period between 2008 and 2010.

Data were collected in the form of project-related documents, interviews, and surveys (30 in total) with a broad representation of actors involved in each URCs. The aim of the surveys was to gain insight into the following URC dimensions:

- **URC Performance:** We sought to assess whether (a) the goals of the URCs were achieved, (b) stakeholders were satisfied with the results, and (c) stakeholders were satisfied with the process. Within the context of Managerial Flow, poor URC performance is indicative of a *strategy gap*, because this outcome represents goals that have been unmet (Vecchi & Brusoni, 2012).

- **URC Organizational Form:** We collected data regarding the URCs relationship to government (disaggregation), their level discretionary power (Pollit, Tablot, Caulfield, & Smullen, 2004), and the strength of relationships among PPP actors within the URC; this is referred to in the literature as "tightness" (Koppenjan & Klijn, 2004). Within the Managerial Flow framework, the organizational form of a URC relates to *governance* and *selection* considerations (Vecchi & Brusoni, 2012).

- **URC Network Management:** Governance literature stresses the importance of horizontal coordination between public and private actors. Coordination takes place in interactions and these have to be managed. Most of the literature stresses that active forms of network management are crucial for good results (Agranoff & McGuire, 2001; Koppenjan & Klijn, 2004; Sørensen & Torfing, 2007). Within the context of Managerial Flow, the managerial strategies at play within the URC networks relates to *coordination* and *communication* considerations (Vecchi & Brusoni, 2012).

RESULTS

We explored these dimensions in three case sites: WOM De Laares in Enschede, De Tarwewijk in Rotterdam, and OMD Delfzijl in Delfzijl. The following provides some contextual information about these case sites.

De Laares in Enschede was built as a new living area for factory workers at the beginning of the 20th century. As the factories disappeared from the city centers through the years the living and housing conditions declined. In 1996 the municipality appointed de Laares as area for urban regeneration. The first initiatives proved unsuccessful. After some years of preparations and deliberations the urban-regeneration PPP, WOM De Laares was established in 2003 to implement an integral urban regeneration approach.

The Tarwewijk in Rotterdam was also built at the beginning of the 20th century as a living area for workers in the port of Rotterdam. As newer and better houses were built in the surrounding areas, more and more people left the Tarwewijk, and regional neglect ensued. In 2004 the URC WOM Tarwewijk was established to turn the tide.

Delfzijl is situated in the northern part of the Netherlands in a region indicated by national government for economic development. A new port and large housing areas were developed, but as a consequence of the crisis of the 1970s, the intended economic growth did not develop. The municipality was unable to transform Delfzijl into an attractive place to live and population started to reduce. In 2001 OMD Delfzijl was created to deliver urban regeneration. Table 13.1 summarizes the profile of these URCs.

Performance of the URCs

There was clear progress in all three of the three studied cases (see Table 13.2 for a summary). However, in all three cases the original specified plans with regard to objectives, functions, and number of houses to be built, were subject of a reorientation.

Table 13.1   The Tasks of the URCs

	WOM de Laares	WOM Tarwewijk	OMD Delfzijl
Planning area	A city neighborhood in the center of Enscheda (+/–2 km²)	A city district in the south part of Rotterdam (+/–3 km²)	The urban core of Delfzijl as a whole
Spatial functions	Housing, public space, and infrastructure (town roads)	Houses, public space	Houses, public space, infrastructure, commercial developments
Houses (before)	400	492	1,850
Houses (after)	460	546	1,414
Planning	6 partly parallel stages	8 projects in the area developed in stages	Subareas are regenerated in stages
Public funding	€17 million	€20 million	€30 million

Table 13.2   Concrete Results Summarized

	WOM de Laares	WOM Tarwewijk	OMD Delfzijl
Results	About 50% of houses delivered. Almost all houses are sold. Plans for remaining projects are finished, and necessary property is acquired.	More than 50% of houses delivered. Sales are far behind (results in financial problems). Plans for remaining projects are finished.	Demolition finished. Construction of houses more than halfway completed. Commercial and health building realized. Plans for remaining area (center) are finished.

Table 13.3   Actors' Satisfaction With the Results of the URCs

	WOM de Laares	WOM Tarwewijk	OMD Delfzijl
Substantive results*	4.0	3.3	3.6
Process results*	3.9	3.3	2.9

*Measured as the average of six items per category on a 5-point scale.

At the completion of the data collection process, WOM de Laares had succeeded in delivering one third of the planned houses. Furthermore, WOM Tarwewijk had begun its acquisition of privately owned properties, and OMD Delfzijl was in the process of acquiring and demolition properties. Thus, the projects had progressed more than halfway.

In order to assess the performance of the URCs we also explored the actors' satisfaction with the project outcomes, and the processes that built these outcomes. For both factors respondents were asked to indicate whether they agreed with six statements on a five point scale (1 = *completely disagree* to 5 = *completely agree*). In Table 13.3 the mean for each category is displayed.

From Table 13.3 we can derive that overall actors' satisfaction with substantive results is above the mean (2.5) in the cases. WOM de Laares has the best score on substantive results. Where actors in all three projects in general agreed on the effectiveness of the proposals and the approach, the opinions differ with respect to their perception on feasibility and realism of the project. With respect to the "satisfaction with process" results, WOM de Laares again held the highest score. OMD Delfzijl scored below the average.

A final point to note is that at the completion of the data collection, all three cases experienced delays and had to reevaluate their time frames. This can been seen as unavoidable responses to changed circumstances (and potentially poor strategic planning at the outset).

URC Organizational Form

The three URCs adopted different organizational forms. In addition, individual URCs had different degrees of discretionary power, disaggregation, and tightness. Table 13.4 outlines the similarities and differences in organizational form.

Disaggregation

The URCs were set at some distance from local governments and their parent organizations to focus on delivery of the regeneration task. In the three cases most interaction and cooperation took place between the URC and various public servants. Also, data derived from document analysis indicate that the distance was not a constant factor in the three cases but varied over

Table 13.4 Organizational Form of URCs

	WOM de Laares	WOM Tarwewijk	OMD Delfzijl
Initiator	Municipality and housing associations	Municipality	Province
Participants	Three housing associations, private developer, and builder–developer on equal basis	Municipality, housing association, and private developer on equal basis	Municipality (49%), housing association (49%), and province (2%)
Focus	Planning, land, and construction development	Planning, land development, and some renovation projects Construction development is in the hands of housing association and developer together	Planning and land development Construction development is done by consortium of housing association and two construction companies
Organization	Project bureau based in the area 5 employees	No project bureau 2 employees	Project bureau based in the area 15 employees 3 supervisors
Employees	Director is external consultant; other staff are hired from participants.	Director and employee are both external consultants.	Director is external consultant; other staff are both external and hired from participants.

the time of the projects as a result of the different project phase and events, including abrupt and unexpected resistance from stakeholders and changes within the local governments and project environment.

Discretionary Powers

In each respective policy document concerning the URCs in this study, the URCs are defined as organizations that have necessary discretionary powers to deliver their regeneration task. Analyzing the cases provides us with the insight that the degree of discretionary powers differs between the three URCs. The OMD Delfzijl had the most discretionary power, and this is perhaps due to the proportionately larger set of tasks the URC had to deliver. Autonomy for this URC was permitted on the condition that it aligned with a preexisting framework set by the City Council. Similarly, WOM de Laares had relative autonomy as long as it operated with its preexisting framework. In contrast, WOM Tarwewijk had almost no discretionary powers at the start of its life, but this increased during the project. The governance structure required all decisions to be supported by all partners prior to implementation; however, this constraint was removed to increase the speed of activity.

Tightness

Theory suggests that more tightly organized PPPs/URCs achieve better results (Klijn & Teisman, 2003). Tightness measures the relation between partners in the PPP.

Within the WOM Tarwewijk the municipality was responsible for the acquisition of property, the housing association delivers the renovation projects and the private developer was involved in developing the plans and managing financial aspects. WOM Delfzijl, in contrast, displayed a more intensive cooperation. The administrative staff employed by this URC were assigned to specific areas instead of different tasks. This facilitated a combination and exchange of knowledge between different partners and areas. Consequently the OMD Delfzijl was the most tightly organized partnership, followed by WOM de Laares and WOM Tarwewijk.

URC Network Management

The degree to which network management was employed was measured using 18 items. In line with Agranoff and McGuire (2001), these items were divided in four categories: (1) the involvement of actors (arranging), (2) the development of ideas and solutions regarding content (exploring content), (3) communication, steering and solving conflicts (coordinating), and (4) binding actors through various process rules. These results are presented in Figure 13.1.

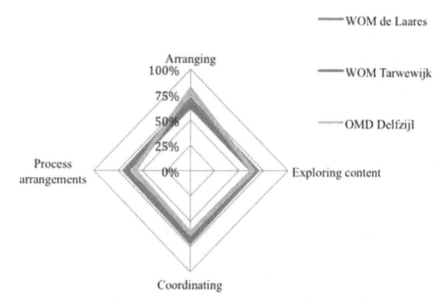

Figure 13.1 Network Management Scores for URCs

In respect to all network management dimensions, WOM de Laares scored the highest (average score of 3.5/5), followed by OMD Delfzijl (3.3/5) and WOM Tarwewijk (3.2). Taking a closer look at management strategies shows that the total intensity of network management strategies is not that different between the cases. Interview partners from each case confirmed that many management efforts were needed to attune the interests of the different stakeholders. If tasks and projects are complex, such regeneration projects that a lot of managerial activity is required to match this complexity.

DISCUSSION

With respect to URC performance, by applying a Managerial Flow lens, some strategy gaps, as well as competencies, can be observed. WOM de Laares performed "better than average" in both process and outcome. This suggests that although there were some delays, the planning involved in the prephase of the project was sufficient to enact the process. Furthermore, in comparison to the other cases, WOM de Laares was proportionately better resourced. This URC had smaller, less ambitious (perhaps more realistic) goals, proportionately more money, and a proportionately more equipped project administrative team in comparison to the other URCs. Thus, the project goals, configurations and resources for WOM de Laares is smaller and perceivably more manageable. In contrast, the poorest performing URC with respect to process—OMD Delfzijl—had a significantly more ambitious goal (i.e., to redevelop and/or demolish nearly four times as many houses as the other URCs), with a disproportionate amount of funds, and a more complex governance structure. While it is possible that economies of scale could have been through this project achieved (which goes some way to explaining the lower proportion of funds assigned to this URC), OMD Delfzijl lacks comprehensive strategic considerations in relation to the other URCs.

The WOM Tarwewijk URC shows acceptable strategic planning and provides a suitable competent benchmark between the two other cases. While process satisfaction and project outcomes are lower than WOM de Laares, the WOM Tarwewijk strategic goals are proportionately slightly more ambitious. Furthermore, the governance structure/network management structure of WOM Tarwewijk is administered by fewer employees (2) than is WOM de Laares (5).

From the perspective of *coordination, communication,* and *governance* considerations within the Managerial Flow Framework, WOM de Laares had the most balanced approach. Although OMD Delfzijl had the highest arranging score (4.0) of all URCs, this is likely, in part, due to the fact that there were more parties involved in this PPP. Furthermore, this URC also had the lowest score for *Process arrangements* (2.9). Thus, OMD Delfzijl shows a higher consideration for *coordination* owing to its more complex, multiparty arrangement; however, this also inhibits the *communication* flows between the groups. From a *governance* perspective, OMD Delfzijl had the most autonomy; again, this is likely due to the amount of actors that comprised the organizational form, which was much larger in comparison to the other URCs.

These results pose a rhetorical question: *Which is more important for project outcomes, organizational form incorporating PPP strategy and resourcing or network management?* Our results here indicate that these two factors are linked, in that the more complex the organizational form of a PPP, the more intense and well resourced the network management processes need to be. Together the network management and organizational form of a PPP provide a foundation for project outcomes. In the case of OMD Delfzijl, which had a lower ranked process performance than the other URCs, it was tasked to do more activities, involving more partners, with proportionately less resources. From a Managerial Flow perspective then, this result shows the importance in aligning the competencies of *strategy, governance, selection, coordination,* and *communication* at the outset of any PPP project. Thus, although OMD Delfzijl had a more comprehensive governance structure, it had a significant strategy gap in that it was required to coordinate more activity, with fewer resources, among more partners. It was given more autonomy to do this; however, we argue that this autonomy needed to be matched with proportional resourcing.

In the case of WOM Tarwewijk, a balanced approach to *strategy, governance, selection, coordination,* and *communication* can be observed, and a satisfactory outcome was achieved. Thus, although targets for the URC were more ambitious than WOM de Laares, there was slightly more funding and governance support for WOM Tarwewijk. In this way, WOM Tarwewijk provides a middle-ground benchmark of Managerial Flow performance for the three cases.

CONCLUSION

This chapter highlights the way in which organizational form and network management combine to contribute to the success of PPPs. Using the Managerial Flow framework, we have highlighted the way in which considerations including *strategy, governance, selection, coordination,* and *communication* manifest within the organizational form and network management of URCs. The total intensity of network management strategies is not that different between the cases. In complex tasks and projects like regeneration projects, a lot of managerial activity is required to match this complexity. Furthermore, when resources are adequate and the organizational form is tight, URC outcomes are positive, as in the case of WOM de Laares. Although we are not suggesting here that "smaller" network configuration are better for PPPs, we reframe our results by offering the conclusion that larger and complex organizational forms within PPPs may require more managerial consideration and more resourcing to be successful. This is an interesting subject for future research.

REFERENCES

Agranoff, R., & McGuire, M. (2001). Big questions in public network management research. *Journal of Public Administration Research and Theory, 11*(3), 295–326.

Cruz, C. O., & Marques, R. C. (2013). *Infrastructure Public-Private Partnerships.* Berlin: Sprinver-Verlag.

Flyvbjerg, B., Bruzelius, N., & Rothengatter, W. (2003). *Megaprojects and Risk: an anatomy of ambition.* New York: Cambridge University Press.

Geddes, A. (2008). Immigration and European Integration: Beyond Fortress Europe? (2nd Edition). Manchester: Manchester University Press.

Ghobadian, A., Gallear, D., O'Regan, N., & Viney, H. (Eds.). (2004). *Public private partnerships: Policy and experience.* Basingstroke, England: Palgrave.

Hodge, G., & Greve, C. (2010). *International handbook of PPP.* Cheltenham, England: Edgar Elgar.

Huxham, C. (2000). The Challenge of Collaborative Advantage. Public Management, 2, 337–357.

Kenniscentrum. (2002). *Ministerie van Financiën, Voortgangsrapportage 2002* [Progress report 2002]. The Hague, the Netherlands: Author.

Klijn, E. H., Steijn, B., & Edelenbos, J. (2010). The impact of network management strategies on the outcomes in governance networks. *Public Administration, 88*(4), 1063–1082.

Klijn, E. H., & Teisman, G. R. (2003). Institutional and strategic barriers to public–private partnership: An analysis of Dutch cases. *Public Money and Management, 23*(3), 137–146.

Koppenjan, J., & Klijn, E-H. (2004). Managing Uncertainties in Networks: Public Private Controversies. New York: Routledge.

Kort, M. B., & Klijn, E. H. (2011). Public–private partnerships in urban renewal: Organizational form or managerial capacity. *Public Administration Review, 71*(4), 618–626.

Mandell, M. P. (Ed.). (2001). *Getting results through collaboration: Networks and network structures for public policy and management.* Westport, CT: Quorum Books.

Marra, A. (2007). Internal regulation by mixed enterprises: the case of the Italian water sector. *Annals of Public and Cooperative Economics. 78*, 245–275.

Meier, K., & O'Toole, L. J. (2007). Modelling public management: Empirical analysis of the management-performance nexus. *Public Administration Review, 9*(4), 503–527.

Ministerie van VROM (2002). Letter of the Dutch Minister of Housing, Spatial Planning and the Environment to the Dutch Parliament, regarding the progress of urban regeneration and the selection of fifty priority urban areas, 2002. KST 28 600 XI, nr. 88.

National Audit Office. (2002). *Managing the relationship to secure a successful partnership in PFI projects.* London, England: Author.

Office of the Deputy Prime Minister. (2004, May). *Urban regeneration companies— guidance and qualification criteria.* London, England: Author.

O'Toole, L. J. (1988). Strategies for intergovernmental management: Implementing programs in interorganizational networks. *Journal of Public Administration, 11*(4), 417–441.

Pierre, J (ed.). (1997). *Participation and democratic theory.* Cambridge: Cambridge University Press.

Pollitt, C., Talbot, C., Caulfield, J., & Smullen, A. (2004). *Agencies: How governments do things through autonomous organizations.* Basingstoke, England: Palgrave Macmillan.

Sørensen, E., & Torfing, J. (2007). *Theories of Democratic Network Governance.* New York: Palgrave MacMillan.

Vecchi, V., & Brusoni, M. (2012). The managerial flow of public local development policies: A conceptual framework. *Singapore Management Review, 32* (Suppl. 2), 5–13.

14 Gaps in Small to Medium-Sized Enterprise Policy Implementation

The Case of the Italian Central Guarantee Fund[1]

Francesca Casalini and Monica Rossolini

INTRODUCTION

In the past, there has been a conceded effort on the part of governments to facilitate access to finance for small to medium-sized enterprises (SMEs) through public policy, as these firms represent the economic backbone of most industrialized countries. However, many attempts have had very little impact on SMEs as a whole. In the search for better policy tools, governments have begun to promote the development of public–private partnerships (PPPs) involving firms, financial institutions, and public managers, to provide a more stable financial structure for SME growth. This chapter uses the Managerial Flow framework to analyze the role of strategy, coordination, selection, governance and knowledge management in the context of SME financing in Italy. The study focuses specifically on the case of the Italian Central Guarantee Fund (CGF), and its partnering role in developing Italian SMEs. We focus on the CGF's guarantee role in the process of bank lending for SMEs. Using the Managerial Flow framework of Vecchi and Brusoni (2012), we identify the gaps in the design and execution of the Italian CGF policy.

BACKGROUND

Small to medium-sized enterprises (SMEs) are the backbone of most economies, accounting for more than 90% of all enterprises in industrialized countries. SMEs contribute significantly to economic growth, job creation, social cohesion, poverty reduction, and regional and local development (Amini, 2004; Beck, Demirguc-Kunt, & Levine, 2005; Drever, Hutchinson, & Morgan, 1999; Storey, 1994). However, the financial structure of SMEs inhibits their development. Thus, owing to their comparatively small resource base, and the lack of alternative funding options, SMEs are very vulnerable to disruptions in their access to financial investment, and this inhibits their growth potential (Beck & Demirguc-Kunt, 2006; Berger & Udell, 2006). In Italy, this limitation is more pronounced, in comparison to the rest of Europe and other Organisation for Economic Co-operation and Development (OECD) countries, as Italian SMEs have a less diversified financial structure, and, as a consequence, they strongly rely on bank loans (Banca d'Italia, 2013; European Commission, 2013).

In the past, there have been many policy failures in supporting the development and growth of SMEs. "Soft" and "hard" government-support programs have often led to a lack of resources for some SMEs and an ever-increasing dependence on public funding for others (Cumming & MacIntosh, 2002). Furthermore, government support can be politically influenced, rather than targeted through an economic assessment of potential SME impact (Florida & Smith, 1993). Finally, the public managers who coordinate SME support can lack management capabilities (Martin & Scott, 2000).

A recent attempt to more effectively facilitate the development of SMEs through public policy has been achieved through PPPs. PPPs bring public and private actors together to undertake joint ventures that have the potential to have a positive impact on all parties and their stakeholders. PPPs also have the ability to reduce governance and functioning costs for SMEs and public bodies operating in partnership, so as to stimulate enhanced effectiveness (Hallberg, 1999; Oakey, 2003).

In Italy, several initiatives have promoted public–private cooperation at a national level. Such programs include

- the Central Guarantee Fund (CGF), where the government provides a guarantee in favor of the intermediary granting loan to a SME;
- the Italian Investment Fund (IIF), where the government supports the capitalization of SMEs; and
- the SME-related Plafond, where Cassa Depositi e Prestiti provides liquidity to banks that grant loans to SMEs.

The PPP involving the Italian CGF and SMEs is complex (Bugno, 2012). This is because between the public-initiated fund and the private SMEs, there are financial intermediaries in the middle. Such intermediaries include banks, mutual guarantee institutions (MGIs), and leasing companies. The financial intermediaries mainly privately liaise directly with the SMEs, as mediators in the granting of credit backed by guarantees by a fund.

Focusing specifically on the role of guarantee funds, Riding and Haines (2001) have identified four main criteria that describe a loan guarantee program, these include

1. the degree of discretion in lending,
2. the type of guarantee and guaranteed amount,
3. the fees, and
4. the eligibility conditions.

By altering these dimensions, in line with the market, guarantee funds assist in financing firms (particularly SMEs) effectively.

The effectiveness of a guarantee program is then generally evaluated exploring different profiles (i.e., Boocock & Shariff, 2005). The first dimension considered by many authors is *financial additionality* (FA), which is essentially aimed at valuing whether SMEs have been able to access loans that would not have been available in the absence of the guarantee scheme (Curran, 2000). FA thus concerns direct benefits to SMEs as a result of intervention by the public program, such as increased access to bank credit, increase in the size of loans, and more favorable conditions in terms of interest rates and/or reduction of transaction costs. Because guarantee recipients should then have utilized the funds to benefit their own companies and to generate positive economic and social benefits, the second dimension of effectiveness is referred as *economic additionality* (EA; Lerner, 2002). These economic gains generally take the form of increased employment and/or production and increased profits for owners and/or wages for workers, which eventually turn into increased tax revenue for the government. *Financial sustainability* (FS) and *overall effectiveness* (OE) of the program are typically indicated as third valuation dimensions, which are strictly related to the way in which the credit guarantee program is organized and managed by the public managers.

In this chapter we focus on the case of the CGF in Italy. We investigate the impact that this policy driven and its dimensionality have had on Italian SMEs.

METHODOLOGY

To examine the impact of the CGF on Italian SMEs we explore different dimensions and analyze data from several sources. In the first instance, a desk review of documents concerning the historical development, the organizational structure, and the role of the CGF within the entire guarantee system is undertaken. This is followed by descriptive quantitative analysis explore the impact of the CGF on participating firms in terms of performance indicators, default rate, and lending rate. These analyses are realized using a sample of a confidential database directly supplied by the CGF and are aimed at providing some insights into the FA, the EA, and the FS of the guarantee program.[2]

We compare the economic and financial results achieved by a sample of firms guaranteed by the CGF in the period between 2007and 2009 with a comparable sample of firms not guaranteed by the CGF in the same period of observation. This analysis explores those indirect improvement generated at the firm performance level, referring to the EA dimension of effectiveness. Then, we carry out an analysis of default rates, comparing CGF data with Banca d'Italia data from 2000 to 2009, and a lending rate analysis on the average lending cost applied to loans guaranteed by CGF from 2009 to

2012 compared to the average cost applied to loans in Italy. The aim of these further two quantitative analysis is to explore the FA and the FS dimension and to verify the existence of prerequisites for opportunistic behaviors that might thwart the future sustainability of the guarantee scheme.

Finally, using the Managerial Flow perspective of Vecchi and Brusoni (2012), we verify the existence of gaps in the design and execution of the public policy and assess the OE of the CGF program.

THE CENTRAL GUARANTEE FUND

The Historical Development of the Fund

During the last financial crisis, bank credit decreased in most countries as a result of reduced resources for banks and a deterioration of the credit quality of firms. In the last years, in fact, the financial conditions of SMEs has weakened, because of an increase in the difficulty in collecting payments from clients and, more generally, a reduction in income flows. The lack of profitability and the rise in insolvencies have an impact on the labor market, with an upward trend in unemployment experienced around the world.

As a response governments have implemented a range of measures capable of facilitating access to credit. This is because credit access is considered a central factor in enabling economic development. The most widely used policy measure worldwide to increase access to finance has been the extension of loan guarantees (OECD, 2011). In Italy, the most important scheme used by the government to respond to the crisis was the CGF.

The CGF has been active since 2000 and has the purpose of facilitating access to credit for SMEs. The fund is an instrument of credit risk mitigation in support of SMEs, operating at the Ministry of Economic Development. It achieves this by granting a public guarantee for loans, which joins together with, or replaces, the guarantees given by the SMEs in order to obtain funding.

Figure 14.1 shows that the number of applications the CGF has approved has increased significantly in the years from 2000 to 2013. In 2000 there were 1,213 applications, while the number skyrocketed to over 77,000 in 2013. Although the trend has been continuously growing, the role of the CGF has become more pronounced starting from 2009. This result is due to both the credit crisis and the introduction of some facilitation in the use of this guarantee scheme. In fact, owing to a series of regulatory changes (see Table 14.1), the CGF has become the main tool of public facility to credit for SMEs used by the Italian government during the global financial crisis.

The comparison between the activity in the period between 2009 and 2013 with that of the previous nine years is significant: Between 2009 and 2013, the CGF has provided guarantees of more than €22 billion and activated almost €41 billion of loans to SMEs, quadrupling the activities of the entire period between 2000 and 2008.

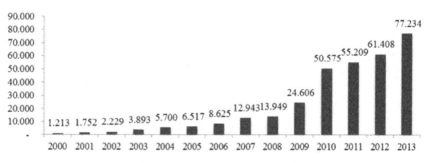

Figure 14.1   Number of Applications Accepted

Table 14.1   Timeline of Main Government Interventions on the CGF

Year	Government Intervention	Reference
1996	Creation of the CGF with an amount of funding up to Lit 400 mm (€206K)	Law 662/96, art 2, par 100
2008	€2 billion additional funding for the years 2008–2012	Law Decree "Anti-crisis" n. 185/2008
2009	Introduction of the guarantee of last resort of the state, which involves the weighting of zero mechanism and resets the capital absorption for lenders	Decree of the Italian Ministry of Economy and Finance dated 25 March 2009
2011	€1.2 billion increase in the funding for the period 2012–2014	Law Decree "Save-Italy" n. 201/2011
2012	Decrease in the percentage of liquidity coverage ratio for the fund by 2%, from 8% to 6% of the guaranteed amount, which significantly leverages the resources available	Decree of the Italian Ministry of Economic Development and the Ministry of Economy and Finance dated July 26, 2012

The Organizational Structure of the CGF

The organizational structure of the CGF is multilayer and characterized by the presence of a Management Committee, which is entrusted the administration of the fund, and a manager, which supports the committee that analyzes and approves applications (see Figure 14.2). The manager of the CGF is currently represented by a group of banks in which Mediocredito Centrale acts as the lead group representative. The function of the manager is to govern the preliminary investigation of the applications received. The Management Committee is composed by the representatives of the central government, local administrations, the Italian Association of Banks, and many others categories. It meets on a weekly basis, with the task of deciding not only the general provisions and the conditions

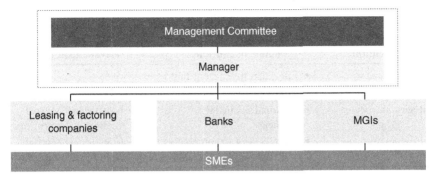

Figure 14.2   The CGF's Organizational Structure

of eligibility, but also with reference to the individual operations, the admission to the guarantee, and the respective amount. The final evaluation of admission to the guarantee of the CGF is always and exclusively by the Management Committee; however, the preliminary stages of the same; they are carried out primarily by banks and MGIs and, then, by the manager.

Applications submitted by banks and MGIs are evaluated and selected through the application of internal scoring models. The assessment of the creditworthiness of individual loans is based on historical quantitative information about the company to be founded.

Despite the complex architecture, a point of strength of the CGF is represented by the slenderness of the decision-making processes, with an average time of management applications for access that is around 30 days from the arrival of the application until the final decision of the Management Committee.

In this logic of public–private partnership, the CGF is designed in such way as to be attractive for the operators and encourage them to use the guarantee with benefits for their own business. The strengths of its attractiveness that distinguish it from other instruments available within the Italian guarantee system can be summarized as follows:

- Since 2009 the CGF has been under the guarantee of the last resort of the Italian Government who involves, according to the Basel Accord, "risk mitigation credit" on direct guarantees and counter-guarantees on first demand granted by the CGF. This guarantee applies, in particular, the zero-weighting mechanism, which resets the capital absorption for lenders for the loans guaranteed.
- SMEs accepted by the fund have access to credit without any additional collaterals: this is what happened in the majority of cases.
- In addition, there are some benefits ranging from reduction of the fees to total gratuity (as envisaged by the "Save Italy" Decree).

Table 14.2   Main Credit Guarantee Institutions in Italy and Their Level of Intervention

Institutional level of intervention	Public institutions	Private institutions
Supranational	• European Investment Fund	
National	• Central Guarantee Fund	
Regional	• Regional Financial Agencies	• I- & II-level Mutual Guarantee Institutions
Provincial	• Chambers of Commerce	• I- & II-level Mutual Guarantee Institutions

The Role of CGF Within the Italian Guarantee System

The Italian guarantee system is one of the largest, and at the same time one of the most fragmented, in all of Europe (European Association of Mutual Guarantee Societies [AECM], 2013). The universe of credit guarantee institutions in Italy tends to form a multipillar system based on a mix of public and private initiatives (see Table 14.2; Zecchini & Ventura, 2009). Despite the presence of numerous private actors, public money is the real engine of the system. Public resources, in fact, on one hand, contribute to the funds of MGIs, while, on the other hand, feed the public funds at central, regional, and provincial levels with the primary objective of allowing a counter-guarantee from the MGIs' guarantee. The system actually works as a multilayer structure, where at the first level, both MGIs and banks provide guarantees, which are then usually reinsured by second-level entities, such as second-tier MGIs and regional agencies; finally, at the high-ground level, the CGF acts as a guarantor of last resort. However, because the CGF provides also direct guarantees, banks can bypass all the levels and apply directly for a state-supported guarantee.

As stated earlier, the recent regulatory interventions have significantly broadened the scope of the CGF, incentivizing all intermediaries to apply at the fund and transforming it into the most prominent guarantee tool within the entire system.

GUARANTEED FIRMS: PERFORMANCE, DEFAULT RATE, AND LENDING RATE

An Analysis of the Performance of Guaranteed Firms

Performance analysis is realized on a confidential database of roughly 15,800 observations, each related to a single firm who received a guarantee by the CGF in the period from 2007 to 2009.[3] We collect some financial and economic data relative to the year of guarantee grant and the 2 years after using the data provider AIDA Bureau Van Dijk.

Table 14.3 shows the main characteristics of loans guaranteed: The average size of the financing is around €245,000, with an average maturity of 46 months and a percentage of guarantee of about 53%; the 75% of guarantees are required by MGIs in the form of a counter guarantee, whereas banks submit about the 25% of applications accepted. As presented in Table 14.4, guaranteed firms are mainly small and micro-size firms, chiefly located in the north and south and operating in manufacturing and service industries.

Table 14.3 Sample of Applications Accepted in 2007–2009

	Year of guarantee granted			
	2007	2008	2009	Mean value
Mean value of financing (€)	238,312	231,806	255,070	244,819
Mean value of guarantee rate	52.0%	51.0%	54.0%	53.0%
Average Maturity (months)	47.8	46.8	44.6	46.0
Type of guarantee				
Direct	23.3%	20.0%	25.0%	23.3%
Co-guarantee	0.0%	0.0%	0.2%	0.1%
Counter-guarantee	76.7%	80.0%	74.8%	76.6%
Intermediary				
MGI	71.8%	76.5%	74.8%	74.5%
Banks	28.1%	23.3%	24.4%	25.0%
Other	0.1%	0.2%	0.8%	0.5%

Table 14.4 The Guaranteed Firms and the Control Sample

	Guaranteed firms	Control sample
Firms (number)	15.775	22.930
Size		
Micro	45.4%	45.9%
Small	41.5%	41.3%
Medium	13.1%	12.8%
Geographical Area		
North	48.0%	54.0%
Center	17.9%	16.6%
South and Islands	34.1%	29.3%
Industry		
Agriculture	0.2%	0.2%
Manufacturing	39.7%	41.3%
Construction	8.6%	8.7%
Service	51.5%	49.7%

We then construct a comparable control group with respect to the guaranteed sample. The criteria considered are firm size, economic sector and geographical area. Using AIDA Bureau Van Dijk, we collect the universe of companies that meet our analysis criteria. To obtain the comparable sample we select about 23,000 observations randomly (for details, see Table 14.4).[4] For these companies we register financial and economic data from 2007 to 2011.

Using data from this sample, we carry out a comparison between the two groups, on the period from 2007 to 2011, based on the following indicators: number of employees, sales, return on equity (ROE), return on investment (ROI), liquidity ratio, and solvency ratio.[5]

The growth rates of employees and of sales give us some information on firm's ability to growth, whereas ROE and ROI provide information on the profitability of the company, respectively, in relation to equity and the entire capital invested. Liquidity ratio gives information about the liquidity of the company, whereas solvency ratio provides important information on the capitalization. Both these ratio provide useful evidence on the riskiness of the firm in terms of its financial structure and ability to repay debts.

We test the presence of differences between the two samples with a *t* test (difference between mean values) and a Wilcoxon rank-sum test (difference between median values).[6]

Table 14.5 compares the economic and financial indicators of the two groups of companies. We can see some important differences. Concerning the number of employees, we can observe a higher value of growth rate for guaranteed companies than others. Guaranteed companies have an employment compounded annual growth rate of 8.02% whereas others companies register a value of 1.82%. The analysis of the growth rate of sales confirms a better situation for guaranteed firms, which achieve a compound annual growth rate (CAGR) of 2.63% whereas nonguaranteed firms realize a 2.15%.

Concerning the ROE we can observe significant differences, guaranteed companies start in 2007 with a value of ROE higher than control sample but at the end of the period of observation, they have a value significantly lower. Considering the average annual growth rate, we observe a –1.92% for guaranteed companies and –0.99% for others. The second profitability ratio analyzed is ROI. Guaranteed companies show an average annual growth rate of –0.61 lower than that of the control sample (–0.43%). Table 14.5 presents also the liquidity and the solvency analyses. Guaranteed companies show in the period a mean value of liquidity ratio of 0.96, compared to 1.80 of others. They show also a lower value of solvency ratio. The guaranteed companies have in the period a mean value of solvency ratio of 15.89%, compared to 28.75% of others.

We can conclude summarizing the main results. Guaranteed companies, in our sample, show a better growth rate in terms of employment and sales; nevertheless, they have some lacks in terms of profitability. The first results

Table 14.5 Descriptive Analysis: A Comparison Between Guaranteed Firms and the Control Sample

	Years					
	2007	2008	2009	2010	2011	
Employees (number)						CAGR
Guaranteed firms	14.1	14.0	13.2	12.7	19.2	8.02%
Control sample	24.0	23.1	22.00	21.8	25.8	1.82%
t test	***	***	***	***	***	
Sales (€000)						CAGR
Guaranteed firms	4.478	4.565	4.055	4.499	4.968	+2.63%
Control sample	5.080	5.254	4.633	5.012	5.531	+2.15%
t test	***	***	***	***	***	
ROE (%)						Average Annual Growth Rate
Guaranteed firms	9.15	5.51	1.34	2.73	1.48	–1.92%
Control sample	5.38	3.06	0.49	2.21	1.72	–0.99%
t test	***	***	***	***	***	–
ROI (%)						Average Annual Growth Rate
Guaranteed firms	7.81	6.15	4.27	4.51	5.39	–0.61%
Control sample	6.60	5.54	4.16	4.80	4.90	–0.43%
t test	***	***	***	***	***	–
LIQUIDITY RATIO (x)						Mean Value
Guaranteed firms	1.02	0.95	0.92	0.96	0.95	0.96
Control sample	1.76	1.74	1.78	1.84	1.87	1.80
t test	***	***	***	***	***	
SOLVENCY RATIO (%)						Mean value
Guaranteed firms	16.37	16.73	15.61	15.51	15.22	15.89%
Control sample	26.49	28.94	29.49	29.40	29.53	28.75%
t test	***	***	***	***	***	–

Note: This table shows the value of number of employees, Sales, ROE, ROI, Liquidity Ratio, Solvency Ratio, for the years 2007–2011 for guaranteed companies and control sample. It reports also results of the mean test (*t* test). "*", "**", "***" indicate 1%, 5%, 10% significance levels, respectively.

seem to sustain the effectiveness of the CGF in term of EA, but lacks in profitability indicate some possible weaknesses. Considering the financial indicators, the value of liquidity and in particular the low value of solvency should be considered with attention. On one hand, we can assume that these results confirm the nature and the aim of the CGF: to improve access to credit for firms that not have direct access to the market. On the other hand, these indicators are very important in assessing the ability of the firms to repay the debt, with obvious impact on the sustainability of the public program.

The Risk of Default Analysis

The analysis of the risk of default has been developed on a database provided directly by the CGF Management Committee about loans granted by the fund and defaulted in the years between 2001 and 2009. Data from CGF are compared to average annual default rate recorded by Banca d'Italia in the same period. To calculate the average default rate of loan facilities for the Italian system we used the Statistical database of the Banca d'Italia (Bankit) "BIP on line."[7] It has been reconstructed considering data related to household producers and nonfinancial corporations.

The CGF default rate is defined as follows:

$$Default\ rate(CGF\ number) = \frac{Number\ of\ defaults(t)}{Number\ of\ credit\ issued(t-1)}.$$

where the nominator is the number of operations that had a default in t (so in this case the CGF activated the guarantee) and the denominator is the number of credit (guaranteed by CGF) used by all borrowers not in default in $t - 1$.[8]

This Banca d'Italia default rate is defined as follows:

$$Default\ rate(Bankit\ number) = \frac{Number\ of\ adjusted\ bad\ barrowers(t)}{Number\ of\ credit\ issued(t-1)}.$$

where the denominator is the number of credit used by all the borrowers covered by the Central Credit Register not classified as "adjusted bad borrowers" (see item on BIP Online) at the end of the previous period and the numerator is the number of credit used by such borrowers who become "adjusted bad borrowers" during the considered period.

Figure 14.3 shows the main results. From 2000 to 2005, the default rates recorded by corporate borrowers from the fund show significantly lowers values than the average, in many cases more than half. Starting from 2006,

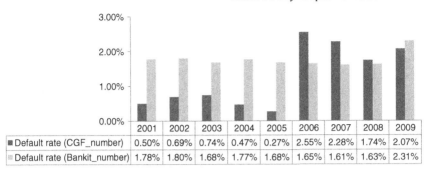

Figure 14.3 The Comparison of CGF and Banca d'Italia Default Rates (number)

there is a reversal of the trends. The differences became lower in 2008 (where CGF is 1.74% and the Italian average is 1.63%), and in 2009 the CGF went back to having a value less than the national average.

The risk of default analysis provides some useful considerations on the FS dimension. The banks' capital requirement imposed by Basel II could explain the increase in the risk of default of guaranteed firms starting from 2006. The presence of collateral and in particular the "risk mitigation effect" may have encouraged intermediaries to claim the guarantee for riskier clients. Furthermore, Figure 14.4 shows that applications submitted by banks have a major risk of default than those of MGIs. Considering the 2007–2009 period, the average risk of default of applications presented by banks is 9.33%, whereas that of MGIs is 2.55%.

Intermediary type	Total application accepted[1]	Number of default[2]	Number of no default[3]	Default rate
MGI	18.477	472	18.005	2,55%
Bank	6.160	575	5.585	9,33%
Total	24.637	1.047	23.590	4,25%

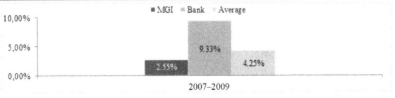

Figure 14.4 The Comparison of CGF Default Rates by Intermediary Type for Applications Accepted between 2007–2009 (number)

The Lending Rate Analysis

The analysis of the lending rate is carried out on a confidential sample of observations from 2009 to 2013 with about 130,000 observations.[9] Some of these loans were fixed rate, and others, floating rate (Euribor + spread).

To calculate the means value of Italian lending rate we used the statistical database of Banca d'Italia "BIP Online." It has been reconstructed considering lending rates on loan facilities. In particular, we collected data on term loans related to household producers and nonfinancial corporations.

Figure 14.6 allows us to draw some conclusions. In 2009 and 2010 the average rates applied to guaranteed loans were lower than the Italian average. Starting to 2011, the situation is reversed and the rates applied to loans with the collateral of the CGF are higher than those of Bankit. These findings allow us to do some considerations on FA. In 2009 and 2010 the presence of the CGF guarantee seem to reduce the lending rate with a positive impact in term of FA, but this effect disappears from 2011. This could also be caused by the worsening of the financial conditions of SMEs in the wake of the economic crisis. In the 2009–2013 period of observation we observe an alignment in the lending rate of guaranteed and counter-guaranteed loans (Figure 14.6).

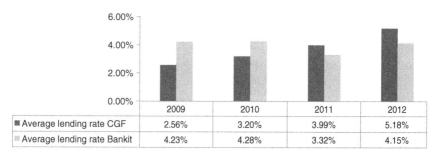

	2009	2010	2011	2012
■ Average lending rate CGF	2.56%	3.20%	3.99%	5.18%
▨ Average lending rate Bankit	4.23%	4.28%	3.32%	4.15%

Figure 14.5   The Comparison of CGF and Banca d'Italia Average Lending Rates

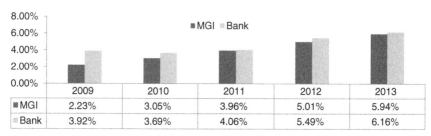

	2009	2010	2011	2012	2013
■ MGI	2.23%	3.05%	3.96%	5.01%	5.94%
▨ Bank	3.92%	3.69%	4.06%	5.49%	6.16%

Estimations refer to the confidential database provided by the Management Committee of the CGF

Figure 14.6   The Comparison of CGF Average Lending Rates by Intermediary Type[10]

USING THE LENS OF MANAGERIAL FLOW TO EVALUATE OVERALL EFFECTIVENESS OF THE CGF

The analysis presented in the section above seems to suggest the existence of shortcomings at the level of FA, EA and FS of the fund. Because there is consensus that the success of a credit guarantee program and the level of FA, EA, and FS generated is strongly influenced by the way in which it is designed and executed, the OE dimension is the most crucial to be explored for the CGF (Demirguc-Kunt, Beck, & Honohan, 2008; Green, 2003). To this end, by adopting a retrospective approach, Managerial Flow offers a useful framework to analyze the overall effectiveness of this state-funded guarantee program (Vecchi & Brusoni, 2012). In particular, Managerial Flow evaluates policy implementation using five main dimensions (*strategy, governance, selection, partnership*, and, finally, *communication and knowledge*), which are going to provide new perspectives into the strengths and drawbacks of the design and implementation of the CGF by the Italian government.

Strategy Gap

Strategy gaps emerge when public programs are defined based on short-term expectations, current fashions, and "announcement effects" or solely to allocate financial resources that otherwise could be diverted toward other policies or programs (Vecchi & Brusoni, 2012).

In the case of CGF, strategy gaps can be found at micro and macro level. At micro level, CGF has been characterized by discontinuous interventions essentially made by the government to respond to contingent situations rather than by systematic, year-by-year resource planning and allocation. As shown in the previous sections, although the number of application has been continuously growing over the years, the fund has had a marginal role until 2008, when it suddenly became the main tool of public facility to credit for SMEs. This result is a consequence of "rescue" interventions aimed at responding to the exacerbated financial instability of Italian enterprises during the crisis. These actions at the CGF level were not actually combined with regulatory initiatives at the macro level of the system.

The Italian guarantee system is extremely fragmented and not outright, because no specific network agreement or legal constraint exists in order to bring together all these entities within the framework of a system (Zecchini & Ventura, 2009). Therefore, although one of the largest in Europe, it is very inefficient (AECM, 2013). While subsidizing the CGF, the government did not actually intervene in order to activate a concentration process of the entire system, resulting in even more fragmented and overlapping initiatives (Vecchi & Brusoni, 2012).

Governance Gap

Also, as far as governance is concerned, gaps can be found both at the fund and the system level. Governance gaps at the system level essentially originate from the strategy gaps described earlier; the fragmentation and the overlapping of guarantee initiatives create confusion over roles, responsibility, and accountability, resulting in coordination problems and inefficiencies (Vecchi & Brusoni, 2012).

At micro level, the CGF's governance structure is characterized by different grounds that prevent the Management Committee to interact directly with beneficiaries. In fact, financial operators and the Manager act as intermediaries between SMEs and the committee, which in the end decides the grant and the amount of any guarantees. Although the process is lean, there is no aligning incentives schemes that involves partners in making careful assessments. As a consequence, moral hazard and adverse selection behaviors can be pursued by both intermediaries and beneficiary entrepreneurs at the expense of CGF (as affirmed also in literature by some authors, such as Benavente, Galetovic, & Sanhueza, 2006, and Lelarge, Sraer, & Thesmar, 2008). However, the amount of guarantee, which is an essential element for the fund's functioning and not actually a governance instrument, can play an important role in reducing agency problems between intermediaries and the CGF.

Selection Gap

The articulated and multilayer governance structure of the fund eventually brings about gaps in the selection process of applications. As stated above, requests accepted are decided on the proposals of banks and MGIs, which are indeed the main interlocutor of the government, which does not have the ability to evaluate and screening for eligible projects and then make use of specialized private institutions (Minelli & Modica, 2009). Intermediaries undoubtedly have the tools to analyze the riskiness of the company and of its investment plan, but a too high level of collateral weakens their incentive to do this analysis carefully, because they are confident to reduce the loss given default (Arping, Lóránth, & Morrison, 2010; Benavente et al., 2006). The results from the CGF seem to show, especially in the last few years, a slight adverse selection by intermediaries. The presence of collateral and in particular the "zero weighting" may have encouraged intermediaries to claim the guarantee for riskier clients. This is demonstrated with the financial characteristics of the firms and the increasing of default rate compared to average data recorded by the Banca d'Italia, as shown earlier.

This is quite physiological and probably falls within the purpose of the CGF; however, the Management Committee should pay close attention to the selection of applications to prevent the CGF become an instrument of rescuing firms that are not economically viable. The increased number of defaults can be also explained by the drastic growth of applications, which has probably destabilized the CGF's expertise to manage a large number of applicants.

Partnership Gap

Even if intermediaries are the main interlocutor of the government, it is important to emphasize that the CGF is not involved in the bank–firm relationship, and therefore, interest rates, repayment terms, any request for additional guarantees on the part not covered by the fund, and so on are established through the free negotiation between banks and enterprises. The lack of any form of control of the CGF on the relationship between intermediaries and SMEs may incentivize banks to act in an opportunistic way. These partnership problems will eventually limit the effectiveness of the policy in delivering it to beneficiaries (Vecchi & Brusoni, 2012).

The presence of partnership gaps can be demonstrated by the lending rate analysis presented before. Because banks can apply the so-called zero weight to the exposures guaranteed by the CGF, thus saving regulatory capital, they should require lower interest rates from borrowers. The lending rate analysis actually shows that in 2009 and 2010 the average rates applied to guaranteed loans were lower than the Italian average, but then, starting from 2011, the situation has reversed, and the rates applied to loans with collateral are higher than those of Bankit. These results confirm the opportunistic behavior theory. In particular, there might have been an adverse selection problem, whether the presence of collateral, and in particular the zero weighting have encouraged intermediaries to request the guarantee for riskier firms, or moral hazard, whether banks have applied a higher interest rate even when not necessary.

A further deepening of the analysis yields that firms affiliated to MGIs demonstrate a lower default rate, as well as paying a lower interest rates for loans, and this confirm that MGIs, by their very nature, are better in peer-screening and peer-monitoring activity of small borrowers (which is also demonstrated in literature by Columba, Gambacorta, & Mistrulli, 2010, and Mistrulli & Vacca, 2001).

Italy's universe of financial intermediaries significantly varies in terms of nature, geographical concentration, volume of operating activity, and degree of capitalization. Because the governance structure of the CGF assigns a key role to intermediaries in the process of granting the guarantee to enterprises, it is suggested that the fund's committee pay attention to those characteristics of intermediaries that allow them to be better partners.

Knowledge and Communication Gap

The data collecting and the monitoring activity of the CGF are carried out by the Observatory of the Management Committee, which communicates the results achieved to the Management Committee and, given that the CGF is an instrument of the Ministry of Economy, periodically also to the Italian parliament.

While the first communications are internal and thus reserved, from the latter, which are publically accessible,[11] the analysis carried out by the Observatory seem to have primarily focused on "spending capacity" measures, such as the number and amount of guarantee issued and the amount of loan financing channeled to SMEs, rather than on outcomes indicators aimed at measuring the real effectiveness of the program in terms of FA, EA, and execution efficiency.

FA and EA are crucial points for policy makers because the government needs ensure that the CGF is able to increase overall welfare by enough to justify the subsidy cost and not merely produce a costly distortion. Furthermore, as also suggested earlier, functioning criteria, such as selection procedures, eligibility criteria, maximum amounts of guarantee, risk-sharing arrangements, default determinants, and intermediaries incentives, should be carefully assessed and, if necessary, better designed.

This analysis should be implemented, disclosed, and shared within all the stakeholders in an effective manner in order to overcome those knowledge and communication gaps that push the different actors of the system to operate on different wavelengths, focusing only within their own silos, and prevent a careful and meaningful resource planning (Vecchi & Brusoni, 2012).

CONCLUSION

The success of a credit guarantee scheme depends largely on its design and on how well it is implemented. To this end, the lens of Managerial Flow has provided new insight into the most important public credit guarantee initiative in Italy, the CGF, exploring the dimension of policy design and execution.

Adopting a retrospective approach, the CGF, although having played a prominent role in facilitating SMEs access to finance during the crisis, has shown some drawbacks that should be carefully evaluated to ensure the future effectiveness and sustainability of the program. These gaps, which have been analyzed at five levels (strategy, governance, selection, partnership, and communication and knowledge), are actually mutually related (see Figure 14.7).

In the main, policy makers have been so far driven by the urgency of expanding access to liquidity for enterprises to avoid their bankruptcy. Now the implementation of a complete and transparent monitoring system should be considered of the utmost importance in order to close those strategy gaps that have prevented a meaningful resource planning and allocation and to activate a reform and concentration process of the entire guarantee

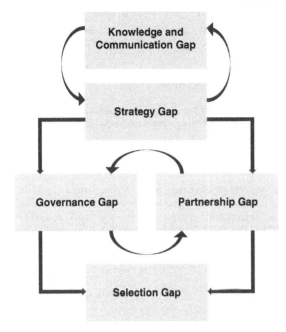

Figure 14.7   Relations Between the Gaps of the CGF

institutions system. This process would improve the governance of the system and facilitate partnership relationships between the fund and the other interlocutors. In the end, this would have a positive influence on the effectiveness of the CGF's selection process, improving the quality of the guarantee portfolio and thus the sustainability of the public program.

Future research will be directed at having a deeper insight into the analysis and providing more specific recommendations to the CGF's Management Committee to design and implement relevant performance indicators.

NOTES

1. The analyses presented in this chapter are developed by the authors within the Bocconi Monitor on Public Private Partnership (MP3), using a confidential database provided by the Management Committee of the Italian Central Guarantee Fund.
2. The descriptive analyses developed in this chapter give us some insights but are not able to definitely assess the effectiveness of the public program. Because the analysis of additionally is very important to evaluate a public program, Caselli, Corbetta, Rossolini, and Vecchi are developing a paper focusing on economic additionality of the CGF using accurate statistical analyses.
3. The sample represents about 50% of the entire population of firms guaranteed by the CGF in the period between 2007 and 2009.
4. We delete from the comparison sample all companies already present in the CGF sample.

5. ROE(%) = (Net income/Shareholders funds)* 100; ROI(%) = (Operative income/Invested Capital)* 100; Liquidity ratio (x) = (Current assets – Stocks)/ Current liabilities; and Solvency ratio (%) = (Shareholders funds/Total assets)* 100.
6. The Wilcoxon rank-sum test on median value confirms the results of the mean test; therefore, it was decided not to report them.
7. See http://bip.bancaditalia.it/.
8. This figure is calculated as number credit not in default at the end of the previous year, plus number of new credit in the year, minus credit in default in the year, minus credit expired in the year.
9. The manager of the CGF has started to collect data on lending rate from 2009.
10. Estimations refer to the confidential database provided by the Management Committee of the CGF.
11. Deposition by Claudia Bugno, former chairman of the Management Committee, to the Senate of the Italian Parliament dated June 5, 2012; see http://www.senato.it/documenti/repository/commissioni/comm10/documenti_acquisiti/IC%20competitivita/2012_06_05%20-%20Fondo%20Centrale%20Garanzia%20PMI%20-%20schede%20di%20sintesi.pdf and http://www.senato.it/documenti/repository/commissioni/comm10/documenti_acquisiti/IC%20competitivita/2012_06_05%20-%20Intervento%20dr.ssa%20Claudia%20Bugno.pdf.

REFERENCES

Amini, A. (2004). The distributional role of small business in development. *International Journal of Social Economics*, 31(4), 370–383.
Arping, S., Lóránth, G., & Morrison, A. D. (2010). Public initiatives to support entrepreneurs: Credit guarantees versus co-funding. *Journal of Financial Stability*, 6(1), 26–35.
Banca d'Italia. (2013). *Relazione Annuale sul 2012*. Retrieved from http://www.bancaditalia.it/pubblicazioni/relazioneannuale/2012/rel_2012.pdf
Beck, T., & Demirguc-Kunt, A. (2006). Small and medium-size enterprises: Access to finance as a growth constraint. *Journal of Banking & Finance*, 30(11), 2931–2943.
Beck, T., Demirguc-Kunt, A., & Levine, R. (2005). SMEs, growth, and poverty: cross-country evidence. *Journal of Economic Growth*, 10(3), 199–229.
Benavente, J. M, Galetovic A., & Sanhueza R. (2006). *Fogape: An economic analysis* (Working Paper 222). Santiago: University of Chile.
Berger, A. N., & Udell, G. F. (2006). A more complete conceptual framework for SME finance. *Journal of Banking & Finance*, 30(11), 2945–2966.
Boocock, G., & Shariff, M. N. M. (2005). Measuring the effectiveness of credit guarantee schemes evidence from Malaysia. *International Small Business Journal*, 23(4), 427–454.
Bugno C. (2012). Il fondo centrale di garanzia tra opportunità e rischi. *Rivista italiana di intelligence, Gnosis*, 1, 49–59.
Columba F., Gambacorta L., & Mistrulli P.E., (2010), Mutual guarantee institutions and small business finance. *Journal of Financial Stability*, 6, 45–54.
Cumming, D. J., & MacIntosh, J. G. 2002. The extent of venture capital exits: evidence from Canada and the United States. In L. D. R. Renneboog & J. McCahery (Eds.), *Venture capital contracting and the valuation of high-tech firms* (pp. 339–371). Oxford, England: Oxford University Press.
Curran, J. (2000). What is small business policy in the UK for? Evaluation and assessing small business policies. *International Small Business Journal*, 18(3), 36–50.

Demirguc-Kunt, A., Beck, T., & Honohan, P. (2008). *Finance for all. Policies and pitfalls in expanding access* (A World Bank Policy Research Report). Washington, DC: World Bank.

Drever, M., Hutchinson, P., & Morgan, B. (1999). *Innovation and economic development: Small business enterprises in Wales (United Kingdom) and New South Wales (Australia)* (Working Paper 12). Naples, Italy: International Council for Small Businesses.

European Commission. (2013). *2013 SBA country fact sheet Italy*. Retrieved from http://ec.europa.eu/enterprise/policies/sme/facts-figures-analysis/performance-review/files/countries-sheets/2013/italy_en.pdf

Florida R., & Smith D. F. (1993), Venture capital formation, investment, and regional industrialization. *Annals of the Associations of American Geographers, 83*(3), 434–451.

Green, A. (2003). *Credit guarantee schemes for small enterprises: an effective instrument to promote private sector-led growth?* (Working Paper No. 10). Vienna, Austria: UNIDO, Programme Development and Technical Cooperation Division.

Hallberg K. (1999). *Small and medium scale enterprises: A framework for intervention, small enterprise unit private sector development department.* Washington, DC: World Bank. http://dx.doi.org/10.1596/0-8213-4727-6

Lelarge, C., Sraer, D. A., & Thesmar, D. (2008). Entrepreneurship and credit constraints-evidence from a French loan guarantee program. In J. Lerner & A. Schoar (Eds.), *International differences in entrepreneurship* (pp.243–273), Chicago, IL: Chicago University Press.

Lerner, J. (2002). When bureaucrats meet entrepreneurs: the design of effective public venture capital programs. *The Economic Journal, 112*(477), F73–F84.

Martin, S., & Scott, J. T. (2000). The nature of innovation market failure and the design of public support for private innovation. *Research Policy, 29*(4), 437–447.

Minelli, E., & Modica, S. (2009). Credit market failures and policy. *Journal of Public Economic Theory, 11*(3), 363–382.

Mistrulli, P., & Vacca, V. (Eds.). (2011). *Mutual guarantee institutions and small business credit during the crisis* (Occasional Paper 105). Rome: Banca d'Italia.

Oakey M. P. (2003). Funding innovation and growth in UK new technology-based firms: Some observations on contributions from the public and private sectors. *Venture Capital: An International Journal of Entrepreneurial Finance, 5*(2), 161–179.

Organisation for Economic Co-operation and Development. (2011). *The impact of the global crisis on SME and entrepreneurship financing and policy responses.* Retrieved from http://www.oecd.org/industry/smes/43183090.pdf

Riding, A. L., & Haines Jr, G. (2001). Loan guarantees: Costs of default and benefits to small firms. Journal of Business Venturing, 16(6), 595–612.

Storey, D. J. (1994). *Understanding the small business sector.* London, England: Routledge.

Vecchi, V., & Brusoni, M. (2012). The managerial flow of public local development policies a conceptual framework. *Singapore Management Review, 34*(Suppl. 2), 5–20.

Zecchini, S., & Ventura, M. (2009). The impact of public guarantees on credit to SMEs. *Small Business Economics, 32*(2), 191–206.

15 Closing Public–Private Partnerships' Gaps in Italy

From Legal Microsurgery to Managerial Flow

Veronica Vecchi, Marco Airoldi, and Stefano Caselli[1]

INTRODUCTION: INFRASTRUCTURE GAP AND PUBLIC–PRIVATE PARTNERSHIP IN ITALY

Despite a level of fixed investment aligned to the European average, Italy shows an infrastructure gap of 15% to 20%, and this comes as a consequence of an inefficient expenditure (Banca d'Italia, 2012). According to the World Economic Forum (2013) the quality of Italian infrastructures is far lower than in other benchmark countries, such as Canada, France, Germany, and UK. The Italian gap is doomed to increase under the effect of the measures dictated by the European Union to reduce its level of debt. This trend has already begun with fixed investments on the gross domestic product (GDP) decreasing from 2.1% in 2010 to 1.9% in 2012, and the Italian National Auditor estimates a further drop to 1.6% by 2017 (Corte dei Conti, 2013).

In Italy, as in many other countries worldwide, there is a common view that the public–private partnership (PPP) can be the solution to close the infrastructure gap and to alleviate governments from budget rigidities (Greve & Hodge, 2013). Successive governments in Italy have promoted the use of PPPs in the delivery of infrastructure (Vecchi, Hellowell, & Longo, 2010). The legal framework for such contracts was established in 2002, and additional elements have been introduced more recently to increase the flexibility of the procurement process and extend the range of officially sanctioned contractual models (Vecchi & Cusumano, 2012).

Because PPPs are based on standard international schemes, they are also seen as a way to attract foreign investment. Thus, according to the Italian Census of 2014, in the last 5 years foreign investments dropped of 58%. Thus, the Italian PPP market appears fragmented and limited in comparison to the other European ones. The average value of a PPP signed contract is 14.5 million euros, while the average value of a PPP request of offers is 4.5 million euros. However, PPPs are used also for large schemes, such as hospitals, motorways, and public utilities; these three sectors represent the 80% of the market value, but only the 22% per number of deals.[2] Actually the average number of tenders per year for PPP projects with a value higher than 50 million euros is only 1.2% (Infopieffe, 2013). Thus, in the last 10 years 40 billion euros have been awarded to PPP projects. Figure 15.1 shows the trend of PPP in Italy.

In the last years an increasing value of public investments has been developed through PPPs (22.5% compound annual growth rate [CAGR]), as shown in Figure 15.2, especially for larger schemes. However, the gap between PPP tenders and awarded contracts remain sizeable, and only the largest schemes achieve closing status.

Even if international comparisons are often problematic, especially when investigating complex contracts such as PPPs that are deeply influenced by national judicial frameworks, some specific features of the application of PPPs in Italy can be recognized:

1. Italian PPP contracts are very small because they are often applied at local level, by authorities, with reduced financial autonomy due to increased and severe fiscal constraints (Anessi-Pessina & Steccolini, 1995).
2. As a consequence of this, in addition to the traditional dominance of small and medium-sized enterprises (SMEs), the market has been dominated by small operators, mainly builders, with limited knowledge of

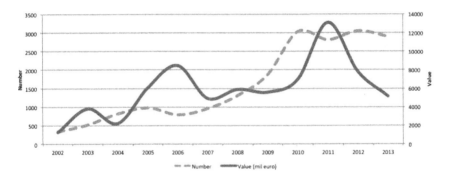

Figure 15.1   PPP Trend (volume and number of PPP in procurement)
Source: Infopieffe (2013).

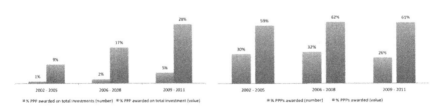

Figure 15.2   PPP Market Dimension (on the left) and Evolution (on the right) on Public Total Investments
Source: Infopieffe (2013).

the process, and a low capacity for innovation. In the health care sector, for example, more than the 80% of Special Purpose Vehicles (SPVs) shares belong to building companies (Vecchi & Cusumano, 2012). Furthermore, the five biggest Italian building companies have aggregated sales of 8 billion euros (Il Sole 24 Ore, 2013).

3. With small numbers and capital values, project financing techniques have remained fixed on a few select projects, while in the majority of cases a corporate financing approach has been applied (Vecchi & Hellowell, 2013). This feature may explain the limited number of financial closes reported by European PPP Expertise Centre (EPEC; 2013) and by Associazione Nazionale Costruttori Edili (ANCE; 2012), as confirmed also by the PPP Italian National Task Force (UTFP; 2012).

PPP: THE MAIN INTERNATIONAL ISSUES IN A NUTSHELL

PPPs have become popular with the rise of new public management in the Anglo-Saxon countries in order to increase the public services efficiency and performance and to reduce the boundaries of the public sector and the public bureaucracy (Broadbent & Laughlin, 2003). It has been applied as an alternative to the pure privatization, often opposed by the public opinion and therefore politically embarrassing (Pollitt, 2005).

PPPs soon became a popular approach worldwide (Greve & Hodge, 2013), and now there are several types of applications, as well as several slightly different definitions for the term *PPP* (Hodge & Greve, 2010; Linder, 1999).

The popularity of the PPP concept is associated with the *off balance sheet* argument; in other words, the opportunity to develop investment without increasing the public debt headings (Savas, 2000; Spackman, 2002), and to develop investments not prioritized by central governments and therefore without public funding (Durkan, 2001).

Research to date has been often critical of the value for money and affordability of PPPs, and this is in spite of a belief by many domestic and international institutions that these configurations lead to more efficient and effective outcomes for policy development (Reeves, 2013; Siemiatycki, 2011; Vecchi & Hellowell, 2013). For example, Shaoul (2009) reported that PPPs have led to wicked results in the UK and elsewhere. Furthermore, Forrer, Kee and Zhang (2002) suggest that PPPs only really transfer risk from the private sector to the public sector, at least in the US. Thus, as noted by Hodge and Greve (2009) much must be done to increase the reliability of the findings.

Beyond the theoretical discussion, there is a wide international consensus that PPPs, in many cases, facilitates the delivery of new infrastructure on time, thereby staving off "megaproject paradoxes" (Flyvbjerg, 2013; Greve & Hodge, 2013). The PPP contract can act as a filter, especially for user fees–based projects, skimming unfeasible and unbankable projects. When PPPs are partially granted by the public sector, the matching fund mechanism can mitigate the misallocation of public money toward unrealistic projects.

Scholars are often critical of the capacity of the public and private sectors to develop PPP contracts based on mutual trust (Rosenau, 1999; Spackman, 2002). Moore (2002) notes that for-profit companies will "treat the performance standards set by government as a constraint and will use any discretionary room that is left to them in the contractual arrangements to maximize their financial returns" (p. 316). The institutional and value-related differences between public and private players has required "contractual enforcement," which remains a critical element due to the information asymmetry between public and private partners and the investment specificities (Parker & Hartley, 2003; Teisman & Klijn, 2002). Furthermore, because PPPs are long-term contracts, it is crucial to find the right balance between completeness and flexibility (Klein, 1998).

The contract complexity, the level of uncertainty, and the oligopolistic features of the market make the value for money a chimera (Reeves, 2013; Saussier, 2013; Siemiatycki, 2011). Furthermore, the high number of actors, the fragmentation of the decisional process and the dichotomy between the public and private sectors make the partnership hard. For example, Teisman and Klijn(2002) described the PPP that they were observing as the "right proposal at the wrong time."

Competences are a crucial element for an efficient and effective application of a PPP (Bloomfield, 2006; Spackman, 2002). Spackman (2002) writes that

> at the level of central administration, a strong central structure, using private-sector expertise, has been needed to promote and guide the policy implementation. This has been provided successfully. However, the benefits and the imaginative development of policy, are weakened by the continuing policy drivers of ideology and off-budget finance.
>
> (p. 299)

Bloomfield (2006) claims that Local governments need sufficient resources to manage, monitor, and enforce PPP contracts. In Kettl's (1993) words,

> government's relationships with the private sector are not self-administering: they require, rather, aggressive management by a strong, competent government.
>
> (p. 6)

Long-term contracts require long-term commitments of resources to manage them. Governments that are unwilling or unable to make such long-term commitments should not use PPP schemes. As Bloomfield (2006) notes,

> the challenge is to locate independent, unbiased specialists who will protect the public interest meticulously and aggressively—as aggressively as

their counterparts in the private sector are working to protect the interests of companies seeking long-term contracts from local governments. In this respect, government should be more like business.

(p. 409)

Recently, a growing body of literature has discussed the importance of institutional framework for supporting an efficient and effective application of PPPs (European Investment Bank [EIB], 2011; Kwak, Chih, & Ibbs, 2009; Public–Private Infrastructure Advisory Facility, 2012). Three appears to be the factors that are crucial for the development of PPPs. They include a clear PPP policy, an appropriate legal and regulatory framework, and dedicated supporting institutions with clear procedures and responsibilities (Verhoest, Petersen, Scherrer, & Murwantara Soecipto, 2014). Often such institutional capacity is ensured through a PPP management body, often termed a *PPP unit* (Dutz, Harris, Dhingra, & Shugart, 2006; Jooste & Scott, 2011; Organisation for Economic Co-operation and Development, 2010; Rachwalski & Ross, 2010; Verhoest et al., 2014). The PPP unit generally covers the following tasks: PPP policy making and dissemination of best practice, project identification, PPP project or program planning and prioritization, provision of guidance and support to contracting authorities, and knowledge dissemination (EIB, 2011). However, because of the variations among PPPs across different jurisdictions, as well as the difficulties in accessing reliable data, it is difficult to clearly measure the effect of institutional enforcement on PPP outcomes.

In sum, theory and practice suggest that the efficiency and the effectiveness of PPPs are influenced by a range of internal and environmental factors. In this chapter we explore the case of Italian PPPs. We identify the main drawbacks affecting the performance of current PPPs and the inhibitors that impede the development of new ones.

GAPS IN THE ITALIAN PPP MARKET

To investigate the factors that affect the operations of Italian PPPs we adopt a qualitative approach to analyze a range of interviews and focus groups, conducted in 2013, with Italian stakeholders connected to PPPs. We used the Managerial Flow framework to inform the coding of our data. Thus, the emerged themes have been grouped under the following five gaps: *planning, governance, selection, partnership,* and *knowledge.* The following outlines our findings.

Planning Gap

The first key finding stemming from our analysis was that the financial instability of the Italian government, manifest also at the local level, inhibits the development of clear and stable infrastructure planning. Thus, our data suggest that recent infrastructure projects, which traditionally would have been developed by the public sector alone, were converted into PPPs. Hence, PPP development in Italy is driven by a fiscal imperative, rather than a strategic one, and PPPs are considered the "only game in town" at the local level. This is because capital expenditure has been completely frozen for local jurisdictions.

The planning gap has strong implication also on the certainty and availability of government grants to PPP projects. Actually, grants to reduce the private capital expenditure are very common in Italy. This represents a further signal of the fact that PPP is used as a "matching fund" strategy to develop investment otherwise not possible. It also confirms that PPP is not considered a new approach to develop service-based infrastructures. This approach to PPP is the main reason of a lack of a pipeline of feasible projects, conceived since the beginning as initiatives to be developed through a PPP model.

This finding goes someway to explaining why Italian PPP initiatives are small in size and are focused at the local level.

Also the private sector, mainly formed by small building companies, perceived the PPP as an alternative procedure to traditional procurement. Furthermore, with the aim of generating business opportunities, they submit unsolicited proposal, thus forcing the public planning procedures. However, these proposals are often unable to overcome the political and or technical barriers because the lack of consensus or knowledge about public interests.

Governance Gap

The Italian PPP Unit was created in 1999; however, its role, aside from the formal tasks assigned to it by law, has been very limited. In particular, it has struggled to provide technical support to procuring authorities. Our research indicates that the lack of an effective supporting unit for PPPs has meant that these partnerships are subject to the main weakness of the Italian administrative and institutional framework (which is complex, involving a large bureaucracy that is underpinned by multiple legal processes).

In this environment, the typical procuring authority, which is often located at the regional or local level, has to deal with many administrative bodies located at different levels of government. These bodies often have conflicting powers and divergent interests. Their actions are also often uncoordinated because of the lack of a PPP policy and a consistent institutional framework assigning clear role and responsibilities to the different competent authorities.

This process presents as a major political risk not only for the private sector but also for procuring authorities.

Our research also indicated that the interest for PPPs amongst business constituencies has generated several lobbying initiatives. These initiatives have been, in the main, oriented to deliver guidelines, standardized contracts, and procedures.

These lobbying initiative have created a "microsurgery effect" within the Italian PPP legal framework, mainly dominated by the *Code of Public Contract*, which regulates public procurement, especially in the field of public works and infrastructures, and therefore with a scarce orientation to public services

Selection Gap

As a consequence of a "short-term approach" to PPPs, and a judicial framework rooted in the public work traditional procurement, Italian PPPs are not primarily used as a way of allocating risks to players who are able to manage them. The risk allocation is often seen as a formal requirement to justify the off-balance-sheet treatment. Thus, so far Italian PPPs haven't been able to skim the market for the benefit of the most innovative and competitive players able to efficiently manage the project life cycle. Our research suggests that this gap has been influenced also by a lack of financial investors. Project financing is limited to few investments: Typically banks step in after the concession is awarded, and the financial closes are often postponed during the construction phase to mitigate the construction risk. Furthermore, equity investors are almost absent. Recently, some micro changes to the Code of Public Contracts, addressed to cope with the bankability issue, have stimulated the participation of banks into the process of project structuring. Precisely, procuring authorities can require PPP bidders to undertake a mandatory bank commitment. Actually, a change in the law cannot produce any effect without any evolution in the ecosystem environment and, especially, in the way in which PPP contracts are applied.

A selection gap emerges also when PPP contracts are used to bypass fiscal rules. These rules are so stringent, especially at the local level, that authorities cannot make any financial strategies, such as to opt for a PPP configuration only when it makes sense. This means that public resources can be allocated to those investments where the operation/service component is weak. As a result, they have no choice and the PPP configuration remains the "only game in town."

Partnership Gap

The application of PPPs to overcome the fiscal rules, in a context in which a traditional culture and legal framework dominate, generates a partnership gap. A PPP is essentially a contract, rather than a partnership, and the unbalanced competences between the public and the private sectors generate a moral hazard and information asymmetry, which inhibits the implementation of a partnership-based relation. On the public sector side, the severe cut to the consultancy, and training expenditure and the hiring freeze have further distanced authority from private players.

On the private-sector side, mainly formed by building companies, there is a scarce knowledge and experiences of PPPs and the short-term vision leads them to push for PPP configurations even when prerequisites are lacking. This comes about as a result of a widespread awareness that the public sector will support the private partners in case of risk of failure.

Knowledge and Communication Gap

Despite information about PPP and public procurement should be of public domain, there is no public database in which stakeholders can find information about procurements and contracts. The competent authority for the monitoring of public contracts provides a database that contains few details related to the procurement and award. Figures seem not to be consistent with those provided by Osservatorio Nazionale sul PPP, which is promoted by the association of chambers of commerce and building company, with the support of PPP task force. However, it releases information and updates only on underpayment, mainly taken from procurement notice and therefore just referred during the preliminary phase of the project and not at its implementation. Even procuring authorities do not release information about their PPP projects; contracts are undisclosed, and the press lacks of an open and balanced debate on PPP. For years, cases that have poor performance have been considered good practices by the press, which has generally echoed only the supporters, such as the concessionaire, the procuring authority, and the consultancies involved. In this context, experience-based learning has been difficult.

The knowledge and communication gap can be referred also to the fact that the procurement process is quite rigid and formal, as in all the countries dominated by civil law. However, it has been further sharpened by a captious approach to appeals to the Administrative Court by private sector. This makes it harder to apply a technical dialogue with the market or road shows that attract investors.

Figure 15.3 shows a synthesis of these gaps.

CLOSING GAPS: MANAGERIAL ACTIONS AND ASSETS

The same stakeholders involved in the gaps analysis were requested to support the identification of possible actions to close the gaps. Four actions were presented to the Italian government at the end of 2013, and two of them have been included in the *Document for the Economic and Financial Planning* for 2014. Therefore, a first step has been done; however the implementation challenge still remain, and the risk is that the envisage solutions remain a so-called announcement effect (Vecchi & Brusoni, 2012).

Figure 15.3   PPP Gaps—a Synthesis

The envisaged solutions are rooted in the awareness that PPP could bring innovation and competition in the public services management, if it is efficiently and effectively conceived, and not only off-balance-sheet investments. The first and core action is the creation of a *national body*, which could also originate from the institutional reorganization currently under management and pillar of Mr. Renzi's government, to whom to assign the following tasks: policy definition, technical support, capacity building, and market interface. Its main role should be the creation of the ecosystem in order to sustain a pipeline of feasible, value for money, and bankable and affordable projects. Afterward, and under the coordination of the PPP national body, it is overriding to implement a dedicated PPP code (corpus of laws) and a system to certify the competences of public and private managers involved in the design and implementation of PPP. Finally, a public–private equity facility may be useful to sustain the project development phase, where private capital may lack.

This flow of actions can be considered a managerial flow (see Figure 15.4), which generates the assets to close the gaps and therefore to create the ecosystem in which PPP can be correctly used to address the shortage of infrastructure to support the competitiveness and the economic recovery of the country.

The Features of the National PPP Body

Based on the literature about and the experiences of PPP task forces, it may play a compulsory advisory role for the development of strategic infrastructures, supporting both the design (feasibility study) and the implementation

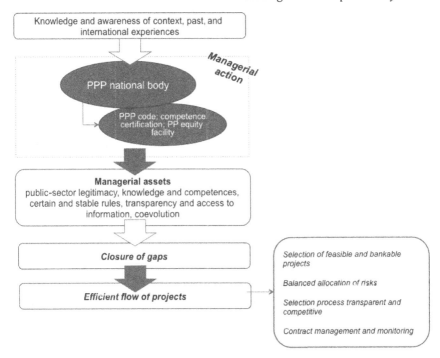

Figure 15.4   The Managerial Flow Approach to Close PPP Gaps

(during the tender and contract phases) of the project. It could also have the power to intervene to unblock some procedures/projects, thanks to its competences and the authority to coordinate other institutions. For minor investments, it may support local authorities or regional agency. It must be influential, independent, competent, and lean. It could be able to attract the most competent professionals available on the national market and to use the best services offered by the market. It may act as a kind of "PPP mastermind": Thanks to its competences and to its institutional position, it may coordinate all the institutions involved into PPP policy design and project implementation, the law system update, the definition of guidelines, and technical notes and methodologies. It may also act as a forum to coordinate the dialogue with the market and the lobbying processes. Last but not the least, it may support the promotion of Italian investments within international markets and therefore the attraction of foreign investors.

The PPP Code

At the beginning of 2014, the European Union approved a new directive on concessions, which is the main judicial framework for PPP contracts. Unlike what happened in the past, it would be of utmost importance to adopt the new directive *tel quel*, without distortion and through a code dedicated to

PPP to help the alignment with the other member state in order to facilitate the attraction of foreign investors. The code could contain other legal, fiscal, and accounting specifications also, which would be useful to apply PPPs in a certain way, both for authorities and for the industrial and financial players.

Certification of Competences

PPP complexity can impede the selection of the appropriate competences to design and implement a feasible, cost effective, bankable and affordable project. Furthermore, in Italy professionals have not been the way to channel project resources outside to feed corruption. Therefore, the certification of competences may be a useful action to skim the market of professionals, to sustain the pipeline of efficient and effective projects, to reduce corruption, and to increase the quality of training, leveraging on the best competences available.

Public–Private Equity Facility

Credit crunch and the new capital requirements for banks introduced by Basel 3 make it harder to fund PPP and have lowered the gearing (the debt–equity ratio). To cope with that situation, the UK government introduced a financial facility to provide a share of public equity to PPP projects. In Italy a public–private equity fund could be useful to provide capital during the construction phase, which is the riskiest phase, to support the bankability of a project. This would also insert into the project a subject interested in choosing the best players enable project efficiency and effectiveness across the whole life cycle.

CONCLUSION: THE BACKSTAGE

This chapter has shown a further application of the Managerial Flow framework to sustain PPP as a way to increase infrastructure and economic development. The Managerial Flow framework has inspired the design of an actionable process. The implementation of this process, which should start from the creation or refoundation of a national PPP body, requires strong political will, which does not add layers of authority but, rather, a new entity able to coordinate a process of institutional redesign and ecosystem development. Furthermore, to be really novel, it needs not only a brand-new name and the approval of a statue, but new people, new competences, and a new culture able to execute the process and to reach measurable results.

NOTES

1. This chapter has been developed within Bocconi Monitor on Public Private Partnership, which the authors acknowledge for the support.
2. These figures are referred to PPP requests of offers.

REFERENCES

Anessi-Pessina, E., & Steccolini, I. (1995). Evolutions and limits of new public management–inspired budgeting practices in Italian local governments. *Public Budgeting & Finance*, 3(2), 1–14.

Associazione Nazionale Costruttori Edili. (2012). *Il Project Financing in Italia— L'indagine ANCE sulla realizzazione delle opere*. Retrieved June 23, 2014, from http://www.ance.it/docs/docDownload.aspx?id=9180

Banca d'Italia. (2012). *L'efficienza della spesa per infrastrutture*. Retrieved from http://www.bancaditalia.it/pubblicazioni/seminari_convegni/conv-10/efficienza_spesa.pdf

Bloomfield, P. (2006). The challenging business of long-term public-private partnerships: Reflections on local experience. *Public Administration Review*, 66(3), 400–411.

Broadbent, J., & Laughlin, R. (2003). Public private partnerships: An introduction. *Accounting, Auditing & Accountability Journal*, 16(3), 332–341.

Corte dei Conti. (2013). *Rapporto 2013 sul coordinamento della finanza pubblica*. Retrieved from http://www.rivistacorteconti.it/export/sites/rivistaweb/Ultimo_fascicolo/2013-Rapporto-2013-finanza-pubblica.pdf

Durkan, M. (2001). A programme for partnership. *PFI J*, 6, 13–14.

Dutz, M., Harris, C., Dhingra, I., & Shugart, C. (2006). Public-private partnership units : What are they, and what do they do? Retrieved from https://openknowledge.worldbank.org/handle/10986/11175

European Investment Bank. (2011). *FEMIP Study on PPP legal & financial frameworks in the Mediterranean partner countries*. Retrieved from http://www.eib.org/infocentre/publications/all/femip-study-on-ppp-legal-and-financial-frameworks-in-the-mediterranean-partner-countries.htm

European PPP Expertise Centre. (2013). *Market update, review of the European PPP market in 2012*. Retrieved from http://www.eib.org/epec/resources/epec_market_update_2012_en.pdf

Flyvbjerg, B. (2013). Mega delusional: The curse of the mega project. *New Scientist*, 220(2945), 28–29.

Forrer, J., Kee, J. E., & Zhang, Z. (2002). Private finance initiative: A better public-private partnership. *Public Manager*, 31(2), 43–47.

Greve, C., & Hodge, G. (2013). *Rethinking public-private partnerships: Strategies for turbulent times*. Abingdon, England: Routledge.

Hodge, G. A., & Greve, C. (2009). PPPs: The passage of time permits a sober reflection. *Economic Affairs*, 29(1), 33–39.

Hodge, G., & Greve, C. (2010). Public-private partnerships: Governance scheme or language game? *Australian Journal of Public Administration*, 69, S8–S22.

Il Sole 24 Ore. (2013). Edilizia e Territorio Dossier—Speciale classifiche : le prime 50 imprese di costruzione. Retrieved from http://www.shopping24.ilsole24ore.com/sh4/catalog/Product.jsp?PRODID=prod1380040

Infopieffe. (2013). *Project financing—Osservatorio Nazionale*. Retrieved from http://www.infopieffe.it/

Italian National Task Force. (2012). *Relazione al CIPE sull'attività svolta nel 2012 dall'Unità Tecnica Finanza di Progetto (UTFP)*. Retrieved from http://www.cipecomitato.it/it/documenti/Relazione_UTFP_2012.pdf

Jooste, S. F., & Scott, W. R. (2011). The public-private partnership enabling field: Evidence from three cases. *Administration & Society*, 44(2), 149–182.

Kettl, D. F. (1993). *Sharing power: Public governance and private markets*. Washington, DC: Brookings Institution Press.

Klein, M. (1998). Bidding for concessions: The impact of contract design. Retrieved from https://openknowledge.worldbank.org/handle/10986/11527

Kwak, Y. H., Chih, Y., & Ibbs, C. W. (2009). Towards a comprehensive understanding of public private partnerships for infrastructure development. *California Management Review, 51*(2), 51–78.

Linder, S. H. (1999). Coming to terms with the public-private partnership: A grammar of multiple meanings. *American Behavioral Scientist, 43*(1), 35–51.

Moore, M. H. (2002). Privatizing public management. In J. D. Donahue & J. S. Nye Jr. (Eds.), *Market-based governance* (pp. 296–322). Washington, DC: Brookings Institution Press.

Organisation for Economic Co-operation and Development. (2010). *Dedicated public-private partnership units: A survey of institutional and governance structures.* Retrieved from http://www.oecd.org/governance/budgeting/dedicatedpublic-private partnershipunitsasurveyofinstitutionalandgovernancestructures.htm

Parker, D., & Hartley, K. (2003). Transaction costs, relational contracting and public private partnerships: A case study of UK defence. *Journal of Purchasing and Supply Management, 9*(3), 97–108.

Pollitt, M. (2005). Learning from UK Private Finance Initiative experience. In G. A. Hodge & C. Greve (Eds.), *The challenge of public-private partnerships: Learning from international experience* (p. 207–230). Cheltenham, England: Edward Elgar.

Public–Private Infrastructure Advisory Facility. (2012). *Developing a public-private partnership framework: Policies and PPP units* (Note 4). Retrieved from http://www.ppiaf.org/sites/ppiaf.org/files/documents/Note-Four-Developing-a-PPP-Framework.pdf

Rachwalski, M. D., & Ross, T. W. (2010). Running a government's P3 program: Special purpose agency or line departments? *Journal of Comparative Policy Analysis: Research and Practice, 12*(3), 275–298.

Reeves, E. (2013). The not so good, the bad and the ugly: Over twelve years of PPP in Ireland. *Local Government Studies, 39*(3), 375–395.

Rosenau, P. V. (1999). Introduction: The strengths and weaknesses of public-private policy partnerships. *American Behavioral Scientist, 43*(1), 10–34.

Saussier, S. (2013). *An economic analysis of the closure of markets and other dysfunctions in the awarding of concession contracts.* Retrieved from http://cadmus.eui.eu/handle/1814/26058

Savas, E. S. (2000). *Privatization and public-private partnerships.* New York, NY: Chatham House.

Shaoul, J. (2009). Using the private sector to finance capital expenditure: the financial realities. In A. Akintoye & M. Beck (Eds.), *Policy, finance & management for public private partnerships* (pp. 27–43). Chichester, England: Wiley.

Siemiatycki, M. (2011). Public-private partnership networks: Exploring business-government relationships in United Kingdom transportation projects. *Economic Geography, 87*(3), 309–334.

Spackman, M. (2002). Public–private partnerships: Lessons from the British approach. *Economic Systems, 26*(3), 283–301.

Teisman, G. R., & Klijn, E.-H. (2002). Partnership arrangements: Governmental rhetoric or governance scheme? *Public Administration Review, 62*(2), 197–205.

Vecchi, V., & Brusoni, M. (2012). The managerial flow of public local development policies: A conceptual framework. *Singapore Management Review, 34*(Suppl. 2), 5–20.

Vecchi, V., & Cusumano, N. (2012). Il Partenariato Pubblico Privato "light" e "limited profit" al crocevia tra sostenibilità, bancabilità e vincoli finanziari. In E. Anessi-Pessina & E. Cantù (Eds.), *Rapporto OASI 2012* (pp. 363-392). Milan, Italy: Egea.

Vecchi, V., & Hellowell, M. (2013). Leasing by public authorities in Italy: Creating economic value from a balance sheet illusion. *Public Money & Management*, *33*(1), 63–70.

Vecchi, V., Hellowell, M., & Longo, F. (2010). Are Italian healthcare organizations paying too much for their public–private partnerships? *Public Money & Management*, *30*(2), 125–132.

Verhoest, K., Petersen, O. H., Scherrer, W., & Murwantara Soecipto, R. (2014). *Policy commitment, legal and regulatory framework, and institutional support for PPP in international comparison: Indexing countries' readiness for taking up PPP* (No. 2014-03, Working Papers in Economics and Finance). Antwerpen: University of Salzburg.

World Economic Forum. (2013). *The global competitiveness report 2013–2014*. Retrieved from http://www.weforum.org/reports/global-competitiveness-report-2013-2014

Contributor Biographies

Marco Airoldi is currently the CEO of Benetton Group. When he contributed to this book he was Senior Partner of The Boston Consulting Group (BCG), where he entered in 1989 working on consulting projects for several leading companies, mainly in Italy, France and Spain. Here, as a member of Global Infrastructure Practice, he actively supported Bocconi Monitor on Public Private Partnership in 2013–2014. During his experience at BCG, in the 1990s he also served as Chief Operating Office and later as General Director of Autogrill Italia.

Kerry Brown is a professor of Human Resource Management in the School of Management at Curtin University, Australia. Her principal research areas are change management; collaboration, networks and business clusters; capability, strategy, management and policy for infrastructure, and asset management; work–life balance; gender and careers in the public sector; public management and policy; government–business–community relations; negotiation and employment relations. She has published widely in these areas. She holds a PhD in industrial relations from Griffith University, Australia.

Professor **Yvonne Brunetto** is Head of Research at Southern Cross Business School. She has led research teams examining the impact of leadership on the behavior and job performance of different types of employees (including nurses, engineers, local government employees, economic development officers, small to medium-sized enterprise employees, and police officers) in Australia, the UK, Italy, Brazil, and the US—especially the impact of workplace relationships. She has published extensively in her career.

Manuela Brusoni is Senior Professor of Public Management and Business Government Relation at Bocconi University School of Management (SDA Bocconi), where she serves also as Director of Accreditation. As Director of Accreditation, she manages the relations with international accreditation bodies and networks, such as European Federation for Management

Development, the Association to Advance Collegiate Schools of Business, and European Association for Quality Assurance in Higher Education. She founded MaSan, an executive program of SDA Bocconi for buyers in the public sector, for which now she is the scientific director. She advises Italian central and local public authorities in the field of public procurement, management education, and local development. She serves as Chair of the Accreditation Committee of ASFOR, the Italian Association for Management Education. She is an active member of the Academy of Management since 2004, and Global Business School Network Ambassador for SDA Bocconi. In 2014 she was appointed Chair of Lombardy Region central purchasing body.

Dr. **Grant Cairncross** is a Senior Lecturer at Southern Cross University in Northern New South Wales, Australia where he has taught and researched for the past 16 years. Grant's prior work experience spans both the private and public sectors, where he was involved in corporate-wide change and change innovation at both individual work-group and departmental levels. Grant's research interests include regional development and innovative public-sector projects, remote area labor markets, and employment strategies and their effects on service quality in service industries and the public sector.

Francesca Casalini is a research assistant and coordinator of the Impact Investing Lab at SDA Bocconi School of Management in Milan, Italy. She was formerly research assistant at Bocconi Monitor on Public Private Partnership, where she performed a research on public credit guarantee schemes and, in particular, the Italian Central Guarantee Fund.

Stefano Caselli is Vice Rector for International Affairs and Full Professor of Banking and Finance at Bocconi University. He is Academic Director of MISB Bocconi—Mumbai International School of Business. He is a member of the board of directors for SDA Bocconi School of Management, where he was Director of Executive Education Custom Program for Banks and Financial Institutions from 2006 to 2012. He is a member of the scientific committee of Centro Europa Ricerche in Rome, European Capital Market Institute in Brussels, European Private Equity and Venture Capital Association for PEREP Group in Brussels, ENTER (the research center for entrepreneurship of Bocconi University) and CARE-FIN (the research center for financial innovation of Bocconi University). He is one of the founder of Bocconi Monitor on Public Private Partnership. He is also serving as independent director in several boards of corporations and financial institutions and consultants for many companies and institutions.

Dr. **Jordi Comas** researches social networks by drawing on organization and social theory. Working with quantitative and qualitative data, he brings these perspectives to differing contexts including virtual worlds, community associations, organizational learning, international development, and terrorism. He has worked with various civil society and community organizations. Next, he plans to bring his blend of network studies and social theory to investigate social entrepreneurship. He earned an MA in sociology from the University of Virginia, followed by a PhD in Management from IESE/Universidad de Navarra. Currently he is an assistant professor in the School of Management of Bucknell University in Lewisburg, Pennsylvania.

Dr. Christina Donnelly O'Connor (LLB, MSc, PhD, PGDTL), is Lecturer and Programme Director for BBS Marketing at the School of Business, National University of Ireland Maynooth. Christina's core research interests include small-business marketing, data analytics (dunnhumby/Tesco Loyalty Card), and public policy. Christina's research to date is interlinked with her work in the Northern Ireland Food Industry, where she spearheaded a government-funded project to analyze and deliver market intelligence data to all small agrifood and drink businesses across the region. Christina's most recent work has been published in the *International Small Business Journal, Marketing Intelligence and Planning*, and *Harvard Business Review* blogs on "Data Into Action."

Ben Farr-Wharton is in the final stages of achieving his doctoral thesis at Southern Cross Business School. His doctoral research focuses on the impact of social networks, business acumen, and performance for people working within the creative industries. He has published in the areas of public management and regional development and has coordinated the Arts Management Workshops at the Academy of Management Conference since 2012.

Rod Farr-Wharton, PhD, is Discipline Leader in Entrepreneurship and Innovation at the University of the Sunshine Coast. Rod's research is in the area of innovation, entrepreneurship, small to medium-sized enterprises, and regional development. He is widely published in the field of innovation, entrepreneurship, and regional development.

Adjunct professor **Stephen Kelly** recently joined M2 Academy in Singapore as Academic Director having most recently been Dean of the School of Business at Southern Cross University. M2 Academy is a new private education institute delivering diploma and degree programs in association with leading universities from Australia, the UK, and the US. Prior to joining academia in 1998 Stephen worked in the building materials and construction industry for CSR, AV Jennings, and Clyde Industries. While in academia he has published more than 70 refereed articles predominantly in the area of innovation and enterprise development and secured in excess of US$1 million in grant, project, and research funding.

Michiel Kort is senior consultant at RebelGroup. He is also lecturer and researcher of public administration at Erasmus University Rotterdam and Delft University of Technology. Michiel Kort studied Systems Engineering, Policy Analysis and Management (specialization management of water infrastructures) at Delft University of Technology. His research interests include management of complex projects, alliances, and partnerships (public–private partnerships, community partnerships, self-organization). In 2011 he obtained his PhD. His dissertation dealt with the question whether it is the organizational form or a management strategy that matters for achieving good outcomes in public–private partnership projects.

Adrian T. H. Kuah is Senior Fellow of the Cairns Institute and Senior Lecturer at James Cook University, Australia. Previously, he was MBA Director at Nottingham Business School and Director of UG Business Studies at Bradford University School of Management in the UK. His research focuses on competitiveness, innovation, and regional development, which has led to research grants in excess of half a million dollars and more than 40 research papers. Adrian holds a PhD from the Manchester Business School, an MBA from Strathclyde Business School, and an ITP from SDA Bocconi. An Advanced Institute of Management Research Scholar, Adrian was named *Financial Times* Professor of the Week in 2013.

Eric Martin is Associate Professor of Management in the Managing for Sustainability Program at Bucknell University in Lewisburg, Pennsylvania. He earned a bachelor's degree in science from the University of Vermont, a master's degree in public administration from Indiana University, and a PhD in Public Administration and Policy from the State University of New York at Albany. Martin's research focuses on interorganizational partnering across the public, private, and nonprofit sectors. A Returned Peace Corps Volunteer and Fulbright Scholar, he has focused much of his work on efforts to improve the delivery of international development and humanitarian assistance. He has spent a great deal of time in Central, Eastern, and Southern Europe studying such changes in many different venues.

Dr. Alyson Nicholds is Senior Lecturer in HRM in the Department of Leadership, Work and Organisations at Middlesex University Business School, London. Her main teaching and research interests are interdisciplinary including public management, leadership of place, and critical reflexivity. She publishes in the area of leadership and multi-discourse approaches with a view to making sense of complexity. She is also coleader of a research cluster on organizational life.

Federica Ricaldi is a junior private sector officer at the African Development Bank. She works on an entrepreneurship program, bringing together multiple actors of the Tunisian private- and public-sector ecosystem, while also collaborating with international development agencies. She has prior experience in international development and the private sector as she worked at the Italian embassy in Dakar, Senegal, and for Archidata Consulting in Milan, Italy. She earned a master's degree in international development at the University of Bologna, during which she participated in a 1-year exchange program at the University of Paris VII. She also holds a postgraduate diploma at the Business School of Sole 24 Ore (Rome) and a certificate on Equity-Focused Evaluation by UNICEF-IOCE (Eval Partners Initiative).

Monica Rossolini is Assistant Professor in Banking and Finance at the Department of Business Administration, Finance, Management and Law of the University of Milan Bicocca (Italy). She is Researcher at the Monitor on Public Private Partnership of Bocconi University. She is SDA Assistant Professor of Banking and Insurance at SDA Bocconi School of Management.

Emanuele Santi is Regional Chief Economist for West Africa at the African Development Bank (AfDB) after nearly 15 years of professional experience in development, mostly gained at the World Bank and the AfDB. He has worked in more than 25 countries in Africa, Latin America, Eastern Europe, and Central Asia. He holds a PhD in development policy from Trieste University/ Paris Sorbonne, a Master in Economic Studies from the College of Europe, and an Executive Program Degree on Public Financial Management from Harvard's Kennedy School of Government.

Jennifer Scott, BSc(Hons), MBA, DBA, originally from Ontario, Canada, began her education in the sciences. Once she started working in private industry, Jennifer realized her desire to learn more about business administration and completed her Master of Business Administration in leadership and project management. She then moved to Australia and entered the higher education sector. Jennifer recently completed her Doctor of Business Administration with a specialization in marketing, focusing on how relationship marketing and networks can be used to recruit international higher degree research students to regional universities. Jennifer looks forward to continuing exploring the value of networks and relationships in the international marketplace as she embarks on the next phase of her career.

Jakob Trischler is a doctoral candidate with the Southern Cross Business School, Australia. He has a background in tourism and service management studies undertaken at the Management Center Innsbruck, Austria, and Dalarna University, Sweden. His research focuses on investigating the development of the service design field, particularly by investigating the effect of user involvement into service design and innovation practices.

Apart from that, he currently works on developing a new service design model, which draws on recent service science developments and proposes value co-creation within service systems as the central concept of service design.

Veronica Vecchi is Professor of Public Management and Business Government Relation at Bocconi University School of Management (SDA Bocconi). Veronica serves as Scientific Coordinator of SDA Bocconi Public Private Factory, an executive education program for public and private managers on public–private partnerships (PPP); she coordinates Bocconi Monitor on Public Private Partnership and SDA Bocconi Lab for Impact Investments; she is Director of MaSan, an executive program of SDA Bocconi for buyers in the public sector. She also serves as Director of executive education at MISB Bocconi (Mumbai International School of Business), where she also teaches Business Government Relations. She is external faculty affiliate at Cornell University for the Cornell Program in Infrastructure Policy. She advises Italian national, regional, and local authorities on PPPs and local development.

Pengji Wang is a lecturer at James Cook University (Singapore Campus). She holds a PhD in strategy and policy from National University of Singapore. Her research interests include corporate governance, the strategy and performance of firms from emerging economies, and cross-cultural leadership.

Natalie Wojtarowicz is a PhD candidate in public policy and sessional academic at Southern Cross Business School, Southern Cross University, Australia. Her research interests lie in public policy and policy networks, on one hand, and highly skilled migration as well as migrant integration, on the other hand. Previously, Natalie was policy advisor in the area of migrant integration with the Austrian Federal Ministry of the Interior. Natalie holds two master's degrees, one in political science and one in Slavonic studies, from the University of Vienna.

Lin Yuan is Assistant Professor of Management at University of Macau. She holds a PhD in business strategy from the National University of Singapore. Her research interests lie at the intersection of strategy and international business, including the process and the determinants of internationalization strategy of multinational corporations (MNCs) and entrepreneurial firms, the innovation strategies of developing country firms, and the organizational learning of emerging market firms. Her current lines of research focused on internationalization strategies of emerging market MNCs.

Index

Printed in the United States
by Baker & Taylor Publisher Services